W9-AMA-833

The Young Composers

Studies in Writing and Rhetoric

In 1980 the Conference on College Composition and Communication established the Studies in Writing and Rhetoric (SWR) series as a forum for monograph-length arguments or presentations that engage general compositionists. SWR encourages extended essays or research reports addressing any issue in composition and rhetoric from any theoretical or research perspective as long as the general significance to the field is clear. Previous SWR publications serve as models for prospective authors; in addition, contributors may propose alternate formats and agendas that inform or extend the field's current debates.

SWR is particularly interested in projects that connect the specific research site or theoretical framework to contemporary classroom and institutional contexts of direct concern to compositionists across the nation. Such connections may come from several approaches, including cultural, theoretical, field-based, gendered, historical, and interdisciplinary. SWR especially encourages monographs by scholars early in their careers, by established scholars who wish to share an insight or exhortation with the field, and by scholars of color.

The SWR series editor and editorial board members are committed to working closely with prospective authors and offering significant developmental advice for encouraged manuscripts and prospectuses. Editorships rotate every five years. Prospective authors intending to submit a prospectus during the 1997 to 2002 editorial appointment should obtain submission guidelines from Robert Brooke, SWR editor, University of Nebraska-Lincoln, Department of English, P.O. Box 880337, 202 Andrews Hall, Lincoln, NE 68588-0337.

General inquiries may also be addressed to Sponsoring Editor, Studies in Writing and Rhetoric, Southern Illinois University Press, P.O. Box 3697, Carbondale, IL 62902-3697.

The Young Composers

Composition's Beginnings
in Nineteenth-Century Schools

Lucille M. Schultz

SOUTHERN ILLINOIS UNIVERSITY PRESS

Carbondale and Edwardsville

Copyright © 1999 by *The Conference on College Composition and Communication of the National Council of Teachers of English*

All rights reserved

Printed in the United States of America

02 01 00 99 4 3 2 1

Publication partially funded by a subvention grant from The Conference on College Composition and Communication of the National Council of Teachers of English.

A previous version of chapter 2 was published as "Elaborating Our History: A Look at Mid-19th Century First Books of Composition" in *College Composition and Communication* 45 (February 1994): 10–30, and a previous version of chapter 3 was published as "Pestalozzi's Mark on Nineteenth-Century Composition Instruction: Ideas Not in Words but in Things" in *Rhetoric Review* 14 (fall 1995): 23–43.

Library of Congress Cataloging-in-Publication Data

Schultz, Lucille M., 1943–
   The young composers : composition's beginnings in nineteenth-century schools / Lucille M. Schultz.
      p.   cm. — (Studies in writing & rhetoric)
   Includes bibliographical references and index.
      1. English language—Rhetoric—Study and teaching—United States—History—19th century. 2. English language—Composition and exercises—Textbooks—History—19th century. I. Title. II. Series.
   PE1405.U6S38 1999
   808'.042'071073—dc21   98-21923
   ISBN 0-8093-2236-6 (pbk.)   CIP

The paper used in this publication meets the minimum requirements of American National Standard for Information Sciences—Permanence of Paper for Printed Library Materials, ANSI Z39.48-1984. ∞

For Mary and Frank Schultz—
in gratitude

Contents

Appendixes

Figures

Acknowledgments

The primary sources that ground this book are composition text-books from nineteenth-century schools and the texts that nineteenth-century students composed. Because not many copies of these text-books or examples of student texts have survived, I have spent a good deal of time in public and private archives, searching them out. It is thus that I owe a heavy and ongoing debt to the many librarians and archivists who have enabled my work in countless ways.

I was privileged to do most of the research for this book at the Library of Congress and at Harvard University's Monroe C. Gutman Library; in both cases, the professional assistance I received was extraordinary. At the Library of Congress, Reference Librarian Kathy Woodrell has been with this project from its first days, helping me find my way through a labyrinth of print materials; problem-solving with me on each of my many visits; and, in between visits, responding to phone calls and E-mail with good cheer, expertise, and unlimited patience. In particular, she allowed me entrance to the Library of Congress stacks when that privilege was still available to researchers, and she helped with the complex process of obtaining illustrations for use in this text. Her colleague, Clark Evans, reference librarian in the Rare Book Room, was also helpful with specialized requests.

At Harvard's Gutman Library, Marylène Altieri, special collections librarian/archivist, allowed me access to Gutman's world-class collections of textbooks and school reports. During my extended summer visits, she enabled my work not only with her expert and detailed guidance through catalogued and uncatalogued materials but also with her uncanny ability to identify and/or locate texts, titles, authors, and dates. In addition, she gave me access to the material resources a researcher needs: carrel space, a library truck, and a system for photocopying fragile materials. Like Kathy Woodrell, she, too, has been only an E-mail or phone call away for the past several years. Also at

Gutman, John W. Collins III, librarian of the Graduate School of Education; Gladys Dratch, collections development librarian; and Mary S. Russell, collections conservator, extended their gracious welcome and generous assistance on each of my working visits.

Many other librarians and archivists helped me to find my way among their nineteenth-century documents. I am grateful to John Blake, director of the National Library of Education; to Sister Mary Virginia Brennan, VHM, archivist, Georgetown Visitation Preparatory School; to James Green, associate librarian, Library Company of Philadelphia; to Robert Eskind, curator of prints, Atwater Kent Museum, Philadelphia; to John H. Platt Jr., executive director, Masonic Library and Museum of Pennsylvania; to Robert Sanders, archivist, Central High School, Philadelphia; to Bonnie Smith, director, and Josephine M. Elliott, manuscripts archivist, New Harmony Workingmen's Institute in New Harmony, Indiana; to Chris Thorkelson, public information officer, and Winfield McChord Jr., executive director, American School for the Deaf; and to R. Eugene Zepp, reference librarian, and Roberta Zonghi, curator of rare books, Boston Public Library. Closer to home, I appreciate help from the interlibrary loan staff at the University of Cincinnati, especially from Judith Moore and Christine L. Mueller.

For research travel funding that helped to support working stints at these libraries and collections and, later, for time to write, I thank the University of Cincinnati's Taft Faculty Memorial Fund. I also thank the University of Cincinnati for the sabbatical leave that marked the beginning of this project; my department head, Jim Hall, for his unflagging and spirited support; and my colleagues and friends in the English department for the everyday joys.

The generosity of several organizations facilitated working trips to Washington, D.C., and Boston. Most significantly, I thank the Sisters of the Order of the Visitation of Holy Mary of Georgetown Visitation Preparatory School; it is the sisters' hospitality that allowed me the luxury of a five-month working stint, followed by shorter research periods, at the Library of Congress, the archive where this work began. The sisters also allowed me to read student work from their school, founded at its current site in 1799; and it was in those records that I saw my first example of a nineteenth-century student text in the student's own hand. For shorter but repeated stays in Boston, I received hospitality from Boston College, from Harvard's Episcopal Divinity School, and from Radcliffe College.

In the late Jim Berlin's 1987 Studies in Writing and Rhetoric publication, *Rhetoric and Reality*, he thanked me for sharing the administrative workload of the first-year writing program with him when he was at the University of Cincinnati. In a text in this same series, it is my great privilege to remember him with no small affection and with deep gratitude for his long-term friendship and for the many unnamed ways in which he and his work continue to inspire me. I am also grateful to colleagues working in nineteenth-century composition history and pedagogy—especially Kate Adams, John Brereton, Jean Ferguson Carr, Bob Connors, Mariolina Salvatori, and Sue Carter Simmons—for their work and for our ongoing conversations.

And I give thanks to Janet Miller, Jennifer Monaghan, and Jane Pomeroy, who have helped with specialized expertise: Janet and Jennifer alerted me to relevant publications in literacy studies; and, with great patience, Jane answered endless questions about nineteenth-century engraving and printing. Director of Communications Suzanne Grant at Georgetown Visitation Preparatory School, Washington, D.C.; photographer Charles Rumpf; Chris Thorkelson from the American School for the Deaf; and Jay Yocis, University of Cincinnati photographer, all assisted with reproducing nineteenth-century text and engravings for this book.

Three people have read, several times, every sentence of this text, both the sentences that remain and many that were pitched along the way. To the members of my writing group—Russel Durst, Maggy Lindgren, and Marjorie Roemer—for their wise words and good humor and staying power—I am enormously grateful. Much of their wisdom is in this text, and the text is better for it.

Finally, long-term personal support for this book has come from many quarters. In particular, and especially, I thank Jane O'Brien, Tom Dyehouse, Trudelle Thomas, Kathryn Rentz, Kathy Doane, Jack

xiv   **Acknowledgments**

Sommer, and David Smith. For family support, I am grateful to Frank Robert Schultz; to Dorothy Baird Schultz; to Dorothy Schultz Rapacz; and to my nieces and nephews, all of whom make me proud.

Marlo Welshons from the National Council of Teachers of English and Tracey Sobol from Southern Illinois University Press were instrumental in helping this manuscript begin its journey from my desk to the larger world. As work progressed, readers from the Studies in Writing and Rhetoric (SWR) editorial board provided helpful suggestions. And composition historian John Brereton generously offered a very close reading of the text that both enriched my understanding of nineteenth-century composition history and saved me from a few stumbles; any errors in the text are, of course, my responsibility. Editor of the SWR series, Robert Brooke, walked through the manuscript with me several times, always with an eye on the big picture as well as on the details; I especially appreciate his critical distance in helping me to think through a number of key decisions and the time, energy, and support he gave this project. Answering our many questions, SIU Press's Carol Burns, John Gehner, Kyle Lake, Angela Reynolds, and Teresa White kept us on course through the many stages of the actual publication process. And Rebecca Spears Schwartz did a superb copyediting job.

In sum, many people helped with the birthing of this book—and in many ways. To all of them, and to the Muse, I extend my warmest thanks.

The Young Composers

Figure 1. "The Young Composers." With this title, this illustration appeared in *The Schoolmate* (1855), "A Reader for Youth at School and at Home." Originally edited by Amos R. Phippen, this children's publication came to be known as *The Student and Schoolmate* and was then coedited by Phippen and Norman A. Calkins. The engraving is signed by Elias James Whitney, Albert H. Jocelyn, and Phineas F. Annin, partners in a wood engraving firm in New York City. The illustration also appears, without a title, on the cover of Phippen's *Illustrated Composition Book* (1854).

Telling Our Stories

> The final belief is to believe in a fiction, which you know to be a fiction, there being nothing else. The exquisite truth is to know that it is a fiction, and that you believe it willingly.
>
> —*Wallace Stevens, Opus Posthumous, 1957*

> Our search for alterity, for rhetorics other than the familiar, can reveal to us alternative possibilities in conceiving discursive practices and their power formations.
>
> —*James Berlin, "Revisionary Histories of Rhetorics," 1994*

For several generations now, scholars in rhetoric and composition have been constructing histories of writing instruction in U.S. colleges. From those histories, we have learned much that is significant about our past: about the rhetoricians to whom we are indebted, about the origins of some of our contemporary paradigms, about the conflicts that midwifed new practices and new perspectives. We have learned something about ourselves as storytellers and the role we play—our agency—in writing history. We have also articulated reasons why we tell our stories: Robert Connors reminds us that telling our stories helps to define us upon the stage of time, helps to locate and name our disciplinarity ("Dreams and Play" 34–35); Andra Makler writes that recounting the past allows us to reclaim it, "to reevaluate ourselves in relation to others" (46); Susan Jarratt argues that we write history to overturn truisms and givens, to see the complexities of evidence, to resist simplifications, to resist a single narrative chain, and thus "to achieve the kind of critical distance which allows for re-vision" (18–20). And, from historians, philosophers, and rhetoricians alike, we have learned that writing history is a rhetorical act, an act that makes visible the differences between history as event and history as account.

Perhaps most importantly, we have articulated some of the dangers of telling our stories. Following Hayden White and Michel Foucault, James Berlin cautions us again and again of the danger in pretending—even for a moment—that there is but one story, one way of reading the past; and of the danger in pretending—even for a moment—that the storyteller can stand in a neutral space or in a space outside the story. In Berlin's words, it is the historian's way of seeing that "makes the historical record readable . . . , influencing what he sees as significant and what he finds to be meaningless" ("Octalog" 11).

A danger I would like our profession to avoid is thinking that the histories we have been reading and writing—primarily the histories of writing instruction in the colleges—are the only important composition histories there are. I would like us to avoid thinking that the way writing instruction was constructed in the colleges is also the way that it was constructed in the schools, that the pedagogies embraced in the colleges were also those uniformly invoked in the schools. Instead, I would like to suggest that at the same time that the history of nineteenth-century school-based writing instruction is a part of a history that embraces all levels of education, it is also its own history, a different history, an alterity. *The Young Composers*, then, is our profession's first history of school-based writing instruction. In it, I argue that the history of writing instruction in the schools is an important and undervalued site in the overall history of writing instruction: it is a site where the voices of the British rhetoricians that dominated college-level instruction were attenuated by the voice of the Swiss reformer Johann Heinrich Pestalozzi; it is a site where what we think of as personal or experience-based writing began; it is a site where the democratization of writing was institutionalized; it is a site where some of our contemporary composition practices were prefigured; and it is the site where composition instruction, as we understand it today, began.

Certainly, the rigid rules that are popularly associated with nineteenth-century writing instruction were visible in some aspects of school-based composition instruction. But to read these rules—with their emphasis, for example, on writing as a vehicle for thought, on error-free writing, on formulaic writing—as an unqualified metonymy for nineteenth-century writing instruction is, I believe, an incomplete reading, even a misreading. Education reformer Johann Heinrich Pestalozzi had an influence on the American composition classroom that we have just begun to elaborate. Like Jean Jacques Rousseau, he believed in the goodness of the child, in the importance of educating the child as a child and not as a miniature adult, and in the primary importance of using objects rather than abstractions to teach a child new concepts. As I demonstrate, when Pestalozzi's thought made its way into composition textbooks—and this happened as early as 1839—children were invited to write about the objects and experiences of their own lives. While this instantiation was significant in itself, it is also significant in a larger sense: this is, I argue, the beginnings of the personal experience essay in composition instruction in the United States. As John Brereton points out, prior to Charles Eliot's inauguration as president of Harvard College in 1869, Harvard students, in a required rhetoric course, studied "principles of effective prose, usually by way of brief examples from the English classics" (9). It is fair to say that in 1839, college students were not, in their college classes, writing directly about their lived experiences. All the more noteworthy, therefore, are the implications of this innovation in the schools: that observation became a heuristic for writing, and that the knowledge that students brought with them to an educational setting from their own lives was valued. In a word, writing instruction was democratized.

That school curricula were not uniform in the early part of the century had many obvious drawbacks; one advantage, however, is that there were unlimited possibilities for innovation. And unfettered by the duty to instruct students in rhetorical principles (as the colleges were doing) or by a universal understanding of the best way to teach students to write (isolation of the schools from each other no doubt played a role here), textbook writers, who themselves often held teaching positions in the schools, prefigured contemporary composition practices in ways that we have not yet recognized. The rigid rules notwithstanding, Thomas Palmer wrote this—in 1843:

> Few are aware how improvable is the faculty of expressing thoughts upon paper. The gigantic increase of the muscles in a blacksmith's arm, from his wielding the hammer so frequently; the proverbial strength of the memory, by exercise; or the miraculous sleight which the juggler acquires, by practice, with his cup and balls; is not more certain, than that he, who daily habituates himself to writing down his ideas with what ease, accuracy, and elegance, he can, will find his improvement advance, with hardly any assignable limit." (*Teacher's Manual* 139–40)

Contemporary writing teachers cannot, I think, read Palmer's statement without hearing the voice of Donald Murray, the writer and writing teacher who repeatedly calls us to exercise our writing muscles on a daily basis so that we might be at the ready when the Muse hovers nearby. Similarly, other nineteenth-century authors, for example, anticipate Peter Elbow's advocacy of free writing; Mike Rose's cautions against premature editing; the work of O'Hare, Daiker, Kerek, and Morenberg with sentence combining. This is not to say that these innovations had the same widespread value they do today or that they functioned in the same way. But what this book argues is that nineteenth-century writing instruction in the schools was a site for tremendous pedagogical innovation—and, in fact, that it was in the schools that composition instruction as we know it had its beginnings.

On a sabbatical in the winter of 1992, before the stacks at the Library of Congress were closed to researchers, I roamed and read the "PE" shelves there—the hundreds and hundreds of shelves that are home to the library's collection of composition texts and rhetorics and grammars. It was there that *The Young Composers* began—when sitting on the floor of a narrow aisle with a flashlight, I pulled John Frost's 1839 *Easy Exercises in Composition* from a shelf and noticed how different it was from so many other composition texts and rhetorics that I was reading. Unlike other texts, Frost's *Easy Exercises* opened with "pictures of objects for description," not with grammar rules; it was illustrated with scenes from children's lives at home and at school; it invited children to write about their own lives; and it advised the young composers to write "freely and boldly." More shelf reading followed, and I found additional "First Books"; it was thus that I turned my attention to school-based writing instruction. Since that winter in Washington, I have worked in more than a dozen libraries and archives and have spent parts of several summers working in Harvard's Gutman Library. I have read two hundred nineteenth-century composition textbooks written for students, both beginners and older students; hundreds of nineteenth-century journal articles; and hundreds of pieces of student writing. And I am keenly aware that I cannot fully represent these texts or the secondary work that surrounds them, and that every reading—and, of course, every history—is contingent, perspectival, partial. I am especially mindful of Kenneth Burke's often-quoted reminder that a way of seeing is a way of not seeing.

My particular interest is in what I perceive to be the margins and the silences. In many ways, the story of school-based writing instruction has itself been marginalized, but even within a marginalized site, there are voices that have been privileged, others that have been muted, and, no doubt, many voices that are irrecoverable. Here I make space for some of the voices that have been muted, not in an attempt "to get the story straight" but, borrowing from historian Hans Kellner, to affirm that "stories" are multivoiced, laced with ironic juxtapositions and contradictions, and necessarily and wonderfully crooked (32–33). I consider, of course, the work of Albert Kitzhaber, Janet Emig, Robert Connors, and others who have written about school-based writing instruction; like them, I include the Parkers and the Quackenboses in my account, but unlike Connors, for example, I concentrate on introducing writers from whom and about whom we have to date heard very little: some of these are textbook and treatise writers; some are nineteenth-century student writers. Frost's is the text with which I began, and it is the text to which I have returned again and again as both fountainhead and benchmark. My goal is to give voice to these texts written for the school-age population and to represent them—and their pedagogy—as a significant chapter in the history of writing instruction in this country.

Recent studies have contributed greatly to our understanding of the history of language arts instruction. Tamara Plakins Thornton's *Handwriting in America: A Cultural History* traces changing pedagogies from the colonial period to the present and the ways these pedagogies "embodied, regulated, and generated notions of the self" (x). Patrick Shannon's *The Struggle to Continue* elaborates stories of reading instruction in nineteenth-century schools. More comprehensively, Miles Myers's *Changing Our Minds* traces the wide-ranging forms of literacy that have been part of American educational practice from the beginnings to the present. In my work, I am interested in the composing that students did in nineteenth-century schools: their essays, their letters, their stories, their contributions to their school newspapers. I hasten to say that this study will not answer all the questions that readers might have; many topics are embedded in writing instruction in the schools that I don't address; many, I'm sure, that I don't even see. My hope is that what I do offer will suggest some of the richness and complexity and significance of school-based writing instruction in the nineteenth century and, as part of the process, will spark others to visit the still-unexplored libraries, museums, historical societies, and private collections in order that we might continue to construct and revise our stories about the nineteenth century's young composers.

To provide a context for understanding developments in nineteenth-century, school-based writing instruction, chapter 1 surveys language instruction in the schools with an emphasis on the transition from valuing and teaching memory-based performance to valuing and teaching the practice of composing original text. Because of the deep-rooted connections between educational practices and cultural forces, this chapter also explores the interanimation of composition's development with the burgeoning of the common school, with the culture's changing understanding of children's educational development, and with the developments in the printing industry that allowed the increased manufacture of books for children.

In chapter 2, I focus on some of the earliest books expressly written to instruct beginning students in composition. When viewed in the context of other early nineteenth-century composition texts—those used in the colleges and the best-known books written for the schools—the composition texts written for young students that are inflected by a romantic sensibility and an understanding of the intellectual development of a child mark a major contribution to the history of nineteenth-century writing instruction. Because these little-known texts—I name them "First Books"—advocate a reform pedagogy, because they anticipate some of the ways we teach writing today, and because they suggest that the body of important textbooks in composition is broader and more diverse than has been assumed, they provide the basis for a revised and broadened understanding of how writing was taught in some settings in mid-nineteenth-century America.

While British rhetoricians were the primary influences on college writing instruction in the nineteenth century, we have only begun to understand that an important influence on the books used with school-age students was the work of Swiss reformer Johann Heinrich Pestalozzi. Chapter 3 explores the ways that Pestalozzi's criticism of rule-based learning and his emphasis on learning from direct experience affected composition instruction in the schools, especially as a conduit for experience-based writing. John Frost is an important figure here. Stemming from his edition of an 1830 text by Elizabeth Mayo that is grounded in Pestalozzian thought, Frost introduced writing assignments that asked students to write about the objects and events of their lives. While Frost was among the earliest textbook writers to represent Pestalozzi's approach to learning, many later nineteenth-century, school-based composition books encouraged students to write about their own experiences.

Partly as a response to the realization that youngsters learn in ways different from adults, illustrations were common in nineteenth-century schoolbooks for almost every discipline. In chapter 4, I explore the iconography of composition textbooks and interrogate the ways in which the illustrations were both freeing and restraining:

freeing in the ways they invited students to write about their own experiences, restraining in the ways they encoded and reproduced nineteenth-century cultural and social values and beliefs.

And in chapter 5, I listen to the voices of the young composers. I read samples of student texts written in school, at home, and in the border space between the classroom and home. And I argue that classroom-based student writing follows the historical contours of textbooks, moving, especially in midcentury, from the abstract to the more specific and experiential. In home-based writing, primarily personal journals and letters to families, students both endorse and resist cultural codes. And in the texts that students composed for school newspapers and literary journals, they reflect on writing and on themselves as writers. Student writing itself, therefore, not only suggests a broader reading of the writing students did than the textbooks can offer, it also provides a kind of evidence for the changes in writing instruction that occurred in nineteenth-century schools.

In the conclusion, I offer my reading of the significance of writing instruction in nineteenth-century schools, arguing that although this pedagogy was derivative, eclectic, and often contradictory, it was also innovative. As I demonstrate, a number of contemporary pedagogical practices were prefigured in nineteenth-century schools; in addition, the practice of teaching students to use experience as a form of evidence began in the schools and contributed to the democratization of writing. My reading of nineteenth-century, school-based writing instruction thus enables a revised understanding of the larger history of writing instruction, an understanding that continues to complicate the stories we tell about who we are.

1 / The Beginnings of Composition in Early Nineteenth-Century Schools

With the emphasis on composing original text in today's schools—visible in the number of teachers who participate in the National Writing Project and in the many classrooms where students draft and revise stories, publish their work for each other, create portfolios of their writing, and are celebrated as "young authors"—it is easy to forget that beginning students in early nineteenth-century U.S. schools were not "writing" as we use that term today. Especially in conversations about the education of young children, *writing* often signified *handwriting*, and in what we would call language arts activities, children were, for the most part, memorizing rules and parsing sentences. As the century progressed, however, significant changes occurred in composition instruction, most notably that students were composing original text in their classrooms and also for their school newspapers and literary journals. To help understand these changes, which I make figural in the remaining chapters of this book, I begin with representing the ground the cultural and especially the educational landscape—in which these changes occurred. In constructing this historical overview, I am particularly interested in framing the beginnings of composition instruction in the American educational system.

The Early National Period and Learning by Rote

"A" or "An" is styled the indefinite article: it is used in a vague sense to point out one single thing of the kind, in other respects indeterminate.

—*Murray's Abridged Grammar*, 1808

During the six years that we studied grammar . . . [in Boston schools about 1800], we were never required to write a sentence

of English, and we never did write one, as a school exercise,
though our grammar masters were all educated at college.

—*Common School Journal*, January 1850

In the first two decades of the century, as during the latter part
of the colonial period, European American children attended infant
schools, dame schools, charity schools, town schools, and/or district schools for their earliest formal lessons. In these independently
run schools, hornbooks and the *New England Primer* were the most
common textbooks, and "reading" and "writing" were the goals. The
primary trope for the instruction of children was religious and biblical, and schools and schoolmasters made no secret of the fact that
while they were engaged in an intellectual enterprise, they were sharing with the pulpit and the family the responsibility for teaching the
child the dominant culture's belief system. So as students learned to
read and write their alphabet letters, they also learned that "In *Adam's*
Fall / We sinned all," and that "*Zacheus* he / Did climb the tree / His
Lord to see." At the end of several years of often irregular and seasonal
attendance at these primary schools, most students had completed
their formal education. For those who, because of their family's stature
or means, were bound for college and careers in the law or ministry,
this first schooling was often followed by time with a private tutor in
preparation for the work to come at a Latin grammar school.[1]

Based on the English model, these schools were specifically intended to prepare students for the university; they focused on instruction in Latin grammar and the classics and on instruction in English
grammar that followed the method for teaching Latin. Thus, the English "language instruction" that students received was in formal
grammar and was most often taught from a version of Lindley
Murray's *English Grammar*, from Noah Webster's *A Grammatical Institute*, or from a grammar by one of their imitators. Written originally
for an adult audience, these grammars were typically divided into sections on orthography, etymology, syntax, and prosody. Replicating the
methods for teaching Latin grammar through drills, the pedagogy was
catechistical, calling for students to memorize and recite answers to
standard questions; according to Rollo Lyman in his classic 1922

study *English Grammar in American Schools Before 1850*, the emphasis of this pedagogy was "slavish memorizing, nothing more nor less" (113). Sometimes the answers students were asked to memorize were to a single question, "Of what does Etymology treat?" or "Of what does Syntax treat?" More often, however, the questions occurred in a predictable and almost chantlike series. Here, for example, is a series of questions from Kirkham's *English Grammar*:

> By what sign may a noun be distinguished?—How many kinds of nouns are there? What belong to nouns?—What is gender?—How many genders have nouns?—What is person?—How many persons have nouns?—What is number?— How many numbers have nouns?—What is case?—How many cases have nouns?—Does case consist in the *inflections* of a noun? (60)

By present-day criteria, missing from this instruction was any form of interactive learning; students were rewarded not for problem solving or for original thinking but for accurate memory. Lyman argues that the first step toward interactive learning was the introduction of parsing, and that although grammar authors Murray and Webster required students to parse, they did so only after the student had a command of etymology and syntax. So in Lyman's work, Samuel Kirkham is valorized because he introduced parsing at the same time that students were studying nouns and verbs. Like the pedagogy of memorization, parsing was a carryover from studying Latin grammar to studying English grammar. Parsing required the student to analyze the components of a sentence and thus, for grammarian Goold Brown it had "more dignity than a school boy's conversation, and more ease than a formal recitation" (qtd. in Lyman 121). In Kirkham's 1831 *English Grammar*, Kirkham's goal was to help students not just to memorize definitions and rules but also to understand what they were learning, or to be able "to enumerate and describe all [of a word's] various properties, and its grammatical relations with respect to other words in a sentence, and trace it through all its inflections or changes" (50). To parse the first noun in the sentence "*Birds repose* on the branches of trees," however, this is what a child would have been expected to recite:

> *Birds* is a noun, the name of a thing or creature—common, the name of a genus or class—masculine and feminine gender, it denotes both males and females—third person, spoken of—plural number, it implies more than one—and in the nominative case, it is the *subject* of the verb "repose" and governs it according to RULE 3. *The nom. case governs the verb.* Declined—Sing. nom. bird, poss. bird's, obj. bird. Plural, nom. birds, poss. birds', obj. birds. (53)

While it is true that parsing called for a student to apply principles, not just memorize, we also know that in prerevolutionary American schools and through the first two decades of the nineteenth century, the pedagogical emphasis was not on practice—and certainly not on composing text. As Lyman explains, these early educators believed that since written and spoken discourse involve the "putting together of parts," so "the taking of them apart is the initial step of the learning process" (122); hence in accord with popular wisdom, the first chapter of many texts taught students individual letters and parts of speech; see, for example, the Quackenbos table of contents in appendix 1.

It is thus remarkable that in the curriculum for his 1751 Philadelphia Academy, Benjamin Franklin advocated—and this was an extraordinarily radical move—the inclusion of composition instruction. In Franklin's *Idea of the English School*, prepared at the request of the trustees of the academy, he detailed the composition instruction he wanted in his school. Franklin wrote,

> The Boys should be put on Writing Letters to each other on any common Occurrences, and on various Subjects, imaginary Business, &c. containing little Stories, Accounts of their late Reading, what Parts of Authors please them, and why. Letters of Congratulation, of Compliment, of Request, of Thanks, of Recommendation, of Admonition, of Consolation,

of Expostulation, Excuse, &c. In these they should be taught to express themselves clearly, concisely, and naturally, without affected Words, or high-flown Phrases. All their Letters to pass through the Master's Hand, who is to point out the Faults, advise the Corrections, and commend what he finds right. (qtd. in Leonard Labaree 106)

While Franklin's academy flourished initially and was later to be regarded as the impulse that gave rise to the University of Pennsylvania, the school as it was founded languished by 1770. And records suggest that the curriculum Franklin proposed was never fully adopted in his school and that his call for composition had no widespread effect. According to an account by John Swett, when Samuel Hall introduced the writing of compositions into the common school in Maine where he was teaching in 1815, he was met with a "storm of protests from parents and pupils" for such a radical idea (*Am Public Schools* 77). And firsthand anecdotes suggest as well that students were not composing original text during the earliest decades of the century. The writer of an editorial in the 1849 *Common School Journal*, recalling his own education decades earlier, lamented, "We were *educated* at one of the best schools . . . but, although we studied English Grammar seven years, and received a silver medal for our proficiency, we never wrote a sentence of English at school, and never did any thing which implied a suspicion on our part that grammar had any thing to do with writing or conversation" ("Preventive Discipline" 250).

The Antebellum Period and the Great Educational Awakening

Our chief object for the first two or three years [of school] would be the acquisition of the English language and the art of expressing ourselves in *written* composition.
—John Keagy, *An Essay on English Education*, 1824

Sec. 10. *And be it further enacted*, That any person or persons who shall endeavor or attempt to teach any free person of color, or slave to spell, read, or write, shall upon conviction thereof by in-

dictment, be fined in a sum not less than two hundred and fifty
dollars nor more than five hundred dollars.

—Alabama law prohibiting the teaching of slaves, 1832

Composing has no difficulties worth naming: after you have practiced awhile, it will be a pleasant and interesting exercise.

—Charles Morley, *Common School Grammar*, 1836

What Jean Ferguson Carr calls "interference"—contradictions,
oppositions, exceptions, and setbacks (93–97)—was occurring during the central decades of the nineteenth century, 1830 to 1860, the
time of the Great Educational Awakening. This "interference" would
ultimately lead to school-based writing instruction as we understand
it; and the transition sprang, I argue, from revisionist thinking in two
interdependent environments: the schools and the public culture in
which those schools were embedded. Partly in response to the needs
for a literate citizenry in a growing democracy and partly in response
to the growing numbers of students attending school on a regular basis, the schools themselves were pressing for instruction in composition; interdependently and concurrently, society's attitudes toward the
child and the child's ways of learning were also undergoing revision.

Before I discuss these two interdependent changes—the call for
composition in the schools and the culture's changing understanding
of childhood—it is important to remember that not all nineteenth-
century children had access to school. Well into the century, most of
the students attending school were European American children, and
most often from middle-class families. R. Freeman Butts and Lawrence
Cremin estimate that by 1840, in New England, more children than
not had some formal schooling; by 1850, in the Midwest and West,
some formal school was the rule rather than the exception for most
children (237). Poor children were less likely to be in school. And
if they were in school in the early decades of the century, they were
often subjected to the Lancasterian system, a factorylike educational
practice characterized by rigid order and discipline that allowed large
numbers of students to attend school because the older students were
used as "monitors" to teach the younger children. African American

children, Native American children, Chinese children, Mexican children, children of working-class immigrants, and children with special needs had limited and, in some cases, no educational opportunities. Historians of education including Carter G. Woodson, Carl Kaestle, and Lawrence Cremin, for example, report that schools for African American children were established considerably later than those for European American children, were many fewer in number, were poorer in quality and resources, and varied in availability from region to region, with the greatest number of opportunities being in the East Coast cities of the North. A report in the *Prize Book* of the Boston Latin School records that in July 1823, 5,863 children were in school in Boston, 71 of whom attended the African School on Belknap Street (56).

John Hope Franklin explains that schools for African American children were often established with the help of religious groups, especially the Society of Friends, or with the help of abolition or manumission societies, and that one of the most celebrated schools for Negroes was established in New York City in 1787. This school opened with forty students, and by 1820, more than five hundred children were enrolled (109–10). In other East Coast locations, schools were established for African American children: a school opened in Philadelphia in 1750 (and Woodson notes that by 1797 there were seven "colored schools" [104] in that city); in Baltimore, a school opened in 1792; and in New Jersey, Rhode Island, Delaware, and Massachusetts, schools for African Americans were opened by 1810. To provide students with a religious education as well as with lessons in "English, French, cyphering and writing, sewing in all its branches, embroidery, washing and ironing" (qtd. in Cohen 1622), "a religious society of colored women" established a school for girls of color in Baltimore in 1829.

Not named by Cohen, the women who founded the school are the Oblate Sisters of Providence, and according to members of the community, their Baltimore school, St. Frances Academy, is the oldest continuous school for children of color in the United States. An example of a midwestern school for children of color was the Union Literary Institute, chartered in 1848 on 184 acres of land in Spartanburg,

Indiana. According to *The Students' Repository* (1864), a periodical published four times a year by the school, beginning in July 1863, the Union Literary Institute was founded "by a few benevolent persons, most of whom were Quakers," as a manual labor school, intended to provide children of color not only with school-based education, but with education and experience in farming as well (96).

While there may have been situations in which black and white students attended school together, the practice was both rare and controversial. When Bronson Alcott admitted an African American child to his Boston Beach Street school in 1839 and refused to comply with a request to dismiss the child, other parents withdrew their children from the school. The school closed, but Alcott continued to privately instruct his own children, the unnamed African American child, and the children of William Russell during the following year (McKuskey 111). Some years later, in 1849, Benjamin Roberts, an African American, was turned away when he tried to enroll his child in a Boston public school attended by white children; the Supreme Court of Massachusetts ruled against Roberts and his attorney Charles Sumner, arguing that separate schools did not violate equal rights, in spite of the fact that financial support for the black schools was meager and the buildings and supplies were generally inferior to those of the white schools (Butts and Cremin 318).

Henry Allen Bullock notes that in the South, Hugh Bryan opened a Negro school in Charleston in 1740, and that by 1755, schools for slaves were opened in Virginia (12). In general, however, while educational opportunities for African American children were available in the second half of the eighteenth century in the South, they were severely curtailed there in the early decades of the nineteenth century. As the Industrial Revolution called for greater supplies of cotton fiber, as the plantation system changed from a patriarchal to an economic base, and as the abolition movement gained ground and published greater numbers of documents, slave owners worried that education would encourage discontent among the slaves. So while community-based education in the slave quarter community and in churches was a powerful force, while some African American children in the South attended what were known as "night schools" (after white students left school, children of color would take their places, sometimes until ten at night), and while some children were taught to read and write by sympathetic slaveholders, many children were forbidden to attend school. A number of Southern states passed laws making illegal the school-based literacy education of people of color. Mississippi, for example, passed legislation forbidding the education of slaves or free Negroes in 1823; Louisiana forbade the teaching of slaves in 1830; North Carolina and Virginia, in 1831; and Alabama, in 1832. The North Carolina legislature explained its reason for the prohibition: "The teaching of slaves to read and write, has a tendency to excite dissatisfaction in their minds, and to produce insurrection and rebellion, to the manifest injury of the citizens of this State" (qtd. in Cohen 1622).[2]

At the same time that formal education was in many cases denied to African American children, it was often imposed on Native American children as a "civilizing" measure. In *American Indian Children at School, 1850–1930*, Michael Coleman explains that before American authorities forced Native American children into missionary or government schools, the community assumed the responsibility for the education of children. From their elders, children learned the stories and work and art of their peoples. Then early in the eighteenth century, various religious groups began to support missionaries to live and work among the Indians, and to instruct them in Christianity. In 1734, for example, with support from the Society for the Propagation of the Gospel, John Sergeant, a tutor at Yale, opened a school for the Housatonic Indians at Stockbridge, Massachusetts. At the end of 1735, forty students attended the school; in 1749, fifty-five students were in school, and 182 of the 218 Indians living in the community had been baptized (U.S. Bureau of Education 90–93). Privately funded schools such as this one, where Jonathan Edwards succeeded Sergeant as minister and teacher, eventually gave way to schools funded by the federal government for the "civilization" and education of Indian children. In 1819, a "civilization fund" was established, and, according to Coleman, each year the president could allocate $10,000 to hiring "capable persons of good moral character, to instruct them [Indians] in the mode of agriculture suited to their situation; and for teaching their children in reading, writing, and arithmetic." Quoting a report of the Indian school superintendent, Coleman notes that by 1824, thirty-two missionary schools enrolled nine hundred children of Indian tribes and that the number of government-supported schools continued to grow, so that by 1900, there were twenty-five off-reservation schools and eighty-one on-reservations schools (39–45). While there were no doubt exceptions, the work of these schools, in addition to educating children in school subjects, was, in the words of historian William Barney, to teach the Indian children to be ashamed of "the religion, customs, and values of their parents" (318).

Common schools and the call for composition. Even as European Americans were in many cases making decisions about the education of Native American or African American children, the move toward a universal common school education—that would really be universal only at the turn of the century—gained momentum during the 1820s and 1830s.[3] Against the irregularities and costs of the privately run schools, educational reformers such as Horace Mann, Henry Barnard, and their colleagues gained significant ground in their efforts to establish "common schools," or what we call "elementary schools." The reformers' goals were to provide universal, public, and free education; to reform the harsh, even abusive, manner in which children were sometimes treated in independent schools; to improve the quality of instruction children received; and to regularize the curriculum in some way, that is, to make certain elements of learning "common" to all children were included. Because the educational reformers perceived that families and churches were no longer as committed to moral education as they had been during the colonial era and because there were signs of poverty and violence in communities, the reformers also saw the common schools as an instrument for promoting the social order, the patriotism, and the Christian morality endorsed by the Jacksonian era. In addition to arguing that educated workers are more productive than uneducated workers, Horace Mann argued that not to support free schools was to invite "the certain vengeance of Heaven" (qtd. in Barney 106). And in the words of an anonymous writer in the January 1827 issue of the *North American Review*, "The grand lever which is to raise up the mighty mass of this community, is *education*. . . . The *schools* hold, in embryo, the future communities of this land. The *schools* are the pillars of the republic" (qtd. in Mattingly 1). By mid-century, progress was made in constructing the educational substructure that would support and reproduce the social structure of society: in 1837, Massachusetts established a state board of education and appointed Horace Mann as secretary of the board; in 1838, Henry Barnard was named secretary of the Connecticut Board of Education; and in 1852, Massachusetts passed the nation's first compulsory attendance law.

As the move toward a universal common school education for European American children gained momentum, so did the move toward the inclusion of composition in a school's curriculum. Occasional signs of instruction in composition were visible early in the century. The curriculum of the New York African free schools shows that in 1820, students there were receiving instruction not only in "the elementary branches of reading, writing, arithmetic, and geography," but also in "astronomy, navigation, advanced composition, plain sewing, knitting, and marking" (qtd. in Woodson 99). Not, however, until the 1830s and 1840s did signs appear in a number of venues that language instruction was expanding its scope to include not just reading and memorizing and parsing text, but also composing text. In 1833, Samuel Hall argued that in addition to arithmetic, grammar, writing, geography, and history, the study of composition should be "pre-eminent" (102). In 1831, Roswell Smith, in his *English Grammar on the Productive System*, asked students to write sentences in conjunction with the study of grammar. In 1832, Richard Green Parker published *Progressive Exercises in Composition*, his enormously popular composition textbook that was among the first to emphasize practice. And in 1836, in the first edition of the first volume of *Common School Assistant*, "A Monthly Paper, for the Improvement of Common School Education," a writer of a letter to the editor lamented the unevenness of composition instruction in the common schools and called for composition to "receive its due share of attention" for the common good ("Composition," letter to the editor 36). Unlike eighteenth- and the earliest nineteenth-century writers—among them Joseph Priestley, David Irving, John Andrews—who used the term *composition* to refer to a genre or a set piece, writers by mid–nineteenth century began to use *composition* to mean the teaching of writing in school.

One of the chief ways educational reformers worked to promote public education and disseminate information was by the founding of educational journals. Prominent at the time and an important resource that today's historians have yet to fully explore were, for example, *American Journal of Education*, *American Annals of Education*, the *Common School Journal*; and the *Connecticut Common School Journal*.[4] It was in the *American Journal of Education*—in 1830—that a writer, lamenting that students were not writing weekly themes, suggested that the painter's rule "to pass no day without a line" should be applied to schools, and specifically to the writing of compositions ("Composition," *Am Journal* 235).[5] It was also in the *American Journal of Education* that Henry Barnard pressed for teachers and students to move beyond what Miles Myers, writing today, describes as "signature literacy" (39–62) to the actual writing of compositions. As part of a major report on Connecticut schools, Barnard listed the questions he had asked of all Connecticut common school teachers between the years 1838 and 1841 about their teaching of composition. Important to note is that while these questions supported instruction in composition, and I highlight them for that reason, they were underwritten by Barnard's interest in graded schools, and teacher responses helped Barnard prepare his 1842 document recommending that "school" be separated into primary grades, intermediate grades, and high school. While the composition questions may not seem innovative or progressive to a contemporary reader, so much language instruction in the early nineteenth century was grounded in rules rather than practice, or in rules without practice, that Barnard's questions are a useful indication that practice was gaining favor among educators. I include all ten questions here because they provide an informative overview of a then-progressive educator's outlook on writing instruction. The questions appeared in the supplement to the 1855–1856 volume of the *American Journal of Education*:

Connections to science?
Empiricism

role of illustrations

ideology

1. Do you classify your pupils in reference to teaching composition?
2. Do you accustom your youngest pupils to write or print words and short sentences on the slate, from your dictation?
3. Do you ask them to print or write something about what they have seen in coming to school, or read in the reading lesson?
4. As a preliminary exercise in composition, do you engage them in familiar talk about something they have seen in their walk, and has happened in and about the school? and when they have got ideas, and can clothe them orally in words, do you allow them as a privilege to write or print the same on the slate or paper?
5. Do you give out a number of words, and then ask your pupils to frame sentences in which those words are used?
6. Do you require your older pupils to keep a journal, or give an account of the occurrences of the day, as an exercise in composition?
7. Do you instruct your pupils as to the most approved form of dating, commencing, and closing a letter, and then of folding and addressing the same for the post-office?
8. Do you require your pupils to write a letter in answer to some supposed inquiries, or about some matter of business?
9. Do you request your older pupils to write out what they can recollect of a sermon or lecture they have heard, or of a book they have been reading?
10. At what age do your pupils usually commence writing easy sentences or compositions? (Barnard, "Educational Labors" 692)

A few years after Barnard asked these questions of Connecticut teachers, similar questions were being asked of candidates for the position of "master" in a Boston grammar school. These questions, focusing like Barnard's on practice and pedagogy, appeared in the *Common School Journal* in 1847 and included the following: "What would be your first exercise in teaching composition?" "When would you require single sentences to be written on the slate?" "When would you require essays?" "Would you converse upon the subject given out?" (Questions to Candidates 380).

For all this increasing interest in and emphasis on including composition in the curriculum, to suggest or assume that this transition was anything but messy or irregular would be mistaken. In 1852, William Fowle repeated a story that appeared in the September 1849 *Common School Journal* about teachers who themselves struggled with composing:

> At an Institute in Massachusetts, we required 117 teachers to write what they could in fifteen minutes, on the subject of "Happiness." At the end of fifteen minutes, but seven teachers had done any thing, and four of these had only requested to be excused from writing. Fifteen minutes more were allowed; then fifteen more; then the fourth fifteen; when but fifteen or twenty teachers gave up any thing, and not one gave up any thing deserving the name of composition. (Fowle 375)

And as Emma Besig notes, although composition entered one New York school as early as 1763, composition was not listed by itself as a New York Regents' subject until 1890 (41–44, 130–42).

The concept of childhood. For all its inconsistencies, the transition from memory-based language instruction to practice-based instruction marked a sea change in nineteenth-century schools. And one important contributing factor to this change was the (re)visionary thinking of some teachers and advocates of public school mass education. An interdependent contributing factor was a major epistemological change that occurred as eighteenth-century neoclassicism gave way to nineteenth-century romanticism and the concept of childhood was reconstructed.

In 1960, social historian Philippe Ariès, author of *Centuries of Childhood*, was among the first writers to argue that childhood is a social and political construction, that the idea of childhood did not exist in the Middle Ages, and that as culture changes, so the concept of childhood changes.[6] Until the second part of the eighteenth century, many peoples believed, for example, that children were born in total depravity and that the work of adults was to regenerate children through rigorous discipline and the taming of their spirits; hence the flogging, the caning, the dunce cap that are so often represented in colonial schoolrooms. As this view toward childhood was replaced by a more benign view, one that stressed the child's innocence rather than the child's depravity, it also incorporated new understandings of child rearing and of the intellectual development of children.

The writers who contributed to a recognition of the intellectual developmental patterns of children and the implications of those patterns on "school" are many and well known; foremost among them, of course, are Enlightenment thinkers Locke and Rousseau, but also included are educational reformers such as Pestalozzi, Johann Herbart, and Friedrich Froebel. Although writing from different perspectives, these are the writers who, in their texts on education, first argued that children are not miniature adults, that children are developmentally different from adults, and that children learn—and need to be taught—in ways consistent with their abilities. Signs of this changing attitude toward children appear in the emergence of popular books that offered mothers nurturing advice for raising their children (I think of Lydia Maria Child's *The Mother's Book* and John Abbott's *The Child at Home*) and in the developing interest in early childhood education.

And signs of change also begin to appear in textbooks written for children. Prior to this understanding of children's development, many early nineteenth-century texts written for children used language of the adult world, their claims to the contrary notwithstanding. The first U.S. edition (1816) of John Rippingham's *Rules for English Composition, and Particularly for Themes* was intended, as the title announces, "for the use of schools, and in aid of self instruction." Indeed, Rippingham writes in his introduction, "Great care has been taken to render this treatise suitable to the capacity of youthful intellect" (x). He goes on, however, to open his text with these sentences: "A theme is only the miniature of a declamation, essay, oration, or sermon. In each of these species of composition a subject is proposed, an inference drawn; and arguments adduced to support and authorise that conclusion" (17). Further, he proposes what he terms "Simple Subjects," such as "Justice," "Adversity," "Pride," "Compassion," and "Avarice" and "Simple Subjects and Their Contrasts," such as

"Parsimony and Prodigality" and "Emulation and Sloth" (32). Like other books of its kind, Rippingham's was written as a small version of an adult book and did not recognize that a child's learning process might be different from that of an adult. Although these books were small in size and thus suited to a child's holding them, they used a very small type font, had long paragraphs and little white space, and few if any illustrations. If there were illustrations, they were likely to appear on the frontispiece, to be decorative rather than instructive or pedagogical, and to feature Alexander Anderson's often-reproduced engraving of "Minerva" rather than an illustration of a school-age child. More importantly, the books used language and concepts that in their level of abstraction were not accessible to a child.

Criticism of using abstract language in texts for young students began as early as 1823 in William Russell's *Suggestions on Education; Relating Particularly to the Method of Instruction Commonly Adopted in Geography, History, Grammar, Logic and the Classics*. In that work, Russell pointed to the absurdity of writing books for beginners in language that they could not comprehend. He quotes one of the easiest parts from Murray's grammar ("A or An is styled the indefinite article: it is used in a vague sense to point out one single thing of the kind, in other respects indeterminate") and argues for the futility of expecting children to comprehend words like *indefinite, vague, indeterminate* (26–27). And, of course, one of the most powerful statements on behalf of educating children as children and not as miniature adults comes from Richard Whately in his 1828 *Elements of Rhetoric*:

> Look at the letter of an intelligent youth to one of his companions . . . describing the scenes he has visited, and the recreations he has enjoyed, during a vacation; and you will see a picture of the youth himself—boyish indeed in looks and stature—in dress and in demeanour; but lively, unfettered, natural. . . . Look at a theme composed by the same youth, on "Virtus est medium vitiorum," or "Natura beatis omnibus esse dedit," and you will see a picture, of the same boy, dressed up in the garb, and absurdly aping the demeanour, of an elderly man. Our ancestors . . . were guilty of the absurd-

ity of dressing up children in wigs, swords, huge buckles, hoops, ruffles, and all the elaborate full-dressed finery of grown up people of that day. It is surely reasonable that the analogous absurdity in greater matters also . . . should be laid aside. (23–24)

Criticism of "learning by rote" was also growing; Thomas Dick, for example, in his 1836 treatise *On the Mental Illumination and Moral Improvement of Mankind*, thought it "absurd" and "preposterous" to ask children to memorize definitions and technical rules of grammar (181).[7]

Concurrent with the growth of common schools, the developing concept of childhood and the criticism of books used for children's education were significant developments in the art of printing. In *The Book in America*, Hellmut Lehmann-Haupt explains that after three centuries of stability, printing changed "from an art to an industry" as a result of three significant changes from 1800 to 1850: the evolution of new principles in type casting and setting, of new designs in press building, and of the capability of manufacturing paper, by machine, in large quantity and in sheets of any size. Embedded in these changes was "stereotyping," the process in which a papier-mâché mold was made from type that was set; a metal plate was made from the mold, and then from the plate, books that required few or no changes could be printed frequently and in large quantities (64, 74, 133). Such books included catechisms, copies of the Bible, the English masterpieces, popular American works, and, of course, textbooks. One result of the tandem changes occurring in education and in printing was a burst of subject-specific textbooks created specifically for children. While primers and hornbooks were available from the earliest days, there were, in the first half of the nineteenth century, as John Nietz points out in *Old Textbooks*, spellers, readers, grammars, arithmetics, geographies, American histories, civil government texts, physiologies, and penmanship, art, and music books. And there were composition texts as well, not just rhetorics, and not just composition texts for secondary students as Nietz suggests, but composition texts for beginning students. Most often produced by printers, who in some cases were also publishers, they were written by clergy, by teachers, and by textbook compilers; and their shelf life spanned a tremendous range. As I will demonstrate in later chapters, the absence of a single curriculum and the absence of a textbook industry to authorize what was published meant that a range of pedagogies was represented in the composition texts and, even more powerfully, that texts were a site for innovation.

In spite of their differences in theory or pedagogy, composition textbooks, like nineteenth-century schoolbooks for all disciplines, were embedded in their culture in a variety of ways. Henry Giroux, Joel Spring, and other contemporary scholars in education have made the case that school is designed to reproduce the dominant culture and work on its behalf; in her study of nineteenth-century textbooks in all school subjects, Ruth Elson argues that textbooks themselves are, as a rule, "guardians of tradition." Miriam Brody both elaborates and illustrates those arguments, claiming that the nineteenth-century school's emphasis on memory and recitation encouraged the "submission to routine," the "rule-following diligence," and the "toleration of monotony" that would prepare students for the transformation of agrarian workers into factory laborers (108).[8]

Regardless of the specific subject matter that examples in textbooks were illustrating, they placed a heavy emphasis on personal discipline, self-sacrifice, duty, obedience, and especially in the earlier decades of the century, on taste. In Thomas Palmer's 1839 award-winning *Teacher's Manual*, he includes a "Table of Virtues, with Their Opposite Vices" (207). Some of these 104 virtues and vices also appeared in the popular nineteenth-century composition books as topics for compositions. "Prudence" and "Rashness," "Obedience" and "Disobedience," "Industry" and "Indolence" are, for example, both in Palmer's list for behavior and in Richard Green Parker's well-known "list of subjects" for theme writing (*Progressive Exercises* [PE] 97–102). In James Currie's *Principles and Practice of Early School Education* (1887), there is a section on the moral training of a child, and once again appear some of the same topics for instruction that Parker uses as writing prompts: kindness, honesty, modesty, and punctuality (82–85).

Elson notes that nineteenth-century texts did not pretend neutrality or even suggest that there were optional modes of behavior: "The value judgment is their stock in trade: love of country, love of God, duty to parents, the necessity to develop habits of thrift, honesty, and hard work in order to accumulate property, the certainty of progress, the perfection of the United States" (338). It is also true, of course, that the century's textbooks represented the values and lives of the European American, Christian *haute bourgeoisie* and were written for its members and that *European American* really signified *Anglo-American*. The families that students read about and saw pictured in their nineteenth-century composition books had summer houses, playrooms, pet kittens and rabbits, and sometimes even ponies; and it wasn't unusual to see a young girl sitting in a rocker with her feet resting on an upholstered footstool. In some ways, the textbooks were written for the children of the citizens who saw their lives represented in popular magazines such as *Harper's* and *Godey's*. The problem with the illustrations is that at least in some districts and in urban areas, the school population was more inclusive than the readership of these magazines, and thus while some students saw their own families represented in the illustrations of a composition book and were left to imagine life on a farm or life in poverty, other students—and Butts and Cremin estimate that before the Civil War, ninety percent of Americans lived on farms (237)—were left to imagine life with upholstered footstools or rocking horses. And children of the poor and children of color were unlikely to see positive representations of their families in textbooks.

Post–Civil War Industrialization and the Turn to the Practical

The history of a language is not the skill of using it; and a boy who is worried a year in obsolescent niceties of punctuation, or carried into the upper heaven of taste, sublimity, beauty, and general metaphysics, without seeing sun, moon, or stars, will probably derive little pleasure or benefit from his study.
—Simon Kerl, *Elements of Composition and Rhetoric*, 1869

I would not assign to a girl of fifteen as a theme for a composition, "Ignatius Loyola," and then advise her to consult Ranke's "History of the Popes" to get the needed information. The girl of fifteen, as I know her, would not do more than transfer something from Ranke to her own pages: she would care nothing for Loyola. You would get a composition; you would mark it; but you must have been asleep if you thought it did the girl any good.

—C. W. Bardeen, *A System of Rhetoric*, 1884

Every schoolboy has written his essay on the virtues, and every schoolgirl has filled her allotted number of pages with vague generalities regarding Sunshine and Shadow. Consign all such subjects to the limbo of Dr. Quackenbos' "Rhetoric."

—Ernest Huffcut, *English in the Preparatory Schools*, 1892

While textbooks at the end of the century no longer devoted entire chapters to "taste," vestiges of "taste" as a cultural trope remained visible. Even when as late as 1887, J. H. Gilmore directed students to "write six sentences containing a noun in the singular number, possessive case," his footnote explained, "The student will, perhaps, need to be reminded that a higher value is put upon illustrations that evince taste and culture than upon illustrations which, however correct, are trashy and common-place" (102).

As the country turned toward industrialization, as greater numbers of students were attending school, and as more students in school were preparing for work, not for further education, many composition books also turned to the practical; this trend is most visible in books written for high school students near the end of the century.[9] John Scott Clark's 1887 *Practical Rhetoric*; Albert N. Raub's 1887 *Practical Rhetoric and Composition*; Alphonso Newcomer's 1893 *A Practical Course in English Composition*; and Grace H. Smithdeal's 1895 *Practical Grammar, Speller and Letter-Writer* are among the many books that emphasize their move to the practical in their titles. Other writers make their case in their prefaces, Charles Bardeen, for example, writing in his 1883 *A System of Rhetoric* for older school-age students, that "the treatment throughout is practical rather than scholastic" (viii). While "practical" may have had an appealing ring to it—and thus, I imagine, have been partly intended to boost sales—these books, as well as those college-level books that stressed the practical, highlighted writing skills for the business world. Instructions for business letter writing and essay topics, such as "Shall I Learn Shorthand?", were highlighted in Benjamin Conklin's 1889 *A Complete Graded Course in English Grammar and Composition* (289), and a suggested topic for argument papers in William D. Hall's 1898 *English Grammar and Composition* was "Manual Training Should Be Introduced Into All Schools" (249).

Late nineteenth-century books for school-age students not only include a turn to the practical, they also begin to position themselves vis-à-vis their own antecedents. In the earliest books of the century, writer after writer made icons of the British rhetoricians; at the end of the century, these icons are of course still visible, but their presence is no longer unquestioned. In 1884, in his book for older students, Charles Bardeen claims that he adds "much that is unusual in textbooks of the kind" and omits "some things that since the time of Campbell and Blair have been considered conventional" (viii); and in 1892, Ernest Huffcut argues that a "discriminating use" of modern authors would be "infinitely more valuable [to students] than the closest study of Campbell, Whately, or Blair" (9).

Also toward the end of the century, many texts reflect the directives of late nineteenth-century manuals for teachers that young students write about the familiar and the concrete, the here and now, rather than about the abstract and the far away.[10] Arguing that pupils should avoid bombast, Bardeen quotes from a student newspaper article in which the editor pokes fun at the student writer's high-flown prose. The student writer begins, "*Night* brings out the *stars*" and goes on to say that "It is only when *sorrow* and *misfortune* have darkened our lives that the *brighter* traits of character, the God-like instincts of man's *nature* shine *forth* amid the surrounding *gloom*." The editor's comment about "night" is that "It also brings out the bugs, but the essay neglected to say so" (306). More directly, Albert Raub said to students, "Leave such subjects as Evolution, Freedom of the Will, and the like to such as understand them more thoroughly" (*Practical Rhetoric and Composition* [PR] 259). Huffcut's comments are among the most pointed I have seen:

> Every schoolboy has written his essay on the virtues, and every schoolgirl has filled her allotted number of pages with vague generalities regarding Sunshine and Shadow. Consign all such subjects to the limbo of Dr. Quackenbos' "Rhetoric." If you doubt that this is the proper place for them, read his list of five hundred and sixty-six subjects for essays, among which one finds such as Spring, Peace, War, Death, Life, Anger, . . . The Comparative Influence of Individuals and Learned Societies in Forming Literary Character in a Nation, and finally, as if neither this world nor the limits of time could confine the knowledge and imagination of a schoolboy, the learned doctor seriously announces as a suitable subject for class-room use, The Immortality of the Soul. We cannot avoid a little disappointment at not finding something about the Kantian Philosophy, Esoteric Buddhism, or Transcendental Physics; but perhaps these omissions are compensated for by the inclusion of the subjects, Mesmerism, Psychology, and Spiritualism. (15–16)

In a genre of texts that in the early part of the century were unflinching in their seriousness, I find the self-reflective use of humor and irony telling: telling about the elaborated understanding of teaching writing to school-age students and telling about the textbook writers' choice to position themselves within the history of writing instruction. I also find that the presence of self-reflection, irony, and humor in a field where at the beginning of the century the memorization and recitation, which characterized instruction, also perpetuated an epistemology that embraced certainty and objectivity, is already a critique, a move to deflate that certainty and objectivity.

In many ways, therefore, school-based language instruction underwent major changes during the nineteenth century; the most significant is that for the first time in history, regular practice in composition became part of a student's school experience: instead of memorizing texts written by adults and then writing what they remembered of those texts, students composed their own texts; instead of writing exclusively about abstract topics, students also wrote about their lived experience; instead of preparing students only for the writing they would do in the university, schools began preparing all students for the writing they would do in their lives. In chapter 2, I turn to one of the major contributing factors to these changes: the "First Books" of composition that were written for young composers.

2 / First Books of Composition

I felt . . . the want of an elementary book of instruction in Composition, suitable for beginners. . . . Those which presented themselves seemed liable to a variety of objections. Some were unintelligible to young pupils; others contained methods of procedure which I considered useless and even pernicious; and others seemed to direct the attention of the learner exclusively to words and phrases, to the entire neglect of *things*; which form the *substratum* of thought, and from which the thoughts should be taught to spring, in order to [assist] the formation of a simple and natural style of expression. It occurred to me, that by making a course of exercises on pictures and real objects the starting point, something might be done towards inculcating a natural and correct, as well as an easy and graceful style of composition.

—John Frost, *Easy Exercises in Composition*, 1839

The early nineteenth-century school-based composition textbooks that contemporary readers are most likely to be familiar with are Richard Green Parker's 1832 *Progressive Exercises* and George Payn Quackenbos's 1851 *First Lessons in Composition*. And with good reason. These are the books that receive most attention from contemporary historians who discuss school-based writing instruction. Sharon Crowley and James Berlin, for example, but also Robert Connors, especially in his "Textbooks and the Evolution of the Discipline," locate the significance of these writers and draw on their work. And these are also the books that were the best-sellers of their day and had a long history in print; for *Progressive Exercises*, for example, the National Union Catalogue lists thirty-three imprint years, from 1832 to 1879.

No full-length biography has been written about either Parker or Quackenbos, but both men are represented in biographical dictionaries. Richard Green Parker was graduated from Harvard in 1817,

George Quackenbos from Columbia in 1843. Both were teachers and founders of schools. Parker was the grammar master in several New England schools, the best known of which were probably Boston's Mayhew School and Franklin School; Quackenbos taught primarily at the Collegiate School in New York City. In addition to their teaching and administrative work, both men wrote prolifically. Often identified as textbook compilers, Parker wrote not only language instruction texts, but also history, geography, philosophy, and physics texts; Quackenbos also wrote philosophy and history texts. The references do not list either of them teaching at the college level, but both of them wrote popular advanced composition texts that they intended for use with college students; Parker's *Aids to English Composition* ("embracing specimens and models of school and college exercises") first appeared in 1844, and Quackenbos's *Advanced Course of Composition and Rhetoric* ("adapted to self-instruction, and the use of schools and colleges") in 1854.

What is remarkable about *Progressive Exercises*, Richard Green Parker's first composition book and the only one intended for school-age students, is this: it is the first full-fledged exercise/activity composition book in our history. That is, unlike the rhetorics of Hugh Blair, George Campbell, and Richard Whately; unlike the early textbooks of say, David Irving or John Rippingham; and unlike the early grammars, it emphasizes practice. In Parker's preface, he writes, "The first exercise or lesson consists in giving the pupil a word, or a number of words, and instead of asking for a definition of them, requiring him to use them in a sentence or idea of *his own*" (iii). Albeit in a limited way, this text marks a milestone in the history of writing instruction. The first thirty-five lessons of the book focus on words, sentences, tropes, and characteristics of style (such as clearness, unity, strength, and harmony), but in lesson 36 (of forty), students are given "directions" for writing simple themes, complex themes, and essays, followed by the often-cited 287-item "List of Subjects" that includes such abstractions as "Clemency," "Compassion," and "Conscience."[1] For Parker's understanding of the principles of composition instruction, he is, as he indicates, indebted to David Booth's *Principles of English Composition*, to George Jardine's *Outlines of a Philosophical Education*, and to John Walker's *Teacher's Assistant*. And these writers are all indebted to the British rhetoricians George Campbell, Hugh Blair, and Richard Whately.

Like Parker's book, Quackenbos's 1851 *First Lessons in Composition* is another book intended for beginning students; like Parker's, it was enormously successful, one source noting that forty thousand copies of *First Lessons* were printed. Like Parker's text, *First Lessons* was also indebted to the British rhetoricians, especially, as Quackenbos himself writes, to Blair. Quackenbos begins his text with lessons on "Letters, Vowels, Consonants, Syllables" and "Words"; he presents sixty-two more lessons on topics such as individual parts of speech, punctuation, different kinds of sentences, and characteristics of style; and then in lesson 63 (of eighty-five), he introduces students to different kinds of compositions. Unlike Parker, Quackenbos begins each lesson catechistically, so just as lesson 1 asks, "What is a letter?" and answers "A letter is a character used to represent a sound of the human voice" (9), lesson 63 asks, "What is Composition?" and answers, "Composition is the means of expressing one's thoughts by means of written language" (130). But like Parker, Quackenbos also emphasizes practice in composing texts. Based for the most part on information the text provides, students are asked, for example, to write letters and descriptions and to imitate a genre such as an historical narrative or a biographical sketch.

I offer this information about texts by Parker and Quackenbos because in many ways these are the texts that have been read as emblems of nineteenth-century, school-based writing instruction, at once those most popular in their day and those most often recognized today. And, in fact, because they introduced the practice of writing into their pedagogy, *Progressive Exercises* and *First Lessons* were and continue to be important texts in the ongoing telling of our story. Here, though, I want to enlarge our story by introducing a different group of texts, texts much less known than those of Parker and Quackenbos, and, importantly, texts that represent an epistemological breakthrough in nineteenth-century writing instruction in the schools; in a word, these were the texts that were written for children as children and that introduced the personal experience essay to composition instruction.

Written between 1838 and 1855, the books I focus on here fall generally into the category that I call "First Books" of composition, that is, books that were intended to introduce students to composition, just as first books in reading or grammar were intended to introduce students to other aspects of the language arts.[2] While students in common schools were most often the audience for these books, sometimes the audience included students in high schools who were not college bound. Unlike the better-known books by Parker and Quackenbos, these books share the following characteristics: they advocate a reform pedagogy, they anticipate some of the ways we teach writing today, and they suggest that the body of important textbooks in composition is broader and more diverse than has been assumed; in sum, they provide the basis for a revised and broadened understanding of how writing was taught in some settings in mid-nineteenth-century America and thus allow us to elaborate the story of our discipline.

The First Books of composition that I draw on most heavily are Charles Morley's *A Practical Guide to Composition* (1838), John Frost's *Easy Exercises in Composition* (1839), Charles Northend's *Young Composer* (1848), Amos R. Phippen's *Illustrated Composition Book* (1854), and F. Brookfield's *First Book in Composition* (1855). These texts have received almost no critical attention, either individually or collectively. Brookfield, Frost, and Morley are briefly discussed in Emma Besig's 1935 Cornell dissertation, "The History of Composition Teaching in Secondary Schools Before 1900." Glen Hess, in his 1949 University of Pittsburgh dissertation, "An Analysis of Early American Rhetoric and Composition Textbooks from 1784–1870," and John Nietz, in his 1966 *Evolution of American Secondary School Textbooks*, mention Northend as well as these writers; Hess refers to the *Illustrated Composition Book* but lists no author for it.[3] Janet Emig lists Frost and Northend in the appendix of a qualifying paper she wrote at Harvard in 1963, entitled "The Relation of Thought and Language Implicit in Some Early American Rhetoric and Composition Texts,"[4] and Edward W. Burrell includes Brookfield and Northend in an "Index of Authors" in his 1964 Harvard dissertation "Authors of English Textbooks Published in the United States, 1845–1855."

In an argument that the reform tradition in nineteenth-century composition teaching began in the lower grades, not in the colleges or high schools, William Woods gives one line of his essay to John Frost but does not discuss the other, lesser-known texts I am working with here. Because Albert Kitzhaber and James Berlin focus on college-level instruction, they do not work with these texts; neither does Connors.

One last preliminary comment about the First Books of composition I am working with is that with the exception of Northend, they rely heavily on illustrations as a teaching tool. In John Nietz's discussion of common school texts in *Old Textbooks*, he shows that very few textbooks before the 1830s were illustrated other than with pictures of alphabet letters (3). By the mid–nineteenth century, it was not uncommon for children's primers or readers to accompany the lessons, or even the stories, with simple engravings not just of letters, but of objects such as a bee or a cat; these illustrations were used primarily as ornament or embellishment, and they most often represented an object, not a scene. Charles Carpenter argues that "quaint pictures that could not fail to catch the eye" were "rare" in language-study books as late as 1876 when Quackenbos's *Illustrated Lessons in Our Language* appeared (107); in fact, neither Richard Green Parker's 1832 *Progressive Exercises* nor Quackenbos's 1851 *First Lessons* uses illustrations in any way. But fairly detailed and complex illustrations were used abundantly in many of the lesser-known, mid-nineteenth-century First Books of composition; in addition to common objects, the illustrations depicted scenes of home life, school life, and work life, and they served as writing prompts for young writers who were asked to describe what they saw in the picture. In these books, the illustrations were not simply embellishment or ornament, they were an integral part of the books' instructional practice: a composing heuristic.

Walker's Pedagogy and the Reform Pedagogies of First Books

In "The Rhetoric of Explanation" and in *Composition-Rhetoric*, Robert Connors argues that the text that most influenced composition books in the early nineteenth century was John Walker's *Teacher's Assistant*. Originally published in London in 1801, the book's 1808

American edition made Walker, according to Connors, "the exemplar for a whole school of composition pedagogy," first in the secondary schools and later at the college level, Walker's principles becoming "the guiding forces in early composition pedagogy" ("Rhetoric" 204–5).

The complete title of Walker's book is *The Teacher's Assistant in English Composition; or Easy Rules for Writing Themes and Composing Exercises on Subjects Proper for the Improvement of Youth of Both Sexes at School.* Like the titles of many early textbooks, Walker's title elaborates (rather than simply names) the goal of his book: giving rules, or what came to be thought of as principles of composition. For each of the book's four main sections—"Themes," "Regular Subjects," "Easy Essays," and "Narrative"—Walker offers a page or two of explanation, then gives a series of sample texts.

In the section on themes, for example, he defines a theme as "the proving of some truth" and then lists the seven-part scheme, which shows his debt to the classical tradition: the proposition, the reason, the confirmation, the simile, the example, the testimony, and the conclusion. The major part of the chapter consists of twenty-one sample themes, with each of the proofs and the conclusion labeled for each theme. Each of the twenty-one themes is based on an aphorism ("Well-begun is half done," "Nip sin in the bud," "No art can be acquired without rules," etc.) and relies on abstract ideas, assumes a shared worldview and moral code, and cites authorities, such as the "moralists of all ages," "wise philosophers," and "ancient moralists." In the section, "Regular Subjects," Walker follows the same organizational plan, but in this chapter, he anticipates what we call expository writing, providing five divisions for regular subjects: "Definition," "Cause," "Antiquity or Novelty," "Universality and Locality," and "Effects."

As Connors points out, Walker is largely responsible for making the distinction between persuasive writing (what Walker calls "themes") and explanatory writing (what Walker calls "regular subjects"). In addition to naming the genres and their distinguishing features, Walker had a further effect on the teaching of writing. Addressing teachers in the eleven pages of his preface and introduction, Walker writes what he terms "Directions to Parents and Preceptors, in the Use of the following Work" (6); it is here that, like so many nine-teenth-century authors, Walker articulates his pedagogical approach to the composing process. For Walker and his followers, students learned to write by learning rules; young writers were not judged capable of inventing their own subject matter; and students wrote about general, abstract topics, not about their personal experiences.

The reform pedagogy, on the other hand, which appeared in the late 1830s and was instantiated in what I am calling First Books, differed from Walker's in three ways. First Book writers began their texts not with rules for writing but with asking students to compose texts; they asked students to generate original text, and they argued that the experience of students' lives was appropriate subject matter for student writing.

Here I interrogate the differences between the Walker pedagogy and the First Books pedagogy on three points: the instructional platform from which students learned to write; the view of young writers' capabilities; and the subject matter deemed appropriate for student texts. I make figural these differences to highlight the onset of the reform tradition and to elaborate the innovation of the little-known First Books.

For Walker, students learned to write by learning rules:

> In the first place, the rules in prose must be written out by the pupil, and explained more fully by the teacher. . . . In the next place, the teacher must read over the Theme distinctly to the pupil, observing the correspondence of each part with the rules. When this is done, the teacher should talk over the Theme to the pupil, by making use of his own words in as familiar a manner as possible; after which he should read the Theme over a second time to the pupil, and then leave him to put it down from memory as well as he is able. (Walker 6)

In Besig's "History of Composition Teaching in Secondary Schools Before 1900," she traces the rule-based beginnings of composition, citing Lindley Murray's dictum in his 1795 grammar, that "English Grammar is the art of speaking and writing the English language with propriety" (qtd. in Besig 23). There was no place for composition until the child, having begun literacy study with the "word," was ready to move to more complex forms, a process that invariably took years. Besig suggests that another reason that the study of composition lagged behind the study of grammar is that the primary teaching method, following the study of Latin, was to memorize and recite rules; a new method would be required for the teaching of composition. Finally, Besig argues that because school masters had so many subjects to teach (she cites one teacher in East New Jersey who was assigned to teach English, Latin, Greek, arithmetic, algebra, trigonometry, and sailing), they of course preferred "hearing rules of grammar to correcting themes" (24).

Given this emphasis on memorizing and rules, it is not surprising that composition began to make its way into the curriculum after the student had spent considerable time on grammar, and as with grammar, composition was to be learned "by the rules." Walker's title includes the phrase, *Easy Rules for Writing Themes and Composing Exercises*. Early in *Rules for Composition, and Particularly for Themes* (1816), Rippingham writes, "The commencement in the art of literary composition, requires nothing more than a gentle exercise of reason. . . . The theory and idiom of the language must be first attained; for who can express his ideas by words the relative dependency of which he has not ascertained" (B2). In a similar vein, in *A Grammar of Composition: Including a Practical Review of the Principles of Rhetoric* (1823), William Russell argues,

> The pupil cannot advantageously commence practical exercises, unless his mind is prepared by recent impressions, and a distinct recollection of those principles of rhetoric, which have a more immediate relation to composition. . . .
>
> When the pupil has reviewed the principles of composition, contained in the rules of rhetoric, he is prepared to apply them; but not, in the first instance, to exercises of his own. Such a transition is too abrupt, and too difficult for the minds of youth, and has generally the effect of embarrassing or of disgusting them. The learner should be permitted first

to trace the application of the rules of rhetoric in the writings of others. (xiii–xiv)

Even in Richard Green Parker's *Progressive Exercises*, a text generally considered to be more forward looking than some of the others written at the time because Parker requires the practice of writing, it is only in lesson 36 (out of forty) that the student begins to write "simple themes." Prior to that, the student has lessons ranging from "Variety in the arrangement of the members of sentences" to "Analysis of compound sentences" to "Allegory" and "Hyperbole." While in Parker's system, students eventually wrote original essays, the standard practice for students in the early nineteenth century was to begin the study of the composing process with rules, not with writing. Walker's text—as well as the texts of other early nineteenth-century writers—is a principal exemplar of that belief.

For First Book writers, students began not with learning rules, but with writing. Two textbook writers who demonstrate this reform are Charles Morley in his *Practical Guide to Composition* (1838) and John Frost in his *Easy Exercises for Composition* (1839). When these books were published, Morley was teaching at Albany's Green Street Seminary and Frost was at Philadelphia's Central High School. Both writers argue for what they call a more natural way of learning to compose than was common in other books. In his preface, Morley writes,

> Children and youth are taught to spell and read what they do not understand, to define without understanding the definitions, and to commit to memory the words of grammar, rhetoric, . . . while scarcely a sentence is understood. . . . The pupil should first gain thoughts, clear conceptions of things, and then proceed to learn their names—this is nature's process with the infant. (*Practical Guide* iv)

Like Morley, Frost also argues against beginning with rules:

> In teaching a child to express himself freely and naturally in conversation, we do not begin by systematically inculcating

the rules of grammar; but by presenting to him subjects suited to his comprehension, and encouraging him to say whatever occurs to him respecting them. Grammar follows afterwards; and he has in a great measure acquired his own language, before he commences the process of analysing it according to scientific principles.

The method which we pursue, in teaching the art of written expression, is founded on the same principle. We have encouraged the pupil to write freely and boldly on a variety of subjects, which we consider well suited to his comprehension, his habits and associations. We trust that he has begun to feel somewhat *at home* in the use of his pen; and we believe that, in consequence of this preparatory course, he will be much less embarrassed and disheartened than he otherwise would on entering upon a systematic course of exercises in the analysis and composition of sentences. (*Easy Exercises* [*EE*] 79–80)

While Morley includes a few pages on figurative language and style at the end of his ninety-six-page book, the major emphasis in his book is on the practice of writing. He doesn't follow the then-common practice of beginning the study of writing with the study of grammar, and he doesn't follow Walker's injunction to begin with memorizing the rules for writing, but he does follow a Walker-like suggestion of beginning with a model text. Unlike Walker, who did not permit the student to see the text, Morley puts the text into the student's hands. The student is asked first to answer questions in response to the text, then to write an essay from a skeleton or ellipsis of the story, then to write the story from memory in the student's own language. Another significant leap from Walker occurs when Morley asks the student to write in response to, "What lesson do you learn from this story?" (*Practical Guide* 9). Following his own advice, Frost also begins with writing, not with rules: the first and major section of his book (seventy-eight pages) is devoted to composing; the second and third sections (thirty-nine pages total), to the rules for sentence structure and figurative language.

Like Morley and Frost, Brookfield also departs from Walker and from the better-known textbook writers of his day, but, in some ways, to an even greater extent. Not only does Brookfield not begin his text with rules for grammar, he omits grammar from his text entirely. Not only does he not give rules for themes or essays, he focuses entirely on description. Brookfield's *First Book in Composition* is, as the title proclaims, "on an entirely new plan." After two short catechistical lessons on composition, Brookfield poses questions to the young student about particular subjects, the answers to which will aid the student "in expressing *your own* thoughts and feelings" and will serve as the basis for the student's description. While Brookfield includes a sample composition that might be written about each subject, he also reminds students to "write *your own answers* to the questions" and thus reminds them that what they write will not exactly replicate the model. Sample questions for "My Kitten" include "Have you a kitten?" "What is its color?" "What kind of a disposition has it?" "What will it do with things it finds on the floor?" (26). Brookfield includes fifty such subjects in his text, his assumption being that students are able to write successful descriptions without first memorizing rules.

The second point on which First Book writers departed from Walker's pedagogy was in the view of the young writers' capabilities. For Walker, young writers were not capable of inventing their own subject matter:

> To order a young beginner to write upon a subject without giving an outline, by laying down some leading points, is the most unreasonable thing in the world. We ought to expect nothing from tender youth but memory; judgment and invention will come by degrees, and ought not to be forced upon the delicate intellects of children too soon. (Walker 4–5)

Memory is thus an important part of Walker's composition pedagogy, and contrary to what we might expect from the second part of the book's title (*Easy Rules for Writing Themes and Composing Exer-*

cises), the student is not—at least as a beginning writer—"writing themes" or "composing exercises" as we understand these writerly activities. In Walker's pedagogy, the pupil copies and memorizes the rules for each kind of text; the teacher then reads a theme selected from the book to the class, discusses the theme, reads it a second time, then instructs the pupil to write down—from memory—what he remembers of the text. The teacher corrects what the pupil has written and has the pupil make a clean copy of the corrected text in order to "imprint the corrections in the pupil's mind, and insensibly make them his own" (7). So persuaded is Walker that students cannot (should not?) begin by writing their own themes that he cautions against students having a copy of the book, for students, knowing that the best text they could produce would be the one that most closely resembled the printed text, might suffer a strong temptation not to memorize what they had heard, but to copy the text that was in the book.

From the rules that Walker lays out for "Regular Subjects," we can assume that he believes students will eventually compose original essays. Connors suggests that the rules, especially as reformulated by Daniel Jaudon, are really an inventional strategy, asking students, for example, to define or explain their subject, to show the cause of it, to show whether the subject was ancient or modern ("Rhetoric" 204–6). While contemporary readers would see this as an inventional strategy, it is nonetheless true that Walker's text—a text intended for young writers—does not suggest that students can begin learning to write by writing. Russell seems to share Walker's opinion that students begin with memorizing rules and studying the writing of others before they begin to write original texts:

> The learner should be permitted first to trace the application of the rules of rhetoric in the writings of others. This stage of practice he finds easy and interesting. It also serves to prepare him for transferring to his own compositions the rules which he has been applying to those of other writers. (*Grammar of Composition* xiv)

It is in the face of directives like these that writers who hold an alternative view stand out. Frost is especially important here because of his pronounced difference.

Frost maintained that at the same time that young students were learning grammatical principles, they could write original compositions. And quoting Shepherd, Joyce, and Carpenter's *Systematic Education*, he pointedly rejects Walker's methods for teaching composing, noting that "Schemes have been given by Walker and others for theme-writing, but we feel strong doubts as to the propriety of shackling the minds of young people with those kinds of forms" (*EE* 120). Instead, *Easy Exercises* contains no elaborate rules for composing, and it does not make memory part of the writing process. Frost begins by asking students to write in response to familiar pictures and scenes, giving what he calls "a few simple directions as to the mode of rendering each object or scene the subject of a short essay in composition" (9). In the first section on animals, for example, one of the pictures is entitled "A Cat that has stolen a Bird." The directions read simply, "You have a very good hint in this picture for a short description and story. A single look at it will set your invention at work" (14). Three engravings of birds—a peacock, a macaw, and a carrier pigeon—ask the students, for example, to "originate some good reflections," to write "a glowing description," to "Describe the process of writing a letter" (figure 2). In a later section, the engravings are more complex. One sketch is named "Scene on the sea shore" and offers these directions: "Describe the scene. The woman appears to be buying a supply of fish from the man who is just returned from a fishing excursion. She will take them to market in her basket to sell. Describe the operations of each of these persons" (54).

Another central feature of Frost's pedagogy is his claim that students could learn to write by writing. Richard Green Parker prescribes beginning with mental gymnastics. He directs students to follow a seven-step "study of the subject" before taking up the pen to record a single idea (*PE* 67–69). Frost, on the other hand, encourages students to begin by writing "freely and boldly," and not to edit prematurely: "the first and most important thing," he writes, "is to be able to originate observations on the subjects presented and to express them in

A Peacock.

Beauty and pride belong to the peacock. You can easily originate some good reflections on his character.

A Macaw.

This beautiful South American bird will furnish occasion for a glowing description.

A Carrier Pigeon.

The peculiar habits of the carrier pigeon and his important uses in some countries should be noticed. Describe the process of writing a letter, tying it under the bird's wing. Give an account of his arrival, and of his return with the answer.

Figure 2. "A Peacock," "A Macaw," "A Carrier Pigeon." John Frost, *Easy Exercises*, 1839, 17.

such language as [the writer's] feelings prompt. If he feel a constant solicitude lest he should make a trifling mistake, this will chill his feelings and give his writing an unpleasant air of stiffness and constraint" (*EE* 58–59). So Frost is not only establishing that a student can write original essays, he is also advocating that students begin the writing process with writing, and he maintains that students can write original compositions, even if their first attempts are very short.

Phippen's 1854 *Illustrated Composition Book* also relies heavily on illustrations to stimulate writing. Instead, however, of using many engravings as Frost does (there are more than 150 engravings in *Easy Exercises*), this writer uses a handful of more elaborate sketches and gives up to eight writing suggestions or prompts for each one. The first engraving, for example, is of an Edenic scene. Like the other engravings in the book, it appears at the top of the page and is encircled by seven writing prompts (the creation story, gardens, animals, Adam and Eve, morning, happiness, and birds); the rest of the 8-by-10-inch page is left blank for the student's original composition.

Both Frost and Phippen offer suggestions for field research as an heuristic. Frost invites students to interview people working in the trades and professions. Phippen tells students: "You must study, converse, observe, go into the fields, into cities, into factories, on board ships, and wherever information can be gained" (1). If students were not memorizing themes, and if they did not have large stores of factual information at hand (they were not all pursuing classical courses of study), they needed to gather information from other sources. Frost and others advocated that students do field research to discover subjects and evidence and then write in response to their observation.

And the third way in which First Book writers departed from John Walker was in the subject matter they judged appropriate for young writers. In Walker's pedagogy, students wrote about general, abstract topics, not about their daily lives or personal experiences. Walker's text directs students in writing exposition, argument, and narrative. From today's vantage point, the absence of any reference to personal writing is conspicuous; even the sample narratives that Walker offers are classical stories rather than stories that would emerge from the writer's life. Two of the sample narratives, for example, that students would memorize and then copy are "Fidelity respected by Enemies" (an account of the battle of Philippi) and "The false Happiness of Tyrants" (an account of Damocles and Dionysus). "Sketches and Outlines" (from which the student would reconstruct a narrative) are given for topics such as these: "Courage and Judgement united in Necessity" (the story of a Roman battle with the Albans) and "Friendship continuing after Death" (an account of the friendship of Titus Volumnius and Marcus Lucullus). In none of the essays the student hears is there any attempt to cite or value personal experience, and certainly not the experience of the student. In Walker's pedagogy, students never do get to what Walker calls "that terrible task of writing their own thoughts" (166).

As Robert Connors points out in "Personal Writing Assignments," Walker's pedagogy was "picked up and used by other authors, especially in the United States, where the common schools were teaching composition to an ever-larger percentage of children" (170). Connors goes on to argue that "newer composition texts also offered lists and lists of potential subject assignments, all of which were completely, utterly, relentlessly impersonal" (170–71); that composition teachers did not begin to reject abstract, impersonal topics until after 1860, that John Hart's 1870 *Manual of Composition and Rhetoric* "opened the floodgates to personal writing in composition courses" (173), and that Hart offers the first statement of the classic "How I Spent My Vacation" assignment.

While it is undeniable that many of the better-known books, like Walker's, focused exclusively on the impersonal, it is also true that in what were then alternative sites and in what are even today little-known books, personal writing was in evidence earlier than Connors shows. In Bronson Alcott's school (founded in 1834 and known as the Temple School because it was conducted in the Masonic Temple on Boston's Tremont Street), Alcott's goals were quintessentially transcendental, quintessentially romantic: he wanted to teach the students self-knowledge, he wanted to awaken the genius in each child. In addition to the traditional subjects (reading, spelling, writing, arithmetic, and geography), he introduced drawing as a way of learning; more importantly, however, he introduced the journal, his purpose, in

Lawrence Cremin's reading, "to occasion the kind of introspection and self-analysis that would lead the youngster to the truth of his own nature" (*Am Ed: National* 88).

The connection between what Alcott meant by a journal and what we mean by personal experience writing emerges in the writings of Elizabeth Palmer Peabody. Perhaps best known for establishing the first English-speaking kindergarten in this country and for her voluminous publications about the education of children, Peabody assisted Alcott with his school for a while, instructing the children in Latin and arithmetic. As part of her work with Alcott, she also conducted an early form of ethnographic research; on a daily basis over a period of time, she observed Alcott teach, recorded what she saw, and published her findings in 1835 and 1836 in her book called *Record of a School*. In her notes, Peabody not only observes that Alcott set aside time for his students to write in their journal every day (she notes that when she arrived in the classroom in the mornings, the children were already working in their journals), but she also explains how Alcott worked with the journals:

> January 3, 1835: At quarter of one, the journals of the scholars were brought up, and Mr. Alcott began to read [aloud] one girl's journal, which described all she had done in school and at home this last week—and some of her thoughts. It proved she had altered and improved a good deal, since she came to school three months ago. A boy's journal was next read; it was a very pleasant account, and contained some good resolutions of conforming to the rules of the school. (Peabody 47)

On January 24, Peabody records,

> [Alcott] told one journalist that he wished he would put more of himself into the journal; the boy of that journal was a mere automaton; he came in, and went out, and did things, but he never felt or thought. . . .
>   Mr. Alcott praised the writing of one of the girls in her

journal, and said that the journal gave something of her mind. (95)

Given Alcott's goal of teaching self-knowledge, it is not surprising that he praised students for recording their personal thoughts and feelings; encouraged them to do so when they weren't; and asked them not to write like automatons. Nor is it difficult for contemporary readers who are studying nineteenth-century writing instruction to contextualize Alcott's work with journals: to read it not as an isolated event, but as a part of a larger historical narrative and in that context, as one of the earliest markers of personal writing in our history. What I find particularly interesting is that Alcott himself recognized that in teaching students to work with personal writing in their journals, he was also providing instruction in composition writing. Peabody wrote in *Record of a School* that while Alcott was using journals to further self-knowledge and self-inspection, he knew that he was also

> assisting [students] in the art of composition, in a way that the rules of Rhetoric would never do. Every one knows that a technical memory of words and of rules of composition, gives very little command of language; while a rich consciousness, a quick imagination, and force of feeling, seem to unlock the treasury. (xxvi)

Forms of experience-based writing, therefore, were taught much earlier in alternative sites than Connors allows; this kind of personal writing also occurred much earlier in First Books of composition than in books for older students. As the accompanying illustration demonstrates (figure 3), John Frost introduced the summer vacation assignment in 1839—thirty years before Hart did—when Frost asked students to "describe your own idea of a pleasant summer holiday" (*EE* 24). Even Quackenbos, in his 1851 *First Lessons in Composition*, asked students to write a letter to their teacher, "giving an account of the manner in which you spent your last vacation" (178).

As I demonstrate in the next chapter, Frost asks students to write out of their personal experience in dozens of places in *Easy Exercises*. The same is true of Charles Northend in *The Young Composer*, of

A summer holiday.

Pleasure of spending holiday in a garden.   Describe your own idea
of a pleasant summer holiday.

Figure 3. "A summer holiday." John Frost, *Easy Exercises*, 1839, 24.

Amos R. Phippen in *Illustrated Composition Book*, and of F. Brookfield
in his *First Book in Composition*. In *The Young Composer*, Northend
asks students to write on such topics as "my school-house and yard,"
or "the street in which I live" (31). In *Illustrated Composition Book*,
students are invited to write about the part of the world they would
like to visit, about their family, about a comet they may have seen,
about the farm where a friend lives. And in Brookfield, to give yet another example of a personal writing assignment: "Subject No. 8" for
writing reads in part, "Almost every one has some pleasant association
with oak-trees and acorns. Should you have such with some particular
oak-tree, give a description of its situation, and of any pleasant scenes
connected with it" (41).

The Beginnings of the Democratization of Writing

In Ann Haley-Oliphant's work on the value of teaching from the
margins in a science class, she draws on Wendell Berry's work about
those places on the earth that are at the edges, the edge of a field or
the edge of the sea, for example. And she shows that these margins

in the natural world are often dismissed as unimportant or irrelevant; that margins represent less stable, less predictable environments; and that margins can only be described in relation to something else. She also demonstrates, however, the freedom of the margins: that new varieties of life are constantly being created in the margins through unanticipated, uncontrolled, and unplanned cross-pollination and intermingling; that the richness in activity, meaning, and responsiveness occurring in the margins may not be easily detected; and that observers must get in deep in the margins to sense the full value of these diverse places (107–42). In this same way, I believe that the little-known, nineteenth-century First Books, like natural margins, were a site for new varieties of life, and that they represented not a monoculture, but a polyculture. They were, in fact, places of possibility.

Albert Kitzhaber notes that by the end of the nineteenth century, secondary and college-level texts were turning to topics based on personal experience and observation; in particular, he cites texts by Fred Newton Scott and Joseph Denney (1897) and by Edward Everett Hale (1896), and paper topics such as "How I learned to like good music," "The First Snowstorm this Year," and "An Early Morning's Fishing" to show that, finally, students were being asked to write "only what [they] knew or could reasonably find out through limited investigation" (106–7). In fact, the authors of some First Books were working with topics such as these as early as 1839.

One factor contributing to the inclusion of concrete, work-related, personal topics in some textbooks was the growing awareness of the need for a literate citizenry in a democracy that accompanied the increased numbers of students attending school. Unlike the college-level books, which were preparing upper-class students for careers in the law and ministry (I think of Samuel P. Newman's 1827 *A Practical System of Rhetoric*, for example), common school and secondary school texts were more often preparing students for trades and professions; and some teachers were registering their frustration with abstract topics that would not facilitate their students' entry into the world of work. Besig quotes this teacher from the 1851 *Massachusetts Teacher*:

We have walked in the churchyard, till we know every epitaph by heart; we have read disquisitions upon patience and virtue; we have perused remarks upon temperance, till it seems that nothing more can possibly be said; and now we ask that our pupils leave these topics, of which they know nothing, and write upon subjects with which they are or may be familiar. Let them write what they *think*, and they will soon find (what is now new to most of them) that they can think with ease. We may not make novelists and poets of all our pupils; it is not desirable we should; the world needs them for nobler purposes; we shall teach them to correspond with propriety, and attend more acceptably through all future life to the demands both of business and friendship. (268–69)

From Frost's *Easy Exercises*, students could write stories and anecdotes about the usefulness of the farmer and the carpenter, about the ways in which haymaking supports all other trades and professions, about beautiful edifices reared by the labor of the stonemason, about "drawing from real objects in order to apply the art to useful purposes" (34). In Northend's *Young Composer*, students are asked to describe the tools and implements of laborers such as the blacksmith, the shoemaker, the tanner, the printer, the carpenter, the mason, and the cabinetmaker (33). In Phippen's *Illustrated Composition Book*, students are told that "all classes of people—farmers, mechanics, merchants, and professional men—must write so many letters, advertisements, notices, agreements," and that "the composition of [these texts] must be accurate to insure success in business" (1). Students are asked to write about "the condition of the factory girls of Lowell" and "the different kinds of mechanics, and the work they do" (figure 4). And in Brookfield's *First Book in Composition*, students are told, "You can describe the display of flowers, fruits, and vegetables, at a Horticultural Fair, and the manner in which this is generally conducted; also, an Agricultural Fair, in which a cattle show is the most prominent feature" (101).

The culture's growing attention to and appreciation of labor and the working class—and to writing as a means of successful participation in a democracy—is one way to explain the use of writing prompts

Figure 4. "Factory Girls. Their employments. Describe the condition of the factory girls of Lowell or some other place; their industry and intelligence.
"The Mechanic. Mention the different kinds of mechanics, and the work they do. What branches of study are necessary for a good mechanic. History of some of the most eminent mechanics.
"The Mechanical Powers. Describe the simple mechanical powers, the lever, inclined plane, and pulley. The screw and wheel and axle. Show how these simple powers compose the most complicated engines." Phippen, *Illustrated Composition Book*, 1854, 15.

different from those advocated and demonstrated by Walker. A second explanation for the occurrence of writing based on students' actual lives is the one I turn to in the next chapter: the place of Johann Heinrich Pestalozzi in nineteenth-century, school-based writing instruction.

3 / "No Ideas but in Things"

In rainy weather toadstools spring up on every dung-heap,
and in the same way merely verbal definitions generate a
mushroom-like wisdom which soon dies in the sunshine. A clear
sky is poison to it.
The power of description must precede definition.
—Pestalozzi, quoted in J. A. Greene's
Pestalozzi's Educational Writings, 1916

What can a child, unaided, say about "Spring," and the beauties of
"Hope," the follies of "Youth," and the comforts of "Age," "Memory" and the like? for such subjects he will surely select for himself; he aims high and wants to bring his teacher something worth
reading, and, all untried, doesn't know but his puny efforts can
grasp them. He doesn't know how far off the moon is, only sees
she's bright and pretty, and so spends himself in vain attempts to
reach her. But show him an apple tree and a ladder, and he will
bring you fruit enough.
—"How To Teach Composition," *Connecticut
Common School Journal*, January 1864

Echoes of romanticism in American composition history are frequently traced to Ralph Waldo Emerson. Before Emerson, however,
Bronson Alcott, in his school and in his teaching espoused what we
have come to think of as Emersonian and certainly romantic beliefs:
in Dorothy McCuskey's words, "teaching children to act in accord
with their spiritual natures, to consider nature as the symbol of spirit,
and to look upon words as symbols of spirit" (92). And audible in
Alcott's emphasis on the benevolent nature of the child and a pedagogy that emphasized experience not memorization is the resonating

voice of Johann Heinrich Pestalozzi, Swiss education reformer who lived from 1746 to 1827. Credited with inspiring the pedagogy that came to be known as "object teaching," Pestalozzi is most often identified with the nineteenth-century normal schools that embraced this pedagogy and with educators such as Henry Barnard, Horace Mann, and Edward Sheldon, who were its primary spokespersons. Like Emerson, Pestalozzi was also a conduit for principles of romanticism to move from philosophical treatise and belletristic writings into the American educational system for beginning students and, important for this study, into the composition classroom; unlike Emerson, however, our composition histories have given him little attention.

In composition instruction, Pestalozzi's echoes are most audible in texts for school-age students, and in texts that, for the most part, are not very well known. In fact, an understanding of Pestalozzi's work and thought help us to understand why some of our earliest examples of writing assignments based on the concrete and the familiar—and in some cases on personal experience—were generated not in the colleges, but in the schools. In addition, and in view of current conversations in our field about the value of experience-based writing for beginning college students, it seems relevant to unearth and understand the history of the earliest site of this genre in our increasingly complex and multilayered story of writing instruction.

Writers have long acknowledged a connection between Pestalozzi and the teaching of writing to school-age children. As early as 1824, J. M. Keagy, in his *Essay on English Education*, acclaimed Pestalozzi's theories and wrote that compositions "should at first be no more than simple descriptions of some article in natural history, or some manufacturing process. . . . The present spelling book system, the unlucky invention of ignorant and barbarous times, will then no more paralyze the energies of the youthful mind" (26–28). In her 1929 *Development of Elementary English Language Textbooks in the United States*, Elizabeth Whitemore Baker points to Pestalozzi's influence in A. H. Weld's 1849 *English Grammar* where students are asked to describe objects such as "a piece of sealing wax," "a book," "a penknife," "a chair." In this century, Emma Besig, Glenn Hess, Albert Kitzhaber, and William Woods cite the influence of Pestalozzi on the lower schools toward the end of the nineteenth century. Kitzhaber, for example, claims that by the end of the century, most composition books for school-age students emphasized observation and experience, a "sign" that Pestalozzi's emphasis on adapting the level of the work to the student's developmental ability was "generally accepted by this time" (106).

But while Pestalozzi is given passing mention by some historians, his influence on the American composition classroom is never elaborated. My goal is to construct an elaboration and to argue for Pestalozzi's importance in our history. To help contextualize Pestalozzi for the reader, I begin with a representation of his life and thought. I then move to my primary interests—to what I call the Pestalozzi-Mayo-Frost connection and what I believe is the first trace of Pestalozzi's thinking in an American composition book; to additional "showings" of his educational philosophy in textbooks; and, finally, to considerations of why his work is important to the history of college writing instruction despite the fact that his thinking had its most visible impact on books for school-age students.

Pestalozzi in the American Classroom

> Let the child not only be acted upon but let him be an agent in intellectual education.
>
> —Pestalozzi, letter to J. P. Greaves, 1819

Unlike George Campbell, Hugh Blair, and Richard Whately, Pestalozzi was an educational reformer, not a rhetorician, and his interest was the education of children, not the spiritual or intellectual development of adults. After he abandoned plans for a career in the ministry or law, he made his lifework the teaching of the young and then, teacher training. He was widely known as an advocate of the poor and started a school for abandoned and orphaned children on what was called the *Neuhof*, his farm near the Swiss town of Brugg in the canton of Berne. For all its potential, however, this first "industrial school for the poor" was not highly regarded by the local community, nor was it financially solvent, and after five years, it closed. During the next several decades, Pestalozzi went to Stanz to work with orphans, to Burgdorf to work as an assistant in the village school, and then to Yverdon. It was in Yverdon, from 1805 to 1825, that he conducted an institute for teacher training that was visited by educators from around the world who were interested in his pedagogy.

Reading the accounts of Pestalozzi's career suggests, though, that it was almost in spite of himself that he was successful. His childhood nickname was "Henry the Odd Fellow from Foolstown" (Jedan 24); he was known for his disheveled appearance and for being a bit of a bumbler (according to one story, he accidentally put a knitting needle through his ear); and he was not, finally, very adept at the administration/management skills needed to run a school over the long haul. But because his ideas caught on—as represented in his own and in his disciples' writings—his teacher training school and his pedagogy received international attention, and even in his day, Pestalozzi was celebrated as a politically progressive educator.

Biographies of Pestalozzi and histories of education often point to Pestalozzi's intellectual similarities to Comenius (and through Comenius to Bacon), to Locke, and to Rousseau.[1] In many ways, these thinkers sprang from different soil and worked on different ground: John Amos Comenius (1592–1670) was a Moravian preacher and educator and the author of the first illustrated textbook for children; John Locke (1632–1704) was a British philosopher and the founder of British empiricism; Jean Jacques Rousseau (1712–78) was a Swiss-French philosopher, political theorist, and the father of romantic sensibility. But like Pestalozzi, these European reformers either anticipated or more fully represented Enlightenment thinking and its place in the emergence of the modern world. In various ways, they had faith in science and in the goodness of the human being; they celebrated reason and experience; they spoke out against social ills and tyranny. And in a variety of specific ways and to different degrees, Pestalozzi's thinking about the education of children shows similarities with their thinking.[2]

Comenius (in Czech, Jan Amos Komensky) was one of the first educational theorists to argue that instructional practice should be based on the natural learning patterns of the child and thus that a

child's education was most profitably begun not with general principles but with concrete objects and/or illustrations, that is, with the
senses. *Orbis Pictus*, his 1658 textbook, was used for two hundred
years as a text and is said to be the only textbook that Goethe ever
had. The National Council of Teachers of English "Orbis Pictus Award
for Outstanding Nonfiction for Children" is an example of a contemporary tribute to this work and a means for keeping alive in our collective memory the innovative work of this seventeenth-century educator. Called an illustrated Latin/English dictionary, a picture book,
and an encyclopedia (its English title is *Visible World* and the subtitle
is *"Or a picture and nomenclature of all the chief things that are in the
world"*), Comenius's book illustrates subjects ranging from "crawling
vermin" to "tennis-play." Comenius himself explains the educational
philosophy that underpins *Orbis Pictus* in his *Didactica Magna* (*The
Great Didactic*):

> [T]he commencement of knowledge must always come
> from the senses. . . . Surely, then, the beginning of wisdom
> should consist, not in the mere learning the names of things,
> but in the actual perception of the things themselves! It is
> when the thing has been grasped by the senses that lan-
> guage should fulfil its function of explaining it still further.
> (337)

Here, of course, is a voice that goes back to Francis Bacon's belief in
induction as a way of knowing and a voice that goes forward to Pestalozzi and object teaching; nineteenth-century educator Norman A.
Calkins goes so far as to say that it is Comenius who first promulgates
"the principles and plans of Object Teaching" ("History" 635). An interesting aside is from Will Monroe's *Comenius*: He notes that according to Cotton Mather's *Magnalia*, when Henry Dunster resigned the
presidency of Harvard College in 1654, Comenius was invited to assume the post, but "the Solicitations of the Swedish Ambassador, di-
verting him another way, that Incomparable Moravian became not an
American" (qtd. in Will Monroe, *Comenius* 78–79). Monroe goes on to
note, however, that no other historian has confirmed Mather's account

of this point (78–80), and it is uncertain if Mather was accurate about the Harvard presidency being offered to Comenius.[3]

Based on John Locke's 1690 *Essay Concerning Human Understanding*, Edward Corbett is perhaps the first historian of rhetoric to systematically argue for Locke's contributions to rhetoric and to explain, for writing teachers, Locke's reliance on experience—as conveyed by the senses—as the source of knowledge. It is, however, in Locke's more pointed educational writings—especially in *Some Thoughts Concerning Education* (1693)—that Locke's thinking about the education of children is most fully displayed. In these works, Locke shows that, like Comenius (and we know that Locke had read Comenius), he also believed that education should proceed according to the child's mental development, beginning with the child's own sense perceptions and experiences of the physical world. Locke criticized teaching that relied too heavily on memorization, for example, or that asked the student to write a Latin theme about a subject unfamiliar to the child. About using a dictum such as "Non licet in bello bis peccare" ("In Warfare, one is not allowed to blunder twice") as a writing prompt, Locke wrote this in *Some Thoughts Concerning Education*:

> And here the poor Lad, who wants Knowledge of those Things he is to speak of, which is to be had only from Time and Observation, must set his Invention on the Rack, to say something where he knows nothing; which is a sort of Egyptian Tyranny, to bid them make Bricks who have not yet any of the Materials. (150)

Simply put, Locke argued that example and practice are better than precept and thus should be the foundations for the child's education.[4]

Perhaps better known for his educational theories than either Comenius or Locke, Jean Jacques Rousseau is, like them, an advocate of the natural learning patterns of a child, going so far as to say that before children are twelve, they have no need for book-centered education and that "experience" is a better teacher than "verbal lessons." In *Émile*, for example, Rousseau writes, "I do not like verbal explanations. Young people pay little heed to them, nor do they remember them. Things! Things! I cannot repeat it too often. We lay too much stress upon words; we teachers babble, and our scholars follow our example" (143).

It would be a mistake to point to similarities among these four writers—Comenius, Locke, Rousseau, and Pestalozzi—and assume they were alike in every aspect of their thinking about a child's education. One important difference between Locke and the others is that Locke's image of the child's growth and development, perhaps because of his emphasis on empiricism, was mechanistic. In one of his most often-quoted sentences, from *Some Thoughts*, Locke refers to the child's mind "only as white Paper, or Wax, to be moulded and fashioned as one pleases" (187); Comenius, on the other hand, offering an organic metaphor, argued, "Nature has implanted within us the seeds of learning, of virtue, and of piety. The object of education is to bring these seeds to perfection" (qtd. in Jeffreys 55–56). And Pestalozzi, like Comenius and certainly like Rousseau who believed in the child's innate abilities, also believed that the child was "a little seed," had the innate potential for maturity, and that "gradual imperceptible advance" was "nature's way" of educating the child (qtd. in Downs 131). According to Pestalozzi's British disciple Charles Mayo, the child is not like a stone that grows by "mechanical deposition of matter on its surface" but is rather like a plant that "grows by the continual expansion of those organs which lie folded up in its germ" (170); a child is "a bud not yet opened," and "when the bud expands every leaf unfolds, not one remains behind" (186).

A key difference between Rousseau and Pestalozzi is that in Rousseau's work on education, he was interested in the Émiles, the children of privilege whose education often had an early and strong beginning in the home and would continue at fine schools, and he did not believe that the poor had a need for education. Pestalozzi, on the other hand, gave his primary attention to the children of the poor who, but for reform, probably would have had no access to formal education; behind this advocacy of popular education or universal education were Pestalozzi's convictions that the goal of education was to provide "useful knowledge" and that social and political reform were, in fact, grounded in education. Hence, he wanted students to have access to what we have come to understand as vocational education. Even though Locke was primarily concerned with a "gentleman's education," he also believed in and advocated what he called "working schools," but the forces that were to become the Industrial Revolution were not yet strong enough in Locke's day to support schools for children of the poor.

So there was a range of individual similarities and differences among these progressive theorists. Their key similarity, however, is what I focus on here: Comenius, Locke, Rousseau, and Pestalozzi shared a concern with tailoring education to coincide with the child's developmental level. Even before the work of contemporary cognitive psychologists, these writers contended that children learned differently from adults and that the starting place for a child's education was not with abstract principles but with concrete experiences.

Of these four theorists, it was Pestalozzi who most carefully articulated his learning theory, and it was he alone who developed instructional practices for the classroom. Central to Pestalozzi's thought and the basis for "object teaching" was the concept of *Anschauung*, the notion that learning is based on observation and experience and, hence, occurs naturally when students have direct contact with the material being studied. As many scholars have noted, there is no exact English equivalent for *Anschauung*; translations include, for example, "observation," "sense experience," "sense impression," "perception," "sense perception." Instead of relying on books for information, Pestalozzi, like Rousseau, routinely took students on excursions and field trips to the countryside, and they used real, concrete objects in their classes. For Pestalozzi, this learning began with the child's mother teaching the child "to observe." She would show the child concrete objects and help the child to see the parts or the qualities of these objects; only then would she offer the word for the object and for its parts or qualities. So that, for example, a child would touch a piece of glass, and based on it, learn words like *artificial, brittle, bright, thin, hard, clear, transparent*, hence the phrase "object teaching." When an actual object could not be brought before a child, Pestalozzi allowed the introduction of pictures, but the actual objects were always preferred. Complementing Pestalozzi's belief in observation and experience was his conviction that the child should play an active role in his or her education and, thus, stand not just as the recipient or the person acted upon but also as an agent in his or her own learning process. Pestalozzi believed that "it is life that educates" and that children should never be told what they can find out for themselves.

Rejecting "the empty chattering of mere words" (Cubberly 264), rejecting "memory and discipline and conformity" to teach young children (Gutek, *Pestalozzi* 12), Pestalozzi criticized rule-based learning and argued that schools were wrong to interfere with a child's natural learning process. In his 1801 *How Gertrude Teaches Her Children*, his most famous work, he complains,

> But consider again for one moment the enormity of this crime! We leave our children in the full enjoyment of Nature until they are five years old. We give free play to their impressions; the children are beginning to feel their own strength. They are steeped in the sensory joys of freedom. . . . Nature has followed with all definiteness the path which she pursues in the development of the sensuously happy wild animal, when suddenly, after five years of blissful sensuous life, we banish all Nature from their eyes; . . . we herd them together like sheep in an evil-smelling room; for hours, days, weeks, months, and years, we chain them unmercifully to the contemplation of miserable and monotonously unexciting alphabets, and condemn them to an existence which, in comparison to their former life, is repulsive in the extreme. (qtd. in J. A. Green 89)

Pestalozzi went even further to say that when children were inattentive to a lesson, teachers should accept the responsibility. In *Letters on Early Education*, he wrote, "[W]hen a child is doomed to listen in silence to lengthy explanations or to go through exercises which have nothing in themselves to relieve or attract the mind, this is a tax upon his spirits which a teacher should . . . abstain from imposing" (152). For Pestalozzi, the path of learning was the path of nature; that is, learning proceeded from the near to the far, from the known to the unknown, from the simple to the complex, and from the concrete to the abstract. And if a child was not able to grasp the concepts of the lesson, it was, in Pestalozzi's language, "absurd" to ask the child to learn by rote what he called "sound without sense."

Most early nineteenth-century writing instruction for children was based on exactly those principles that Pestalozzi rejected. As Robert Connors points out in *Composition-Rhetoric*, the best-known texts for school-age children were based on John Walker's work and embraced a pedagogy of rules, memory, and abstractions. Pestalozzi was not a writing teacher, and I find no evidence that his students wrote compositions, but through his influence on some nineteenth-century composition texts, a new space was created in writing instruction for students to write about the objects and, in some cases, the experiences of their own lives.

The Pestalozzi-Mayo-Frost Connection

In chapter 2, I introduced John Frost's *Easy Exercises* as one of several texts that broke new ground in composition pedagogy. In this chapter, I feature Frost (1800–1859) and his work because, while many nineteenth-century texts for school-age children have visible signs of Pestalozzi's thinking, it is in Frost's work that I find the first and the most detailed traces. After studying at Bowdoin College for a year, Frost went on to Harvard where he was graduated in 1822. At Harvard, he studied with Edward T. Channing, Boylston Professor of Rhetoric and Oratory, and he won the Bowdoin Prize for original dissertations in 1822 (Ralph Waldo Emerson won this same prize in 1821). Frost spent his career teaching and serving as principal at Boston's Mayhew School, as principal of a girls' school in Philadelphia, and as professor of belles lettres at Philadelphia's Central High School (the second oldest public school in the United States, a school that still exists, and a school that has an elaborate archive and a part-time archivist on its staff). In 1843, he received an honorary LL.D. from Franklin and Marshall College; and then, in 1845, he left teaching to work full-time compiling books. With assistance from other writers, and from engravers and designers, he compiled more than three hundred books, primarily histories and biographies, on subjects as diverse as American generals and ancient Greece. John Frost is among the significant personages included in an essay on "autography" in the November 1841 issue of *Graham's Magazine*, he was a member of the American Institute of Instruction, and his obituaries in the Philadelphia dailies (December 1859 and January 1860) refer to him as a "familiar face" in literary and social circles in Philadelphia. The fullest biographical account I have seen of Frost's life appears in Joseph Palmer's *Necrology of Alumni of Harvard College* (1864).

Among his many works, Frost published three grammars: in 1828, *Five Hundred Progressive Exercises in Parsing*; in 1829, *Elements of English Grammar*; and in 1842, *A Practical English Grammar* (*PEG*). Like *Easy Exercises in Composition*, Frost's 1842 *Practical English Grammar* is also illustrated. To practice their knowledge of a grammatical concept or rule, students were asked to write sentences describing what they saw in a picture, so, for example, for the engraving entitled "The Travellers," students were instructed, "Write *simple* sentences illustrative of this picture" (*PEG* 130).

Easy Exercises in Composition is Frost's only composition book. The second and stereotyped edition (published in March 1839, one month after the first edition in February 1839, and the edition I quote from throughout this text) was reprinted through eight editions, the last appearing in 1841. The book is 120 pages long and uses copious illustrations as writing prompts; it was intended, as the title indicates, "for the use of beginners"; and it was used, among other places, at Philadelphia's Central High where Frost was professor of belles lettres from 1838 to 1845. At a March 26, 1839, meeting of the Board of Controllers of Public Schools, First School District of Pennsylvania, the board agreed that *Easy Exercises* would "be introduced as a Class Book to be used at the discretion of the Teachers in all the Public Schools, including the High School and Model School" (*EE* 4).

Two central features distinguish *Easy Exercises* from better-known, comparable books of its day and mark its connection to Pestalozzian thought. First, like a number of other First Books, this one begins with writing practice, not, as was customary in nineteenth-century texts, with grammar and rules. Second, the text asks students to write essays about the objects and scenes in the book's illustrations. Of the book's three sections, "Introductory Course of Easy Exercises," "Structure of Sentences," and "Figurative Language," the section on composition appears first and is the longest. The more common pattern for a mid-nineteenth-century text, the pattern evident in texts by Richard Green Parker and George Quackenbos, for example, is that the author begins with parts of speech and extensive grammatical and sentence-level exercises, and then gradually moves to a few pages of instruction about composition writing. Not so with Frost. Frost begins not with rules, not with sentence-level exercises; rather, offering very few models and very little explanation or prescription, he begins by asking the students to write essays. In the text, students are shown illustrations of objects and/or scenes and asked to write descriptive or, in some cases, narrative accounts in response to them. The first writing task of the book, for example, appears in conjunction with an engraving of a deer and reads, "Describe the picture. Write what you know concerning the animal, its habits, its native countries, and its uses" (*EE* 10). (See appendix 1 for examples of the two different approaches to writing instruction: Frost begins *Easy Exercises* with writing; Quackenbos begins *First Lessons* with rules.)

In addition to this Pestalozzi-like emphasis on learning to write by writing, not by memorizing rules, there is an even more pronounced link to the Swiss educator in John Frost's book. Naming Elizabeth Mayo (1793–1865) as one of his sources, Frost borrows material from her book on Pestalozzian object lessons and transforms that material into writing assignments that are grounded in observation and experience. Here I trace the path that illuminates this second way in which Frost is indebted to Pestalozzi. The path proceeds from Elizabeth Mayo's teaching in her brother Charles Mayo's Pestalozzian school and the publication, in London, of her 1830 text, *Lessons on Objects*; to Frost's 1835 edition of Elizabeth Mayo's book which he called *Lessons on Common Things*; and finally to Frost's 1839 *Easy Exercises in Composition*.

During the late 1820s, Elizabeth Mayo was a teacher in a Pestalozzian school in Cheam, England, run by her brother Charles, who, along with many other teachers from European countries and the United States, studied with Pestalozzi at Yverdon, then returned home to implement Pestalozzi's principles in his educational practices. Elizabeth Mayo did not write her classroom lessons for publication, but in 1830, in London, she published her classroom-based instructional/pedagogical materials in a book she called *Lessons on Objects as Given in a Pestalozzian School at Cheam, Surrey*. This book, which came to be known as *Lessons on Objects*, contains five series of lessons, arranged in increasing order of difficulty, designed to replicate the child's natural learning order. When John Frost edited the first American edition of this book in 1831 as *Lessons on Things*, he extended the title's description to "Intended To Improve Children in the Practice of Observation, Reflection, and Description; on the System of Pestalozzi." With the exception of the title change and minor editing, this edition of Mayo's work is almost identical to her London edition and, like the London edition, contains no illustrations. Frost's 1835 edition, however, which he called *Lessons on Common Things; Their Origin, Nature, and Uses*, shows a significant change from Mayo's work—and from Frost's own earlier edition. To the 1835 edition, Frost added fifty-two engravings to illustrate the objects and, in some cases, wrote captions for the engravings. One significance of these engravings is that a number of them reappear in *Easy Exercises* as the basis for writing assignments, assignments based sometimes on objects themselves and sometimes on an experience the student had that was related to the object.

Mayo writes in the 1832 edition of her work that the goal of her book is to "bring education more into contact with the child's own experience and observation, and to find in *him* the first link in the chain of his instruction" (viii). As Mayo explains in her preface, the first series (with objects such as glass, leather, wool, bread, and a piece of the bark of the oak tree) invites the students to exercise their perceptive faculties by focusing on qualities of the objects recognized by the senses, that the object "Indian rubber," for example, is "opaque," "elastic," and "tough." The second and third series focus on recalling impressions or qualities of objects when they are out of sight and on moving from the natural to the artificial, for example, from quill to pen, from metal to bell. In the fourth series, students focus on similarities and differences and on classifying objects with others that are similar; in studying liquids and their qualities, for example, students might work with properties that are common and unique to water, oil, beer, white wine, vinegar, ink, and milk. And finally, in the fifth series, students, presented with an object, are encouraged to make their own observations, observations that might rely on reason and judgment and take into account cause/effect, use/adaptation, and that the student would arrange and record in a narrative. Some of the objects in this section might be the same as in earlier sections, but the student's work with them would be fuller and more complex and would sometimes culminate in a written piece.

Working with Mayo's original text, Frost built on it in two ways: In *Lessons on Common Things*, he added illustrations for some of the objects, and in *Easy Exercises*, he used these same illustrations as writing prompts. Consider how he treats the object glass. To Mayo's written lists on the properties and qualities of glass, Frost adds an engraving of a greenhouse to show the utility of glass in his 1835 *Lessons on Common Things*. The caption Frost writes for the engraving explains that the greenhouse allows spring flowers, summer and autumn fruits, and in northern climates, produce from the tropical climates. In the 1839 *Easy Exercises*, Frost uses this same illustration of a greenhouse as a writing prompt. His directions to the student on page 49 read: "Description of the picture. Description of the interior of a greenhouse. Its uses. The pleasure to be derived from visiting it; or from owning it." (See figures 5A, 5B, 5C, which trace "glass" from Mayo's explanation to Frost's use of a "glasshouse" as a writing prompt.)

Two other examples of Mayo's objects that Frost illustrated and transformed into writing prompts are "apple" and "leather." In *Easy Exercises*, Frost includes the apple engraving he introduced into *Lessons on Common Things*, and he directs the student to "describe the different kinds of apples you have seen and their uses" (*EE* 28). To Mayo's work with the object "leather," Frost added an engraving of a sleigh ride, again focusing on utility when he captioned the engraving,

LESSON I.

GLASS.

GLASS has been selected as the first substance to be presented to the children, because the qualities which characterize it are quite obvious to the senses. The pupils should be arranged before a black board or slate, upon which the result of their observation should be written. The utility of having the lesson presented to the eyes of each child, with the power of thus recalling attention to what has occurred, will very soon be appreciated by the instructor.

The glass should be passed round the party to be examined by each individual.*

TEACHER. What is that which I hold in my hand?

CHILDREN. A piece of glass.

TEACHER. Can you spell the word "glass"? (The teacher then writes the word "glass" upon the slate, which is thus presented to the whole class as the subject of the lesson.) You have all examined this glass; what do you observe? What can you say that it is?†

CHILDREN. It is bright.

---

* By this means each individual in the class is called upon to exercise his own powers on the object presented ; the subsequent questions of the teacher tend only to draw out the ideas of the children, and to correct them if wrong.

† This question is put instead of asking, " What are its qualities ?" because the children would not yet, in all probability, understand the meaning of the term, but by its frequent application to the answers to this question, they will shortly become familiarized with it.

Figure 5A. Elizabeth Mayo's lesson on glass. Mayo, *Lessons on Objects*, 1832, 12.

FIRST SERIES.

GLASS.

Nothing illustrates the utility of glass more finely than the green-house. By this happy contrivance we are enabled to enjoy, in the depths of winter, the flowers of spring, and the fruits of summer and autumn, and to bring to perfection in our northern climates the productions of the tropical regions.

Figure 5B. With an engraving of a greenhouse, John Frost illustrates Mayo's lesson on glass in his edition of her text. Mayo, *Lessons on Common Things*, 1835, 17.

"Not only our riding-caps and boots, but many other parts of our dress, as well as our whip and harness, are made of this material" (*Common Things* 12). As with the greenhouse and the apple, he used the same illustration in *Easy Exercises*, making the move from teaching the child the qualities of an object to asking the child to use his or her experience as the basis for an essay. The caption for the sleigh in *Easy Exercises*, page 36, thus reads, "Describe the picture, and any similar party of pleasure in which you may remember to have taken a

A green-house.

Description of the picture. Description of the interior of a green-house. Its uses. The pleasure to be derived from visiting it; or from owning it.

Figure 5C. Using the same greenhouse engraving, Frost creates a writing prompt based on Mayo's lesson on glass. John Frost, *Easy Exercises*, 1839, 49.

LESSON III.

LEATHER.

Ideas to be developed by the examination of this substance—*flexible, odorous, durable.*

Qualities of Leather.

It is flexible.
odorous.
tough.
smooth.
durable.
opaque.

Uses.—For shoes, gloves, reins, saddles, portmanteaus—for binding books—covering trunks.

Figure 6A. Elizabeth Mayo's lesson on leather. Mayo, *Lessons on Objects*, 1832, 15.

FIRST SERIES.

LEATHER.

WHEN enjoying the pleasures of a sleigh-ride, we may be forcibly reminded of the many uses of leather. Not only our riding-caps and boots, but many other parts of our dress, as well as our whip and harness, are made of this material ; and their presence suggests many other applications of this every-day article, which will readily occur to the youthful reader.

Figure 6B. With an engraving of a sleigh, John Frost illustrates Mayo's lesson on leather in his edition of her text. Mayo, *Lessons on Common Things*, 1835, 12.

part; or describe just such a sleigh ride as you would like to enjoy" (figures 6A, 6B, 6C).

Thus, in Pestalozzi's pedagogy—as it was represented by Elizabeth Mayo—students began their education with concrete objects; as that pedagogy was then represented by John Frost, it became a way for

A sleigh ride.

Describe the picture, and any similar party of pleasure in which you may remember to have taken a part; or describe just such a sleigh ride as you would like to enjoy.

Figure 6C. Using the same sleigh engraving, Frost creates a writing prompt based on Mayo's lesson on leather. John Frost, *Easy Exercises*, 1839, 36.

students to write about concrete objects and, in some cases, to make the transition to writing firsthand accounts of their own experiences.

Other Pestalozzian "Showings"

> to Pestalossi—
> On Pestalossis sacred brow
> The modest chesnut wreath
> Green yesterday but fadeing now
> And pasing as a breath.
> —Louisa May Alcott, *Journals*, September 1, 1843[5]

Even in the first half of the nineteenth century, a number of American schools identified themselves as "Pestalozzian." Resettling in this country from France, Joseph Neef, for example, started a Pestalozzian school near Philadelphia as early as 1809. In 1825, the Scotsman William Maclure sought the help of Neef and other disciples of the Swiss reformer to begin a Pestalozzian school in the utopian community in New Harmony, Indiana, where for Maclure, "the great or fundamental principle" was "never to attempt to teach children what they cannot comprehend" (qtd. in W. Monroe, *History* 110).

By 1834, Bronson Alcott had established the Temple School, which was grounded in Pestalozzian thought; and in 1849, William Russell opened a private training school for teachers in Lancaster, Massachusetts, on Pestalozzian principles. It was not until the second half of the century, though, that pedagogy grounded in Pestalozzian thought really flourished, perhaps most visibly in the kindergarten-training schools supported by Elizabeth Palmer Peabody and at the Oswego Normal School, the teacher-training institute where Edward Sheldon was a prominent teacher and spokesperson for the Pestalozzian-based method of instruction. In common, these schools promoted a benevolent classroom environment and a pedagogy that moved from the simple and concrete to the complex and abstract. Enabling the work of these schools, a flush of books about "object teaching" also appeared toward the end of the nineteenth century.[6] Most of them, including Edward Sheldon's teacher-training editions of Elizabeth Mayo's work (*Lessons on Objects, Graduated Series; Designed for Children Between the ages of Six and Fourteen Years; Containing, also Information on Common Objects*) focused on all the school subjects; that is, they weren't focusing exclusively on the use of objects for writing instruction.

A number of composition books, however, used "object teaching" as their principal pedagogy; best known, perhaps is M. E. Lilienthal and Robert Allyn's 1862 *Things Taught: Systematic Instruction in Composition and Object Lessons*. Part of the "Preface to Teachers" reads:

> This little volume differs widely from the usual textbooks. It is a book of questions without direct answers. It does not address itself to the memory alone, but to all the faculties of a pupil's mind; nor does it confine the learner within the straight-jacket of a text-book, but seeks to acquaint him with the world. . . .
> The present book, compiled after the most successful works used in the Old World, combines a systematic course of instruction in Object Lessons and Composition. (3)

The table of contents shows a heavy emphasis on observation, reflection, and description of natural bodies, all leading to theme writing about such topics as "Incidents of my last vacation," "My visit to Mount Vernon," "My parents' home," "My faithful friend." To be fair, not all the topics are this concrete, but certainly the swinging of the pendulum away from the abstract and toward the concrete and the familiar is marked. And at least one grammar text acknowledges its underpinnings in Pestalozzian thought. In Roswell Smith's 1829 *Intellectual and Practical Grammar, in a Series of Inductive Questions, Connected with Exercises in Composition*, Smith criticizes memory as a way of studying grammar and in support of his method—predicated on the assumption that students should understand what they learn, not just memorize rules—writes, "The author's views on the subject of teaching English Grammar, are perfectly coincident with Pestalozzi's general method of instruction " (viii).

More commonly, some nineteenth-century composition texts devoted a chunk of their instruction to "objects" and, in some cases, mention their debt to Pestalozzi and/or Mayo. Allen Weld's 1849 *English Grammar* has a "Composition" section which, Weld acknowledges, he borrows from William and Robert Chambers's 1842 *Introduction to English Composition* (201).[7] The Chambers text, published in Edinburgh, borrows extensively and unmistakably from Mayo's pedagogy; on the first page, a list of objects reads "pen," "book," "bottle," "letter," "wax," "knife," and so on. But the Chambers text goes beyond Elizabeth Mayo's by making writing more of a focus than she does. In one lesson, for example, students are directed, "Place an object before you. Examine it carefully by your sense of sight. You must neither touch, taste, nor smell it. Then write what you have learned by sight." Another directive reads, "Taste the object, unless it be dangerous to do so, and write the result" (*Lessons on Objects* 35). Sidney Norton's 1863 revision of Weld, published as *The Progressive English Grammar*, with, interestingly enough, a preface by George Quackenbos, has even more elaborate writing instruction based on objects and a section called "Simple Description." And Henry Day, in his 1870 *The Young Composer*, celebrates the use of object lessons in his preface (vii).

On through the nineteenth century, it was not uncommon for texts to include a section asking students to write about their experience of objects. In 1871, James Boyd included a short lesson in *Ele-*

ments of English Composition called "Elementary Exercises in Original Composition" and asked students, for example, to "enumerate all the parts of your own dwelling-house and out-houses, also of your school-edifice and surroundings" (290). Also in 1871, Hiram Hadley included "object" lessons about, for example, "the apple," "water," "bread," "glass," and "a chair" in his *Lessons in Language*. And in 1895, Alonzo Reed and Brainerd Kellogg, in their *One-Book Course in English*, noted that one of the advantages of using "object lessons" is that material is always available, and "the best is easily furnished in every school-room" (4).

Pestalozzi's Significance

A Sort of a Song

Let the snake wait under
his weed
and the writing
be of words, slow and quick, sharp
to strike, quiet to wait,
sleepless.

—through metaphor to reconcile
the people and the stones.
Compose. (No ideas
but in things) Invent!
Saxifrage is my flower that splits
the rocks.

—William Carlos Williams, 1944

When signs of Pestalozzi's educational thought began to appear in composition texts, a road opened to a new kind of writing assignment: an assignment that asked students to write about a concrete object such as those first listed by Elizabeth Mayo and including, for example, water, bread, sealing wax, India rubber, ivory, paper, and rice.

The objects of ordinary life became worthy of school-based writing, the students' own lives became resources for information about these objects, and thus students had an investment in their writing that they did not when they were writing memorized themes or themes about adult subjects. As an inventional strategy, some textbook authors asked students to write about objects in Elizabeth Mayo's terms for object analysis, that is, in terms of an object's parts, uses, qualities, and properties. Quackenbos did this, for example, in his 1876 *Illustrated Lessons in Our Language*; Simon Kerl used a similar strategy in his 1869 *Elements of Composition and Rhetoric*, and T. S. Pinneo did, too, in his 1877 *Guide to Composition*. A caution is this: by putting a positive value on the introduction of object description into composition instruction, I do not mean to suggest that this approach had no drawbacks or pitfalls. In Pinneo and Quackenbos, for example, students were given a plan listing the qualities of an object and asked to write their essay according to the plan. At its best, the plan serves as an heuristic; at its worst, the plan becomes a formula and anticipates one of the faults more commonly attributed to current-traditional instruction. Other writers, like John Frost for example, relied heavily on illustrations to prompt a student to write about an object. In either case, students were using an associational-inventional strategy that Sharon Crowley describes as "introspective," writers drawing on their "accumulated experience of the world," in contrast to relying on classical invention strategies (62).

John Frost argued that one advantage of a student writing about familiar objects and scenes, even in a very short composition, is that the student "has thus begun to learn the art of original composition" (*EE* 9). A second advantage he attached to object-based writing was its ability to serve as preparation for two other kinds of writing: argumentative and narrative. He recommended that after students had learned to describe a single object, they could begin to study two different objects for their similarities and differences, and, thus, make "a beginning in that species of composition which is called *argumentative*, since all reasoning or argument is founded on the discernment of those relations of things which are discovered by comparison" (*EE* 68). So, for example, drawing on objects from nineteenth-century American life, he asked students to find resemblances and differences between "a canal and a railroad," "a pair of spectacles and a spyglass," "a kite and a balloon." Then he asked students to describe the analogies between, for example, "the wings of a bird and the paddles of a steamboat," "a school and a ship's crew," "painting and engraving" (*EE* 70).

Frost also believed that object-based writing was effective preparation for a lesson he called "Narration of Real Incidents Founded on Personal Observation." Following his claim that "the careful examination and description of real objects, taken singly, forms a good preparation for observing and describing objects and incidents in succession or in connection, which constitutes the essential part of narration" (*EE* 70), Frost lists a number of topics that would allow the student to use the experience of writing about single objects as a stepping-stone to writing contextualized description or narration. He presents, for example, an illustration of a bat accompanied by this writing prompt: "A Bat. The bat is a good subject. After describing him, perhaps you may recollect some adventure which you have had, with one flying into the parlor-window, on a summer evening. If so, narrate the whole affair" (*EE* 12). After listing many additional prompts for the writer (for example, "Narrative of a journey from home to the school house, including a description of matters and things observed in the way"; "A visit to a farm house, with description of subjects seen"), Frost notes that his topics will help students to generate additional topics from their own experience. For Frost, therefore, writing about objects led to what he called narrative writing, a form of writing we also call personal writing, that is, writing based on some experience in the writer's life. As far as I know, Frost is the first American textbook writer to make extensive use of experience-based assignments and, certainly, the first American that I can document who links personal writing with object-based writing.

At the same time that there were clear signs of Pestalozzi's spirit in many composition texts for school-age children, Pestalozzi was not a major player in most college-level texts. The most obvious exceptions occur in the exercise-based texts (as opposed to rhetorics) that were popular in midcentury and part of the later work of Richard Green Parker and Quackenbos. But because writers of these books—as they themselves told us—often borrowed liberally and silently from other writers without giving us chapter and verse, the Pestalozzi and/or the Pestalozzi-Mayo-Frost connection can easily go unnoticed by contemporary readers. In, for example, Sharon Crowley's discussion of Parker's *Aids to English Composition*, she writes that Parker, as a "gesture toward supplying students with ideas about which they could write," asked students, "to enumerate the parts of visible objects," "to enumerate the qualities and uses of objects," to enumerate objects' "parts, qualities, properties, uses, and appendages" (64). While the gesture may have been Parker's, the language he uses for the analysis of objects comes from Elizabeth Mayo's work on Pestalozzi. Similarly, Robert Connors notes that Simon Kerl asks students to describe objects with reference to their appearance, qualities, and uses (*Composition-Rhetoric* [*CR*] 310); again, the gesture was Kerl's, but the unnamed source is Mayo's work on Pestalozzi. Throughout Mayo's *Lessons on Objects* (and Parker lists Mayo in his acknowledgments) and throughout Frost's editions of Mayo's text, *Lessons on Things* and *Lessons on Common Things*, students study objects in terms of their parts, qualities, uses, and properties.

Another instance in which the pedagogy of Pestalozzi—as filtered through Mayo and/or Frost—is unacknowledged but present in a college-level book occurs in James R. Boyd's 1844 *Elements of Rhetoric and Literary Criticism*. In his section on descriptive writing, he instructs students, "Compare one object with another, pointing out the things in which they agree and in which they differ." He then lists twelve pairs of objects for comparison—pairs like "water and air," "canal and railroad," "pin and needle" (175–76). Of the twelve pairs he lists, I find that six of the pairs are identical with those John Frost lists in a section called "Comparison and Distinction of Objects" in the 1839 *Easy Exercises* (68–69).[8]

Professor of logic and English at the University of Aberdeen from 1860 to 1880, Alexander Bain was familiar with Pestalozzi and object teaching and discusses object teaching as an important teaching method in his *Education as a Science*.[9] In this text, though, Bain's focus is on the education of children, not college students, and on the use of object teaching in the section of the text he calls "Natural History, Physical Science, and the Useful Arts" (249). While I do not see elaborated signs of object teaching in Bain's section, "Description," in his

1866 American edition of *English Composition and Rhetoric*, or in the section, "Picturesqueness," in his enlarged 1887 *English Composition and Rhetoric*, or in Bain's 1887 *On Teaching English*, and although Bain announces that his debt is to Blair, Campbell, and Whately, it nonetheless seems reasonable to speculate, the absence of an articulated link to Pestalozzi notwithstanding, that Bain's admiration for Pestalozzi would have spilled over, however subtly, into his thinking about writing instruction. It is also true, however, that Bain was a powerful spokesperson for the separation between writing and thinking (Brereton 305–6), and this would run counter to Pestalozzian-based writing instruction.

In discussions of Pestalozzi's nineteenth-century disciples in the United States, a name that often appears is Louis Agassiz, Swiss-American naturalist who was professor of zoology and geology at Harvard from 1848 until his death in 1911. Agassiz began his teaching career at Switzerland's University of Neufchâtel where, according to nineteenth-century Pestalozzian biographer Hermann Krusi, Agassiz was "imbued" with the same spirit that characterized Pestalozzi's teaching. Remembered and celebrated as a great teacher, Agassiz's hallmark was his insistence that students learn by observing. When Agassiz gave a talk in 1847 to a teacher's institute conducted by Horace Mann in Newton, Massachusetts, his subject was insects. Agassiz himself reports:

> I thought the best way to proceed would be to place the objects in the hands of the teachers, for I knew that mere verbal instruction would not be transformed into actual knowledge. I therefore went out and collected several hundred grasshoppers, brought them in, and gave one into the hands of everyone present. It created universal laughter; yet the examination of these objects had not been carried on long before every one was interested, and, instead of looking at me, looked at the thing. And they began to examine, and to appreciate what it was to see, and see carefully. At first I pointed out the things which no one could see. "We can't see them," they said. "But look again," said I, "for I can see things ten

times smaller than these"; and they finally discerned them. (qtd. in Swett, *Methods* 168)

More familiar to many of us are the personal accounts of Agassiz's students, and, especially the essay by Samuel Scudder called "In the Laboratory with Agassiz." First published in 1874, this essay is popularly known as "Take This Fish and Look at It" and is frequently anthologized in composition readers as a model for teaching first-year writing students how "to observe."[10] In the essay and in Agassiz's philosophy are echoes of Pestalozzi's emphasis on experience-based learning, Agassiz writing, "the worst service a teacher could render a pupil was to give him a ready-made answer" (qtd. in Swett, *Methods* 7).

However subtly or circuitously Pestalozzi's work did (and does) inflect college writing instruction, Pestalozzi's presence is nonetheless more apparent in nineteenth-century texts for school-age students than in nineteenth-century texts for college students. Crowley reminds us that even in the early years of that century, the university professors of rhetoric and composition "were, for the most part, either clergymen or gentlemen of leisure who were hired by the college president to pass on . . . the best that had been thought and said in Western culture" (71). And certainly the best that was known and thought in rhetoric was derived from the classical tradition and from British rhetoricians Campbell, Blair, and Whately and their intellectual heirs that we associate with what we call current-traditional rhetoric. It is hard to find a nineteenth-century textbook writer who does not acknowledge the British rhetoricians; and even writers like John Frost, whose pedagogy is innovative, acknowledge the influence of their own education; Frost, for example, recommends that students pursuing further work in composition, that is, "inquiries into the principles on which the art of composition is founded," should read the rhetoricians he would have studied at Harvard (*EE* 118).

It is also true that observation and description became important in college-level texts and continue to be a part of many texts today. In the center chapters of *The Methodical Memory*, Sharon Crowley points out that the lineage of what we know as "description" goes back to

George Campbell, Adam Smith, and Joseph Priestley; that as early as 1827, Samuel Newman mentioned "description" as a kind of writing in his *Practical System of Rhetoric*; and that Quackenbos, Richard Green Parker, and Day all worked with description in some way in their texts. But Crowley further notes that it was not until Alexander Bain's popularization of current-traditional genre theory later in the century that description routinely appeared in college texts as a distinct genre. Embracing "EDNA" (Crowley's emblem for what we know as the modes of discourse—exposition, description, narration, and argumentation), Gertrude Buck and Elisabeth Woodbridge, John Genung, and David J. Hill, for example, are among the many authors who include a section on descriptive writing in their late nineteenth-century texts for college students. In Hill's chapter on description in the *Science of Rhetoric*, he even has a short section on "describable objects," but both his understanding of description as part of a taxonomy and his explanation of how to write a description (including the four general "laws" which he claims every description should follow—the laws of purpose, unity, completeness and brevity) point to a link to current-traditional rhetoric and not to Pestalozzi.

So while both school and college texts came to view observation-based writing as important, an enhanced understanding of the developmental abilities and needs of school-age children led to an emphasis on description and experience-based writing earlier in nineteenth-century schools than in the colleges and universities. I would further argue that while the British rhetoricians were the primary energy source for nineteenth-century composition instruction at every level, the immediate ductwork that carried description to school and college texts was different. Just as a knowledge of the British tradition helps to explain nineteenth-century college texts and, indeed, many dimensions of nineteenth-century texts for school-age students (including EDNA's presence in some of those texts late in the century; see Huffcut, for example), it is the additional knowledge of Pestalozzi and his reform pedagogy that helps to explain the presence and significance of description in the schools.

In the long poem "Patterson," William Carlos Williams gave voice to twentieth-century American pragmatic democratizing style when he wrote, "Say it, no ideas but in things." In Pestalozzi's explanation of his educational practice—a practice that represented some aspects of the epistemologies of Comenius, Locke, and Rousseau and in some ways democratized writing instruction—he wrote, "There are two ways of instructing: either we go from words to things, or from things to words. Mine is the second method" (qtd. in Holman 198). In the early to mid–nineteenth century, John Frost and other composition textbook authors broke with a long-standing tradition in this country: These writers adapted Pestalozzi's "method" to composition instruction and, decades before personal writing appeared in texts for college students, they invited school-age students to write about concrete and familiar objects and, in some cases, about the realities of their own lives. This reform, a change that affects composition classes even today, marked a watershed in composition instruction and merits Pestalozzi, Swiss educator and humanitarian, a place in our discipline's pantheon of significant ancestors.

4 / The Agency of Textbook Iconography

Pictures are indeed a far more natural language—a vehicle of instruction much more adapted to the nature of children, than the artificial language of letters; and so far as they can be used, they are effective instruments of education. The best method of communicating knowledge is to place before the child the objects of knowledge. If you would give the most accurate idea of a lion, bring the lion himself. If you cannot do this, give a picture of him.

—"On the Use of Pictures in School Books,"
American Annals of Education, 1834

Present an engraved landscape to a boy of four or five years of age. . . . he will at once recognize and describe, in his own way, the houses, the streets, the men, the women, the roads and carriages, and the land and water of which it is composed, and express his opinion respecting them. Present well-executed engravings of a horse, a cow, a lion, an elephant, or a monkey, and he will soon learn to distinguish the one from the other, and he will feel delighted with every new exhibition that is made to him of the objects of nature or of art.

—Thomas Dick, *On the Mental Illumination
and Moral Improvement of Mankind*, 1855

For Pestalozzi and his most devoted American followers, the ideal way to teach children was experientially. Instead of sitting in a schoolroom with their charges and reading about waterfalls and streams and hills, schoolmasters would take their pupils to the nearby woods of Pennsylvania or Kentucky or Massachusetts for their lessons in natural history and geography. Responding to a similar impulse, many teachers in the second quarter of the nineteenth century brought visual aids—natural objects, maps, and pictures—into their classroom. It was also at this time that a growing national economy and technological advances in printing and engraving contributed to a growth spurt in children's textbooks—many of which were illustrated.

In composition texts for school-age students, illustrations appeared as early as 1838 in Charles Morley's *Practical Guide to Composition* and were popular in many First Books of composition. As an industry, textbook production slowed down before, during, and immediately after the Civil War, and so only a handful of composition texts were illustrated between 1862 and 1876; by the end of the century, however, as schools proliferated and curricula moved toward regularization, illustrations were commonplace in composition texts for school-age students. In histories and geographies and readers, the illustrations represented the subject of the written text or the context for the subject under discussion. In the composition books, however, the illustration itself became the subject; that is, the illustration of an object or scene became the prompt for the writing assignment. In dozens of nineteenth-century composition texts for schools, students were asked to write, using W. J. T. Mitchell's phrase from *Picture Theory*, a "verbal representation of a visual representation": a description of the illustration, an imagined story about it, or a narrative from their own life suggested by the actions in the illustration.

In Elizabeth Baker's work with selected nineteenth-century rhetoric and composition texts, she points out that illustrations were used as writing prompts, and Glenn Hess charts the composition books (not always accurately) from 1784 to 1870 that include illustrations. Unlike these earlier writers for whom the power of illustrations was muted, I foreground the iconography of nineteenth-century composition texts and read the illustrations for a significance with which they have not yet been inscribed. Within an historical representation of the pedagogical uses of illustrations and a discussion of the technology that generated them, I argue that the rhetoric of textbook illustrations in school-based composition books is twofold and paradoxical, that the iconography both frees and restrains: On the one hand, the illustrations serve as heuristics for essays about the concrete and the personal and, thus, collaborated in a new approach to composition instruction; on the other hand, the illustrations and their attached framing text serve as agents of acculturation, reproducing and representing as transcendent the culture's dominant norms and values. School in the nineteenth century was dedicated to instruction in both "knowledge" and "virtue." Although inflected by social realities, the knowledge that the illustrations asked students to call on was located in the experience of their own lives; the virtue, however, that the illustrations taught was that of the dominant and then unassailable social codes.

The History and Technology of Illustrations in Children's Books

The history of illustrations in children's textbooks is generally acknowledged to have begun with John Amos Comenius, the seventeenth century Moravian bishop and educator who argued, as I noted in chapter 3, that because the senses were the doorways to understanding, education should begin with everyday life, especially with concrete objects in the child's environment. When the objects themselves were not available, Comenius recommended that models could be constructed, and in the absence of the actual objects or models, the items could be represented by means of pictures. Comenius believed that "pictures are the most intelligible books that children can look upon" (qtd. in Feaver 7), and his 1658 *Orbis Pictus*, translated into English in 1672 as *Visible World*, or in some translations as *A World of Things Obvious to the Senses Drawn in Pictures*, is considered the first deliberately illustrated children's book. For a hundred years, it was the best-known children's textbook in Europe, and was translated into fourteen languages; records indicate twenty-one editions in the seventeenth century, forty-three in the eighteenth, and thirty-two in the nineteenth century.[1] Throughout the book, woodcuts either of an object or of a scene are accompanied by two columns of brief text, one in Latin and one in High Dutch. Later translated into many other languages, including English, the text both identifies the subject of the cut and, in many cases, offers guidelines for behavior. In the first lesson, for example, a dialogue between teacher and pupil, the pupil learns that to be wise, he must "understand rightly," "speak rightly," and "do rightly" and that his teacher will lead him to that wisdom in the name of God. In the illustration, the teacher stands in front of a church, and the rays of heaven shine over the church and the teacher and, through the teacher, in the boy's direction. The book then goes on to illustrate scenes from daily life, a barbershop, for example, and to teach words like *hair, beard, scissors, razor, soap, towel,* and *comb* in the text for the illustration.

Toward the end of the seventeenth century, the empiricist philosopher John Locke commented directly about the value of pictures in educating children in *Some Thoughts Concerning Education*:

> If [the child's] *Aesop* has *Pictures* in it, it will entertain him much the better, and encourage him to read. . . . For such visible Objects Children hear talked of in vain and without any Satisfaction whilst they have no Ideas of them; those Ideas being not to be had from Sounds, but from the Things themselves or their Pictures. And therefore I think as soon as he begins to spell, as many Pictures of Animals should be got him as can be found, with the printed Names to them, which at the same Time will invite him to read, and afford him Matter of Enquiry and Knowledge. (133)

In U.S. education, simple woodcuts were used from the late seventeenth century in hornbooks, in the *New England Primer*, alphabet books, spelling books, and readers.[2] The purpose of the illustrations was pedagogical, extending the limits of the children's knowledge and helping them to connect with a world larger than that of their immediate circumstances, but it was also psychological: to infuse the learning process with pleasure. Not everyone, of course, agreed with the use of pictures in school; in an 1834 issue of the *Annals of Education and Instruction*, a writer identified only as "X" argued that the use of too many pictures overstated the playful aspects of school and undermined the seriousness of the educational enterprise ("Influence of the 'Picture System' " 206–7). But this criticism notwithstanding, when books for teachers began to appear in the late 1830s, they articulated this importance of using "visible illustrations" in educating children, Emerson Davis, for example, arguing that the best access to a child's mind was through the child's eye (71).

Also in the second and third decades of the century, the United States began a time of dramatic economic growth, historians noting that the economy was growing faster than the population. The westward expansion continued, the "transportation revolution" gave industry access to supplies and markets and enabled a national market economy, and technological advances enabled increased production. Significantly, part of the technological and industrial expansion occurred in the world of printing and engraving as an increasing demand for everyday reading materials, decreasing costs of printing, greater availability of wood pulp paper, and lower postal rates allowed printers to increase the number of jobs they could manage and improve the quality of the finished product.

Prior to the work of Thomas Bewick (1753–1828) in England at the end of the eighteenth century, relief engraving on wood was executed on the plank or lateral side of the wood; the engraving that resulted was called a woodcut. Bewick, however, revolutionized engraving on wood by using, instead of the plank side, the grain side, that is, the end of the wood; the result of this work was a wood engraving. In the white-line technique popularized by Bewick and his school, shapes were determined more by darks placed against whites than by free-standing black lines, which have a tendency to break down under pressure from printing presses. For this work, boxwood was the wood of choice: its resiliency under pressure and its almost grainless surface allowed the engraver to make curved lines without interference from the grain. One advantage of a wood engraving on boxwood versus a wood cut on the vertical grain of the wood was the fineness of the lines that could be engraved on the surface. A visual difference between the woodcut and the wood engraving is that the engraving, because of the possibility of more detailed cutting, is less "flat" and reportorial than the woodcut and more representational.

Following the style of Bewick, Alexander Anderson, M.D. (1775–1870), "the father of American wood engraving," introduced and popularized wood engraving in the United States in the nineteenth century.[3] Giving up medicine for full-time engraving, Anderson illustrated more than two thousand books in his career, and his work appears in the earliest editions of *Webster's Spelling Book*. While Anderson had only four students—one being his daughter—he had many followers. Benson Lossing, in his work on Anderson, notes that from 1838 to 1870, the number of professional wood engravers in the United States grew from "not twenty" to "about four hundred" (qtd. in Hamilton xlviii). While other engraving techniques were available and used for high-end publications, wood engraving became the technique most commonly used in inexpensive nineteenth-century publications, publications that included magazines, newspapers, and, not surprisingly, schoolbooks.[4] Anderson is important to this discussion because he popularized the technique that made wood engravings so readily available for textbooks.

For a number of reasons, then, when textbooks beyond the level of primers began to appear in the 1830s that were written deliberately for children and not as an imitation of adult texts, they included illustrations. While there were exceptions, the engravings for the books in the first half of the century were not commissioned, for the most part, for individual works or even signed by the designer or engraver.[5] It was not unusual, especially in the 1830s and 1840s, for printers to own large lots of stereotypes of unsigned engravings and to use them in various works. Twenty of the illustrations in John Frost's *Easy Exercises* (1839), for example, also appear in *Robert Ramble's Picture Gallery, or Lessons on Pictures and Stories* (1838), a book that Frost published under the pseudonym of Ramble. Some of the same illustrations also appear in his 1835 edition of Elizabeth Mayo's work and in the education journal he published for a few years, from 1836 to 1838 (with W. R. Johnson, J. M. Keagy, W. Russell, and J. B. Walker), called *The School Master, and Advocate of Education*. And perhaps even more interestingly, some of the illustrations in Frost's work also appear in Thomas Palmer's *Moral Instructor; or Culture of the Heart, Affections, and Intellect while Learning to Read* (1841). In addition to being used in more than one text, the engravings were occasionally mismanaged, appearing upside down, for instance, or facing east-west rather than north-south; in, for example, Charles Morley's *Common School Grammar*, many pages require turning the book to see the engraving "right side up," as it were. Even, on occasion, an engraving did not correspond with the text it was intended to illustrate; in *The Little One's First Book*, for example, a lesson using grass and outdoor pets as the text is illustrated by a family grouping of children and their mother in front of a fireplace (19).

By the third quarter of the century, the status attached to individual engravings and their handling had grown. Engravings no longer routinely appeared in more than one book, and they were accurately placed on the page; in addition, they were often signed, sometimes by the designer, more often by the engraver, sometimes by both people, and the signatures were from recognized, even celebrated, artists/artisans, such as James Carter Beard, William Croome, and W. Roberts. The detail of the engravings also changed in the second half of the century. In the early 1800s, an engraving had 15 to 20 lines to the inch; by the end of the century, 60 lines to the inch were possible and not uncommon. As a result, the illustrations toward the end of the century were more elaborate, more lifelike, and more likely to have multiple figures in a scene and in motion than the earlier stiff, posed representations. As a further result, it was no doubt easier for children to make the leap from the represented life to their own life.[6]

Illustrations in Composition Texts

> Sensible objects suggests ideas promptly; and we therefore try the experiment of presenting to the pupil a series of pictures of familiar objects and scenes with a few simple directions as to the mode of rendering each object or scene the subject of a short essay in composition.
>
> —John Frost, *Easy Exercises*, 1839

> Pictures and text work harmoniously together. The natural result is the development of such an interest in the subject-matter of composition, that its painful features quite disappear.
>
> —Charles DeGarmo, *Language Lessons, Book One*, 1897

When early writers of composition texts broke with tradition by including illustrations in their texts and asking students for personal writing, they did so, in Frost's words, as an "experiment." Of his book "embellished with cuts," Morley writes that the purpose is to make composing "pleasant and interesting" (iii, *Practical Guide*); Phippen writes that his use of "beautiful pictures" in *Illustrated Composition Book* is to "furnish a great variety of subjects . . . about which you can think and write" (1); Bullions doesn't include illustrations in his text, but asks that teachers direct students to seek out pictures in their spellers or geographies and "to write a description of the picture" (131).

Many composition textbook illustrations represented, as did the illustrations in the primers, a single item: a bird, insect, fish, plant, or a simple household object such as a button. Many, however, especially later in the century, represented a scene from a child's life: children at play, children at school, children with their parents, children with animals. In the early decades, boys wore ruffled shirts and waistcoats, girls wore ruffled dresses and high-top shoes; in the house were formal draperies, upholstered chairs, elaborate tea sets. Occasionally, the setting was rural and the children wore straw hats and plaid shirts and were barefoot. Occasionally, the setting was work-related, and illustrated were places of work, such as the apothecary shop or the grocer's shop; tools, such as a loom or a plow; or items related to transportation or navigation, such as a ship or a canal. And occasionally, the illustrations, like those in the histories and geographies, were of peoples from distant lands or of people participating in a specific historic event, like the execution of Lady Jane Grey or the signing of the Magna Carta. In outdoor scenes, it was not unusual for a church or church steeple to stand in the background or on the horizon, and for a stream of light to emanate from the steeple and to shine on the figures in the engraving. It is perhaps not surprising that especially in the early years of the century, there was little fantasy or humor depicted in the illustrations.

As the century progressed, the arrangement of many rhetorics and composition texts, both for older and younger students, was likely to be predictable, especially in the books that embraced the taxonomy of exposition, description, narration, and argumentation as an organizing principle. In the early part of the century, however, when composition texts for younger students were a new genre, the conventions of the genre were not yet defined; in other words, there was no agreement about either the content of these books or the arrangement of that content. So, too, the number and use and placement of illustrations also varied widely from text to text, even among First Books. Morley, author of the earliest composition book I have found to use illustrations, does not include a table of contents, and his book moves randomly from topic to topic. He begins with a section he calls "Stories," then moves to punctuation, to description, to letter writing, to analytical exercises. In his text, he uses illustrations as prompts for concrete descriptions students might write of animals, birds, insects, or plants; he also uses illustrations as a visual model of an action or behavior that students themselves might imitate. In the section, "Letter-Writing," for example, an illustration shows a girl seated at a desk writing a letter.

For midcentury writers Frost and Phippen, illustrations are the controlling trope of their book's pedagogy. Frost's slender volume includes more than 150 illustrations and is loosely arranged by genre; he begins with chapters titled "Pictures of Objects for Description" (these are primarily animals and birds), and then includes "Pictures of Scenes for Description" (domestic scenes, school scenes, recreational scenes, scenes of various trades and professions, and scenes of peoples of other cultures) and illustrations for narrative writing. Phippen's *Illustrated Composition Book*, as the title suggests, is also based on illustrations and not arranged by genre or rhetorical feature.

Even as illustrations became more common in the second half of the century, they continued to be unpredictably placed and to vary greatly in number from book to book. What the illustrations share— and this is their strength—is that, they enabled textbook writers to move away from John Walker's advocacy of "writing in your own words what you remember of a memorized text written by an adult" and toward teaching students to compose original text. With few exceptions, they played a major role in allowing students to develop their skills of observation and imagination by serving as an heuristic for descriptive and narrative essays, and thus they collaborated in a new instantiation of writing instruction.

Even in the description of animals, John Frost invited students to compose original text: the framing text under the illustration of the opossum clutching a dove reads, "Describe the picture. Notice the dove; and you may infer from seeing it there that the Opossum, when wild, kills and eats doves. You may set your ingenuity at work to conjecture how he catches them" (*EE* 11). When Frost moved to illustrations of children, he invited students to write about their school experiences. For an illustration of a boy standing before his seated father that is entitled "Boy telling about his studies at school," the assignment reads, "You can here describe the picture, and then give an account of your own studies at school." An illustration on the same page of Frost's text asked students to describe a girl learning her lesson— without being distracted by her pets (figure 7). Like Frost, Phippen also used illustrations as a bridge to personal writing; in his self-published edition of *Illustrated Composition Book* (which does not list him as author), he offers a choice of nine writing assignments for a family scene; one of the assignments reads, "Write a letter to your friend, giving an account of the persons composing your family; their daily occupations and pleasures" (13).

By the end of the century, many textbook writers asked students to write original text based on observation or experience. In 1882, W. B. Powell's text entitled *How to Write* announced on the title page that it was illustrated with 150 engravings. The framing text for the engravings of a bird or animal asks students for a description: "Write a description of the crane, referring to the picture and making an outline before beginning to write" (79); another text in Powell's book directs students, "Write an account of the events of a day spent with your cousin, as suggested by the following pictures"; those pictures are entitled "Feeding the chickens" and "Fishing" (133–35). In an 1894 text, Albert Raub includes an untitled illustration of a rural setting, a farmhouse in the background, an open carriage with two adults and one young person in the foreground; the four prompts Raub poses to the writer are these: "Write all you can about this picture. Write a story which the picture may illustrate. Write a short description of a visit to the country. Write a short description of life on a farm" (*Lessons in English* 82). Toward the end of the century, the writing prompt sometimes asked students to compose a "picture-story," an imagined story, in response to a series of questions. In a typical exam-

Boy telling about his studies at school.
You can here describe the picture, and then give an account of your own studies at school.

Girl learning her lesson.
Description of picture. Old-fashioned furniture. Girl's attention not diverted by her pets. She seems to have nearly learned her lesson and to be just ready to start for her school.

Figure 7. "Boy telling about his studies at school," "Girl learning her lesson." John Frost, *Easy Exercises*, 1839, 21.

ple, this one appears on page 11 of Edward Gideon's *Lessons in Language*, the text for an untitled illustration of a little girl sitting among her toys, holding the head of a doll in one hand, the body of the doll in the other, reads: "What do you see in this picture? What do you think her name is? How old do you think she is? What has she been doing? What has she done? Is she a good girl? Why do you think so?"

(figure 8). Yet a further indication of the popularity of illustrations as writing prompts for a picture story is that in 1891, the journal *Common School Education* sponsored a writing contest for children. The April issue published an illustration (without a title or caption) and students were invited to write a story about what they saw ("Our Best Prize Offers" 148–49); the May issue published the prize essay from a primary student and from an intermediate student ("Our Prize Reproduction Stories" 194).

As I noted in chapter 3, the inventional strategy being called for here is what Sharon Crowley calls "associative"; that is, unlike classical invention, which evaluates an argument not only in terms of its effectiveness and appropriateness but also in terms of audience reception, the strategy here calls writers to draw on their accumulated knowledge of the world, gained either from reading or from experience (62). While it is important for students to have a repertoire of heuristics in hand, and while classical invention may be particularly important for older students, the associative method allowed beginning students to write original compositions.

Unremarkable as these assignments may seem to a contemporary audience—asking children to write about a doll or a fishing trip—they were groundbreaking in the mid–nineteenth century in that they represented a change from the literary to the popular and from knowledge grounded in authority to knowledge grounded in experience. In the unillustrated *Progressive Exercises*, the book that dominated nineteenth-century composition instruction, Richard Green Parker suggested that for an assignment combining description and narration, students present "*the history and character of the patriarch Joseph,*—of king David,—of Solomon,—of Job,—of the Apostle Paul" (*PE* 46). In Quackenbos's brief section on description in *First Lessons*, a text intended for students from nine to twelve years old, he required students to begin their description with an analysis of the subject, and as models for student writing he included descriptions of "The Great Clock of Strasburg" and of a Sir Walter Scott forest scene. By 1876, Quackenbos himself asked students to write in response to pictures in his *Illustrated Lessons*, even commissioning the illustrations for his text. The more noteworthy use of illustrations in composition texts

5. What do you see in this picture?
   What do you think her name is?
   How old do you think she is?
   What has she been doing?
   What has she done?
   Is she a good girl?
   Why do you think so?

Write a story about the picture, using all or a part of your answers.

Figure 8. Illustration of a child and the text of a prompt for a picture story. Gideon, *Lessons in Language*, 1888, 11.

occurred, however, almost forty years earlier with those writers who were breaking new ground.[7]

While illustrations as writing prompts became standard practice in many nineteenth-century composition texts for school-age students, they had a particular enabling agency at a specific nineteenth-century school site. Founded in 1817 by Thomas Hopkins Gallaudet and Laurent Clerc to educate deaf children and youth, the American School for the Deaf in Hartford, Connecticut, is the oldest school for the deaf in the United States and the oldest special education facility in this country. Motivated by his desire to help a neighbor's deaf daughter learn to communicate with her siblings and the neighborhood children, Gallaudet, sponsored by Mason Cogswell and other wealthy businesspeople in Hartford, traveled to Europe to observe schools for the deaf. There, he recruited Clerc, a deaf Frenchman and teacher of the deaf, to move to the United States. Clerc taught Gallaudet "the natural language of signs" and together, they opened a boarding school in Connecticut; they introduced signing to the teachers who assisted them in the school; they taught signing to the students who enrolled in the school; and they used signing as a means of instructing students in school subjects.

The use of visual aids has long been important in deaf education. In Harvey Peet's 1851 essay "Memoir on the Origin and Early History of the Art of Instructing the Deaf and Dumb," he documents the use of pictures to instruct deaf persons in "the truths of religion" in the sixteenth century (141). In 1850, Gallaudet wrote specifically about schoolroom arrangements for deaf students, and even more specifically about the use of illustrations in composition instruction. He recommended that the schoolrooms house ample numbers of picture books, "the more pictures the better" (78), including charts, maps, diagrams, and graphs. In particular, he advocated that teachers have a portfolio of engravings, and that students "could often engage in writing descriptions of these engravings and pictures" (79). Important to remember is that in 1851 only a handful of composition texts included illustrations and that while Frost and a number of other textbook writers argued the benefits of the use of illustrations in the preface to their books, there is no midcentury pedagogical work for teachers that

I know of that recommends that students write descriptions of illustrations with the specificity that Gallaudet does.

As early as 1842, a student essay entitled "A Description of a Picture" (*Annual Report*, 1842, 27) appears in the school's archives. An 1860 American School for the Deaf (ASD) *Annual Report* explains to parents that "original composition and instruction in the use of language" was a part of the curriculum every Friday evening; and sample essays written by students provide ample evidence that at least some of what the students wrote was prompted by an illustration (*Annual Report*, 1860, 7–37). A highlight occurs in the school records of 1886: included are not only essays written by three different students in response to each of two illustrations, but also the illustrations themselves. What the writing demonstrates is that writers create their texts not to capture an "objective reality," but to produce what Phyllis Frus McCord would call, "a convincing version of ideas and events, of which there are many other possible versions" (751). In the first text, for example, the adult female figure is a "grandma"; in the second text, she is a "mother"; and in the third text, she is first "an old woman" and later "grandma." In the first text, the writer notes that "grandma" "likes to knit," that "her hair is gray and she has no teeth." In the second text, the mother "is sewing." In the third text, grandmother "sewed a little cloth." But in all three texts, the writers focus on the activities of the children, not the adult, even though the adult is the largest figure in the illustration (*Annual Report*, 1886, 42–44). Here, then, is a representation of writing instruction in which children write "what they see," and what they see is affected not only by their socially constructed language and culture, but also by their individual experience and perspective. (See appendix 2 for the illustration and the text of the children's essays.)

One last note about composition at the American School for the Deaf: The first language of deaf students in this school was sign, a language that at every level—lexical, grammatical, syntactic—makes a linguistic use of space. For the deaf community, written text was evidence that students had used this natural language of sign to learn the lexicon, the grammar, and the syntax of written English, for these students a second language. For composition historians, the attention to written text at the American School for the Deaf—the early publication of student writing, the composing of original texts, and the inflection of text with a personal bias—is evidence of the ongoing need to reshape our historical narratives in the light of new findings, to be ever vigilant that our historical narratives are not closed but open systems. Student writing archived in the records of the ASD is evidence of the ways in which a linguistic subculture is fertile ground for pedagogical innovation and a reminder that not only is the story of writing instruction of nineteenth-century school-age students not contained within the covers of the textbooks, neither is it contained within the dominant culture's sites of composition instruction.

Framing Text and Cultural Codes

> If, therefore, a way can be devised to bring the ideas we wish to communicate to a child to the window of vision, we are very sure they will get admission.
> —Emerson Davis, *The Teacher Taught*, 1839

> The pictorial illustration in these books . . . is so arranged as more vividly to show the development of the subject-matter. The text guides the thought; the pictures stimulate the imagination.
> —Charles DeGarmo, *Language Lessons*, 1897

Occasionally, as in the illustrations used at the American School for the Deaf, illustrations occur without any authorial comment about the subject. And in Phippen's unsigned edition (see note 3 to chapter 2), one assignment reads, "The last picture you observe, has no title, and no subjects, accompanying it. You may study it attentively, and write what you please about it" (*Illustrated Composition Book* 8). For the most part, though, the engravings are accompanied by what I call a framing text. Intended as a prompt for student writing, sometimes this text is as brief as a title or caption; sometimes it is a list of specific directives to the student or a list of questions for the student to answer. In addition to prompting the student's writing, this framing text also prompts the student's reading of the illustration; that is, the framing text defines what the student sees (or doesn't) in the picture. In *Another Way of Telling*, John Berger and Jean Mohr write that all photographs are ambiguous and taken out of a continuity. The authors continue:

> If the event [in the photograph] is a public event, this continuity is history; if it is personal, the continuity, which has been broken, is a life story. Even a pure landscape breaks a continuity: that of the light and weather. Discontinuity always produces ambiguity. Yet often this ambiguity is not obvious, for as soon as photographs are used with words, they produce together an effect of certainty, even of dogmatic assertion.
>
> In the relation between a photograph and words, the photograph begs for an interpretation, and the words usually supply it. The photograph, irrefutable as evidence but weak in meaning, is given a meaning by the words. And the words, which by themselves remain at the level of generalisation, are given specific authenticity by the irrefutability of the photograph. Together the two become very powerful; an open question appears to have been fully answered. (91–92)

While the illustrations in these nineteenth-century texts are engravings, not photographs, the words that frame the text have the effect Berger and Mohr describe: they produce an effect of certainty, even of dogmatic assertion. More specifically, in these nineteenth-century texts, the words transform the illustrations into agents of acculturation, reproducing and representing as transcendent—and closed to question or scrutiny—the values and behaviors of the dominant social order. Often, for example, this framing text encodes the nineteenth century's "ethic of growth," praising obedience, duty, diligence, and industry, and discouraging anger, tardiness, and laziness. The framing text for the illustration in figure 7 entitled "Girl learning her lesson," reads, "Girl's attention not diverted by her pets. She seems to have nearly learned her lesson and to be just ready to start for her school" (John Frost, *EE* 21). The text for an illustration entitled "Boy giving a letter to his father" reads, "Boy probably wishes to have his mistakes corrected. Pleasures and advantages of letter-writing" (*EE* 26). While the illustrations are pictures of the girl learning her lesson and the boy writing a letter, they are also—and just as importantly—pictures of how the readers of the textbook were expected to behave.

In other cases, the framing text reflects the dominant culture's attitude toward other cultures. For an illustration entitled "Arabs listening to a story," students are invited to write about any one or all of the following topics: "Description of the scene. Arabs. Their customs. Fondness for stories. Their wandering mode of life. Their fondness for coffee and tobacco. Their hostility to other nations. Description of a caravan. Fondness of the Arabians for their horses" (*EE* 53). The framing text for an illustration entitled "The Gipsies" reads, "Describe the fortune-telling scene, and the character and habits of the gipsies as far as they may be known to you" (*EE* 55). And the framing text qua assignment attached to an illustration of a European American, wearing a jacket and cravat, preaching to Native Americans reads in part, "Savage Life. Compare it with civilized life; by describing the dress, dwellings, occupations, religion, & etc. Mention some of the nations still in a savage state. How some savage nations have become civilized, and what evils among highly civilized nations may reduce them again to barbarism." Another piece of the framing text for that same illustration reads, "The Heathen. Mention some of the heathen nations, and their religious opinions. Why their idolatry makes them miserable and degraded. How they can be reclaimed" (Phippen [signed edition] 20).

While the framing text accompanying an illustration directed students how to read the illustration, it also directed them how not to read it. Consider the illustration entitled "Cotton" in an 1894 textbook (Metcalf and Bright 143). In the picture, African American women and men are working in a cotton field; in the background is a European American overseer in a suit, and behind him are "the big house" and a row of slave cabins. In the framing text, which includes "Topics for Study and Conversation," students read about the beginnings of cotton farming in this country, about the planting season, and about the uses of cotton. But no human agency is assigned to any of this work; in fact the only person mentioned in the entire "Cotton" lesson is Eli Whitney. Absent is any mention of the people in the illustration, either the workers who plant or harvest the cotton or the overseer; in addition, there is no mention of the injustice of slavery or of difficulties that faced freed men. For the composition assignment, students are directed, "Write about cotton, following the order of the Topics," that is, without any attention to the workers or slavery. In this case, the framing text renders a race invisible even when members of the race are the primary subjects of the illustration (figure 9). This erasure illustrates W. J. T. Mitchell's argument that text can interfere with "seeing"; that just as the wall labels in museums can take more of the visitor's time than the objects themselves, the verbal text can work as "a substitute for seeing, replacing the material, visual presence of the picture with labels, anecdotes" (209).

The peoples who, in the eyes of a contemporary reader, were either marginalized or made invisible by the illustrations and their accompanying framing texts included not only peoples of other races or cultures, but also "the country boy" and the poor: anyone, in other words, who was not the presumed reader of the text. In Frost, for example, in response to an illustration of three ruffle-collared boys holding hoops and sticks in a garden setting, students were asked to write "an account of your latest adventures, in hoop-driving, and ball-playing" (EE 38), while in response to an illustration of a boy walking barefoot on a farm lane with a rake over his shoulder and a basket in his hand, the student was asked to write, "Habits, occupations and pleasures of the country boy. The useful life he leads in the summer. His fondness for school in the winter" (EE 34).

Especially toward the end of the century, a number of illustrations depicted the lives of the poor. In Robert Metcalf and Orville Bright's 1894 Language Lessons, for example, most of the illustrations show well-dressed children at play with their wagons and dolls and pets; in one illustration, however, a different family is represented. In the engraving, a mother washes clothes outdoors in a wash bucket, a child sleeps nearby in a cradle, a boy carries kindling, a girl playing in the background is barefoot, and a rundown house appears in the background. In the text accompanying the illustration on page 118, the student is told, "Describe the inside of the house as you imagine it, and the family of which you see a part" (figure 10). On the facing page

Figure 9. "Topics for Study and Conversation. When and where was cotton first raised in this country? Finest variety—where from—why so called. Planting seeds—blossom—pod, or boll. Cotton seeds—cotton gins—Eli Whitney. Uses of cotton—cotton clothing—cotton factories."

"Composition. Write about cotton, following the order of the Topics." Metcalf and Bright, *Language Lessons, Part One*, 1894, 143–44.

is another assignment: students are asked to read a poem and then write a composition about its lesson. Entitled "Say No," the poem is tractlike: it paints a number of unhappy domestic scenes, attributes them to rum, and ends each verse with some form of the refrain, "say 'No.' " With its overall message (and it does have a message), but also

SUGGESTIONS.

Figure 10. "Suggestions. Describe the picture; that is, tell exactly what you see in it. Describe the inside of the house as you imagine it, and the family of which you see a part. Give a history of the family, or a story suggested by the picture. Every person in the picture must have a name, and also a place in your story." Metcalf and Bright, *Language Lessons, Part One*, 1894, 118.

with specific lines, I believe the poem suggests—and unmistakably— that the domestic poverty the student has been asked to describe in the illustration is a result of the demon rum. The fourth stanza reads:

> Think too of manhood with rum-tainted breath,
> Think of its end and the terrible death.
> Think of the homes that, now shadowed with woe,
> Might have been heaven had the answer been "No."
>
> (Metcalf and Bright 119)

Although more children were attending school at the end of the century, and children of the poor were more likely to be among the student population than they would have been earlier in the century, the reader of this text is still invited "to imagine" the inside of the house of the poor family. The student reading the text is also being taught more than one kind of language lesson: on the one hand, the student is being invited to write original composition; on the other hand, the student is asked to pass judgment on the family living in poverty, with the implication being that "you, too, can turn out like this if you give in to the demon rum." In this particular case, the moral lesson seems to loom larger than the composition lesson.

In Michael Halloran's work on the history of writing instruction, he notes the impact of nineteenth-century technologies on writing; he points to the increased availability of pens, ink, and pencils and the consequences of that availability for instruction. He also notes that because nineteenth-century audiences were likely to be readers of text rather than listeners, an emphasis "to represent discourse visually" emerged: new attention was given to sentences and paragraphs as elements of discourse; the outline gained in stature; and structure of written discourse took on new importance (171–76). Here I have argued that the technology of wood engraving had a particular impact on writing instruction in the schools: as educational reformers came to understand that children learned more readily from things than from words, visual representations of objects and scenes became increasingly important in schools. These visual representations and their framing texts provide contemporary readers of nineteenth-century composition texts with a window on the dominant culture's life and values in the nineteenth century; they provided nineteenth-century students with guidelines for good behavior and good living. More importantly, however, they served as prompts for original writing, and in so doing, they represented a self-conscious break with an earlier pedagogy based on memorization or abstractions.

5 / Textual Practices of the Young Composers

The habit of preserving copies of letters and compositions will be very valuable, and the gratification afforded, by the possession and occasional examination of such copies, will amply compensate for all the time and attention that may be given.
—Charles Northend, *The Young Composer*, 1848

In the schools of New York and New England, compositions vary, in length, from one page to five pages of foolscap: they are written daily, weekly, bi-weekly, monthly, or quarterly; and the subjects are given by the teacher, or selected by the pupils.
—Simon Kerl, *Elements of Composition and Rhetoric*, 1869

One child writes funny stories, and laughs herself as she writes; another gives descriptions of natural scenery, in the midst of which her characters find themselves. One writes about wolves and other horrors. I have a variety of pictures hanging on the walls, and I sometimes propose that they should write stories about them.
—Mary Peabody Mann and Elizabeth Peabody, *Moral Culture of Infancy*, 1869

As I have been arguing, the history of school-based writing instruction is richer and more nuanced than our stories have yet allowed. First Books and their little-known authors; the influence of Pestalozzian thought on composition practice; the role of illustrations in the democratization of writing—these are among the aspects of the story that thus far have gone almost unnoticed. Even to attend to these players and these events, however, is to miss part of the story, for what they represent are the instructional and institutional voices: the voices of rhetoricians, of teachers, of textbook writers, of educational reformers, of philosophers, of clergy. Perhaps more forcefully, they represent one part of the teaching/learning practice, in Kathleen McCormick's words, "what the teacher is supposedly teaching." What they cannot represent—what is absent from an interrogation of the institutional voices and texts—is "what the student is supposedly learning" (104). Reading a list of topics for student papers, after all, doesn't reveal if students wrote on those topics or what qualities they displayed in their writing. Neither do textbooks, for example, open a window on nineteenth-century students' extracurricular writing: on the letters or memoirs or diaries they wrote at home, or on the writing they generated in the liminal space between private writing and classroom-assigned writing. Most significantly, classroom textbooks can never reveal the ways in which students wrote within, against, or beyond the limits set by their school books.

In Carol Gilligan's work, she argues—over and again—that to be human is to have a voice; and to have a voice, you need to have a listener. Here I carve out a space to listen to the voices of the young composers: the receivers rather than the deliverers of instruction, the authors of texts that to date have received the least attention from composition historians. My argument is that student texts contribute to an understanding of nineteenth-century writing instruction in two ways. First, the texts that students wrote in school, what I call classroom-based texts, represent the changes that occurred in composition texts: that is, over the century, assigned student writing began to include not just abstract and distant topics, but also topics that were concrete and familiar. In addition and however gradually, the writing became less distanced and more particularly circumscribed by the particularities of the student's own life. Secondly, extracurricular texts that students composed, either outside of school or at the edges of school, reveal that in these peripheral spaces, students wrote in ways that went beyond textbook directives: they assumed the persona of a writer and wrote with attendant authority about their own experience of writing. While it is important, therefore, to survey not just textbooks but also student writing, it is particularly important to look at the student writing that was produced at the edges of school or out-

Boy writing composition.

Description. Observe that the father and mother are both assisting their son, by giving him information. But neither of them is writing his exercise for him.

Figure 11. "Boy writing composition." John Frost, *Easy Exercises*, 1839, 25.

side of school. It is here that students were most likely to write outside the lines, and it is here that the journey from what Linda Brodkey calls "writing as ritual performance" to "writing on the bias" (30–51)—a journey that is ongoing even in the writing classrooms of today—took its first steps.

Few systems exist for locating texts composed by students. As the work of JoAnn Campbell, David Jolliffe, Sue Carter Simmons, and others verifies, a number of university archives hold writing from college students. As far as I can tell, neither schools nor libraries routinely saved bundles of loose compositions from school-age students. But neither is what Alvina Treut Burrows reported in a 1977 International Reading Association publication accurate: that very little "actual writing by children and adolescents" is available (21) before the end of the nineteenth century, or that very little writing was done; John Frost's 1839 *Easy Exercises* even illustrates and describes a child writing a composition (figure 11). Nonpublished student texts that I have located include handwritten essays in school composition books and letters. Published student writing I have surveyed includes letters, journals, and memoirs; model essays in textbooks and in education journals; award-winning essays in prize books, in annual examination reports, and in commencement programs; and writing in a range of genres in student newspapers and student literary journals.[1]

More difficult than locating the student texts is creating a context in which to read them. For loose student essays, such as those found in a family's papers, it is possible to know, for example, the name of the writer's family, the date of the essay, the school the writer attended, and even something of the family's economic or social circumstances. For student writing that is published, it is sometimes possible to represent an institutional context, that is, to know the name of the writer, her school, and the date of the writing, and also to know how many essays were submitted in a prize category in a particular year, for example, or what the judges' criteria were for awarding prizes. For neither nonpublished nor published writing, however, is it possible to know much about the instructional context for a particular essay or about the student's instruction in writing in broader terms. We rarely have access to the details of a school's curriculum, the textbooks a student used, the parameters of a given assignment, the teacher's approach to writing instruction, what the teacher actually said to the student about writing, what process the student followed in writing his or her paper, what writing the student did outside of school—or any of the many other contingencies that would be helpful in creating a thick description of a piece of student writing. Much of the context for reading student texts, therefore, comes, as in the case of published prize writing, from the larger document of which the models are a part and from the representations of writing instruction that appear in nineteenth-century textbooks and surrounding pedagogical materials.

Textbook Instruction and Classroom-Based Writing

> When we take a survey of mankind, and observe their different persuits, we find that perseverance and industry are necessary to success in them all. No object is so easily attained, as to preclude the necessity of these virtues; and scarcely any, however difficult,

is placed beyond their reach. Peseverance overcomes the greatest difficulties; nature itself bends to its power; and the very elements own its sway.

—Cazneau Palfrey, *Prize Book of the Publick Latin School*, 1821

It was but yesterday that the news came of another terrible battle. All day long had brothers been fighting; all day the cannon had been booming across the field, and Death had been busy claiming his victims, while we sat peacefully at home, little thinking of the hard struggle that was going on in our sister State.

—Wilhelmina Walbridge, student at Buffalo Female Academy, 1862

Consistent with the shift in the larger culture that began to privilege the individual voice, one of the most significant changes that occurred in the nineteenth-century composition textbook is what students were taught about the locus of authority. In the beginning of the century, students learned that authority resided in a shared repository of knowledge, and they were taught to compose their school texts out of their understanding of and participation in that repository. Demonstrating the impersonality of classical rhetoric and the debt of early composition instruction in this country to that tradition, Robert Connors argues that "even children were expected to read and argue from myth, history, and contemporary questions" and that "proofs of argument were impersonal" ("Personal Writing" 167). The result is that children were taught to write about a world populated by adults and distanced from their own lives, and they were taught to write not as children, but as if they were adults. During the century, the locus of authority began to shift: instead of residing in a collective and unassailable voice, authority was extended to include individual voices, including individual voices of children and of young women. And thus, textbook practice changed as well. At the beginning of the century, most texts asked students to write imitative/memorized text (in a "pure and flowing" style); by the end of the century, more texts asked them to write original and experience-based text (that was "fresh" and "clear"). Like any emerging practice, this shift was not clean or simple—or without detours, interruptions, doublings-back, and sidetracks—but it is without a doubt visible. I begin here by pointing to this shift in textbooks, then demonstrating that it is also a visible move in classroom-based writing.

Like the college texts by Samuel P. Newman, Henry Noble Day, and others, school-based composition textbooks were both derivative and eclectic; they were also experimental in many ways and did not, at least in the early part of the century, fit a single mold. The very earliest nineteenth-century composition books for students, those that were written as imitations of adult texts, were, as I substantiate in chapter 2, based on John Walker's *Teacher's Assistant*;[2] these books, and I think of Richard Green Parker's 1832 *Progressive Exercises* as an example, often excerpted lengthy passages from Walker or used his language and/or his framework. As late as 1853, Ebenezer Brewer celebrated Walker's plan in his *Guide to English Composition*. As I point out in chapter 3, some books diverged from that model as early as 1838; these are the books that specifically targeted beginning writers and often grounded their pedagogy in Pestalozzian thought. Many books, both early and late in the century, exhibit traces of Hugh Blair's emphasis on taste or "rules" and traces of George Campbell's aims, later represented as genres; and books from the latter part of the century that focus on older school students reflect the modes of discourse that we have come to think of as Alexander Bain's categories.[3]

Of the British rhetoricians, the writer who most specifically addressed composing of school-age students is Richard Whately. In section 5 of his "Introduction" to the *Elements of Rhetoric*, he writes that young students should compose themes not about "Virtus est medium vitiorum," but about subjects more suited to their age and experience. In particular, he recommends subjects drawn from the student's schoolwork; subjects drawn from conversations that the student may have listened to; and subjects drawn from the student's own "amusements, familiar occurrences, and every-day transactions" (21). More than one nineteenth-century writer includes portions of this section from Whately; some writers borrow silently (J. Orville Taylor's 1838 *A Help to Young Writers*, for instance, includes a long passage of Whately's without any acknowledgment), while others confirm that Whately is their source; J. R. Boyd, for example, in his 1844 *Ele-*

ments of Rhetoric and Literary Criticism and J. M. D. Meiklejohn, in the
composition chapter in his 1894 *English Grammar*, both quote from
Whately's work.[4]

Given that textbook writers turned to a range of sources for their
position on writing instruction and given that, at least for the greatest
part of the century, school board mandates did not determine the content and form of these books, the books display marked pedagogical
differences. Some writers, for example, argued that students were not
capable of original thought until they were twelve or thirteen years old
and, therefore, should not begin composing until then; others disagreed. Some writers thought students should be well-versed in grammar before they began the task of composing; others disagreed. Some
writers held on to a catechistical format well into the midcentury; others broke from that format in the 1830s. Some writers specifically targeted beginning writers and, thus, produced First Books, often fewer
than one hundred pages long; others wrote for both beginning and
advanced students and produced tomes of many hundreds of pages,
compendiums, as it were, of grammar, rhetoric, composition, and
belles lettres. And as I point out in chapter 4, some writers used illustrations early in the century; others did not. Complicating a reading
of writing instruction based on textbooks is that well into the second
half of the century, there was no guarantee that all students in a classroom were using the same text. In *Pillars of the Republic*, Carl Kaestle's
1983 account of common schools, he notes that before uniform textbooks and uniform textbook adoptions, it was a time-honored tradition for students to bring family-owned books to school to be used
as a student's textbook; Kaestle quotes a Wisconsin historian who observed that "there were sometimes as many different textbooks in use
in a school as there were children in attendance" (17). And an 1837
list in the *American Annals of Education* entitled "Fifty Troubles of a
Teacher" includes "Scanty supply of school books," "Great variety of
authors," "Variety of editions," "Books badly printed or badly bound,"
and "Books left at home by the pupils" among those troubles ("Fifty
Troubles" 409–10).

In spite of these and many other differences, what stands out is
this pattern: that the move toward the democratization of writing that

began in the late 1830s continued and grew in the second half of the century. By the end of the century, it was commonplace for textbook writers to ask students to write original text rather than memorized text; to ask students to write about concrete objects before tackling abstract topics; and to invite students to write about their own socially and historically and culturally situated lives rather than about the lives of the ancients.

In "Prefaces" or "Introductions" to their late nineteenth-century texts, many writers themselves commented about this historical shift from the abstract to the concrete, from the impersonal to the personal. Addressing the readers of his 1893 text, Alphonso Newcomer, for example, wrote,

> A thousand aspiring, or, it may be, driven and desperate, young essayists have written upon the genius of Napoleon and the pleasures of hope and the blessings of civilization; but ten to one nobody has ever yet written about your grandfather's barn with all its denizens from the calves in the basement to the pigeons in the roof, with its pulley-fork and grain chutes, its harness room and machinery sheds, and the inexhaustible resources for fun in its spacious carriage room and haymow on a rainy day. The loving and truthful touches which you are sure to give to descriptions of this character will be worth more than all the artificial glamor your fancy may throw over "cloud-capped towers and gorgeous palaces." (11)

This growing emphasis on the daily life of the student was also reflected in the changing nature of the "list of topics for compositions" that was a standard feature in many nineteenth-century texts.[5] The abstract topics in the early nineteenth-century lists did not completely disappear; in John Hart's 1886 text, for example, he still included "The importance of perseverance" and "The evils of carelessness" in his list (*First Lessons* 102–3). And what came to be called "exposition" and "argument" remained a part of the writing curriculum. But abstract topics and impersonally voiced writing no longer prevailed. Introducing a list of "miscellaneous subjects" in 1869 that included "A Year on a Farm," "A Year in a City," "A Year in a Factory," "A Year at School" (364), Simon Kerl wrote, "Unusually abstruse or abstract subjects should also be generally avoided; because most people can not easily understand what is said on such subjects, or they care but little for what can be said" (363). More common in the end-of-the-century lists, such as those that appeared in Shaw's and Hart's texts for young writers, were concrete topics that invited descriptive or narrative renderings or expository text about a familiar subject: "A description of the service you attended last Sunday," "A description of a character— the Peanut Man, the Scissors Grinder, etc." (Shaw 105); "What I can recollect of the first school that I attended," "My first schoolbook," "Some account of the oldest person I ever knew," "How candles are made," "The influence of circus exhibitions" (Hart, *First Lessons* 102–5).

Student models in textbooks. Just as textbooks asked students for personal writing by the end of the century, the models of writing they included (often called "specimens") for students to imitate also reflected this change. John Rippingham's 1816 text "designed for the use of schools," for example, contains essays by Dr. Johnson, Addison, and Hume. When composition books appeared that were, in fact, really written for children, one of their innovations was the use of models not written by celebrated intellectuals. In some cases, these models were written, I suspect, by the textbook author to appear as if they were written by a student. In other cases, the models have a student's name or initials attached and, according to the textbook author, are the work of his or her pupils.

The change to using student models was, like any change, inflected with what Raymond Williams would call both residual and emergent practice (40–42). One year before John Frost, Charles Morley asked students to respond to an illustration from their own experience ("Describe the elephant, and other animals that you have seen or read of," [*Practical Guide* 22]). Yet when he includes sample writing, it is based on the more traditional directive to "write a story from memory," that is, a story based on what the student remembered of an essay read by the teacher. And the sample student writing

Morley includes reflects not the new edge of his pedagogy, directing students to write from their own experience, but the listen-memorize-write pedagogy that was dominant at the beginning of the century. Morley credits a nine-year-old, for example, with writing a fable about a picture book and an arithmetic book: the student's text argued that although the picture book was more attractive than the arithmetic, it was "an empty show," while the arithmetic furnished "much valuable knowledge" (*Practical Guide* 54); and the accompanying moral remonstrated, "The proud make a good outward appearance, but that is all; for their covering only conceals their deformity from public view" (54). The point is that if indeed a child "wrote" that text, as Morley claims, it was first written by an adult, memorized by the child, and then written back, as it were, to the adult.

By the second half of the century, at least some of the models in textbooks were grounded in the personal experience of the young writer. In Hiram Hadley's 1871 *Lessons in Language*, he includes an example of an impromptu theme written by "Jennie." Hadley notes that the theme was written in fifteen minutes on an assigned topic and "is printed . . . without the slightest correction." Entitled "A Garden," the theme reads in part:

> The garden of which I think first, is, of course, my own.
>
> In my garden I have my particular favorites, a moss-rose bush and a large pansy bed. Sitting under the shade of the apple-tree, by the pansies, I talk to them by the hour, and they nod their bright little heads and say sweet things to me. The river is but a little distance from my garden, and its gentle ripple is always heard, adding much to the sweet influence of the spot.
>
> How many bouquets I have gathered from that garden, for friends whom I dearly love.
>
> Now and then a tiny flower to place in a letter that should tell more sweet things than I could write.
>
> Blue forgetmenots I gather for the graves of those who live with the angels, and rose buds for the hair of those

who live with us. A treasure is my garden, and I am longing
for it to-day with a tender yearning which shall soon be gratified. (129)

In a footnote to Jennie's essay, Hadley told his readers that because it
was near the end of the school year, Jennie's yearning to see her garden
would indeed soon be gratified. The implication is that Jennie's "I,"
unlike the "I" character in earlier textbook examples, was a real girl,
not an invented character. To a reader today, Jennie was also invented
in Barthe's sense of "already written" or "always already spoken" because she was, of course, constructed by nineteenth-century cultural
codes that governed children. But for all her constructedness, "Jennie"
was also an actual child and not an authorial composite or a product
of the author's imaginary. And Hadley was among the first of many
textbook writers in the second half of the nineteenth-century, especially writers of language series books, to include model texts written
by children about their own lives.

Belletristic models do not disappear from textbooks, but, in the
second half of the century, they are more likely to be found in books
for older students or in books that are intended for multiple audiences; Kerl's 1869 text, for example, was intended for both beginning and advanced students, and for the advanced students, he offered
models by writers such as Addison, Carlyle, and Dickens. Newcomer,
writing for younger students, argued that "the ludicrously wild flight
of many a young writer's eagle feathered shaft" is evidence that it
was "useless" to give students "a description from Ruskin" or "an essay of De Quincy"; whereas, Newcomer wrote, "If the models are
within [the student's] reach, if he can hope to equal or even excel
them, he will obtain from them not only profit but an encouragement
that is worth more than any false or over-wrought inspiration" (viii).
In fact, Newcomer makes extensive use of student writing in his text.

Student essays from the Latin School prize books. This shift—from
the abstract and the distant to the personal and the familiar—that was
grounded in a changing school population and a changing textbook
pedagogy and reflected in student models included in textbooks was

also reflected in the "prize essays" published in commencement programs or in schools' annual reports. The earliest published classroom-based writing by school-age students that I have found, other than that which occurs in textbooks, occurs in the *Prize Book of the Publick Latin School* (1820–1827). Boston Latin, as the school was popularly known, was a five-year classical school for boys, admitting students who were at least nine years old, who were "acquainted with the stops and marks used in writing" and with the "various sounds and powers of letters," and who could read and write fluently (*Prize Book*, 1820, 14–15). Following the thinking of Vicesimus Knox, D.D., whose essay "On Writing Exercises" was included in the 1822 *Prize Book*, boys were not considered able to compose original essays before they were twelve or thirteen; prior to that, their composing in English consisted of writing Aesop's fables from memory and writing letters to family and friends. Among the English themes that won prizes during this time period were J. T. Sargent's "Carpe Diem" (*Prize Book*, 1823, 88); an unnamed fourteen-year-old's "On Classical Learning" (*Prize Book*, 1824, 24); George Chapman's "On Industry" (*Prize Book*, 1824, 28); William W. Sturgis's "On Firmness of Purpose" (*Prize Book*, 1826, 20); and William H. Simmons's "On Education" (*Prize Book*, 1826, 23).

As the importance of formal education grew in the national consciousness, many of the essays celebrated education, in some cases, privileging knowledge gained in school over knowledge gained from experience or from the land. In Simmons's essay, "On Education," for example, he contrasted the "rustic" with the "philosopher," as he argued that education elevates the person:

Around the rustic's cottage perhaps nature has spread her treasures; but they are lost on his narrow and uncultivated mind; while the philosopher makes scientific discoveries in the stone upon his wall, or the flower by his wayside. [The rustic] stands unmoved and uninstructed by the silent language of nature; while the man of cultivation and refinement, as he sits down on Nature's lap, feels himself at peace with all around him; his passions are calm; his mind is elevated; his heart is melted; and he reposes, as it were, in the bosom of his God. (*Prize Book*, 1826, 24–25)

Later in his essay, Simmons praised the new nation's political and religious knowledge, especially celebrating "industry, sobriety, and virtue" (29). In addition to "cultivation and refinement," these were among the qualities that were valued by the new nation, listed in the early nineteenth-century texts as writing topics, and reproduced in the schools; it is not surprising that they were also the qualities that were represented in prize-winning student texts.

Even, however, as these topics were the norm, early if small signs of emerging differences also appeared. In 1824, a fourteen-year-old wrote a prize-winning essay entitled "On Classical Learning" in which he argued the value of reading a text in its original language:

I know not how others feel; for myself, (although it is said a schoolboy never felt any pleasure in the perusal of a classical author,) I can say, that I receive much more satisfaction, and pay more attention to a beautiful thought in reading it in the original, than if I had received it through the cold and distant medium of a translation. (*Prize Book*, 1824, 25)

But at a time when most of the categories in the *Prize Book* were for works in Latin or Greek (Latin poems in hexameters, Latin odes, Greek odes, Latin themes—or were from Latin translations) and only two categories, English poems and English themes, were in English, this student, while defending the importance of studying Latin and Greek, wrote his theme in English.[6]

Student writing from two girls' academies. As academies and seminaries for girls became more numerous in the second half of the century, these schools, like other private schools, often published annual reports, catalogues, and commencement programs, both to celebrate their faculty and student accomplishments and to encourage new enrollments. These annual publications from two nineteenth-century schools for girls and young women, Albany Female Academy (founded in 1814) and Buffalo Female Academy (founded in 1851), are valuable not only because they include student writing over a period of years and from a range of age groups, but also because they provide a more elaborate context for reading that writing, including the school's position on composition instruction as well as commentary from the committees that made the awards for the year's best essays.

An 1857 edition of the Albany Female Academy's *Annual Examination Report* notes that their students ranged in age from five to eighteen and were divided, by age, into four departments, the first for the oldest students, the fourth for the youngest. The catalogue also notes that along with spelling, reading, grammar, geography, history, and arithmetic, one of the primary branches of study at the school was composition, and of the subjects named in the catalogue, composition is described at greatest length.[7] I include the entire description here because while it doesn't provide the details of a particular classroom, it elaborates the school's approach to composition instruction at a level of detail that is rarely available for mid-nineteenth-century schools:

COMPOSITION
Careful attention is given to this very important branch of female education. Exercises in oral and written compositions are begun in the youngest department, and kept up constantly during the whole course. In addition to this, essays, etc., are written once in two weeks by all the pupils. The compositions are submitted to a teacher whose time is exclusively devoted to composition and criticism. After careful correction and revision, each essay is returned to the writer, with such oral strictures and criticisms as may be deemed necessary and useful. The productions are then rewritten, and copies preserved in the Institution. A portion of each week is devoted to the reading of essays in each Department, and the patrons of the Academy are invited to be present at these exercises. (*Annual Examination Report*, 1857, 6)

The annual publications from both Albany and Buffalo include
the names of the prize-winning essays for each division and some of
the prize-winning essays; a significant gap is that they did not publish
the prize-winning essays from the youngest students. What the titles
suggest, though, is not surprising: that by midcentury, the younger
students were writing, for the most part, themes about concrete topics, while older students, for the most part, were writing about
more abstract and more difficult topics. In 1854, the winning essay
titles for the younger girls at Buffalo Female Academy were "Youth,"
"Our Home Wreath," "Visit to a Grave Yard," "Pets," and "Trees." That
same year, the titles of the prize-winning essays of the older girls included "Nature, the Mirror in Which God Is Seen" and "The Mission
of Genius."

Perhaps more interesting are the comments from awards committees about the style of the writing. In the closing remarks about the
1854 prize essays for the youngest girls at Buffalo, Mary E. Mixer and
Mary L. Norton, on behalf of the awards committee, wrote that they
were

> especially gratified to notice in all the compositions a truly
> feminine style and a love of simplicity and nature, rather than
> a striving after "strong-minded" and far-fetched themes,
> which is so popular a style among the young pupils of many
> of our literary Institutions;—the absence of which is very
> creditable to those who have had the training of the impres-
> sible young minds. (*Annual Circular*, 1854, 37)

While readers today would find the designation "truly feminine" in
need of further definition and, I believe, would resist its easy equation
with "natural and graceful," it is important to note that it is in this
setting—a school for girls—and with this population—the youngest
students—that a change to "natural and graceful" writing is named
and celebrated.[8] Within a few years, students at all levels were praised
for their "absence of all attempt at something fine" (*Annual Circular*,
1856, 33), and an 1859 committee praised essays for their "native

good sense, which promises usefulness in the world" and criticized essays which "savored too much of the mystical, or transcendental" (*Annual Circular*, 1859, 27). In 1858, a committee at Albany wrote,

> Those who themselves are but beginning to learn, assume to teach. They choose as themes the great subjects of the philosophy of history, and the metaphysical problems which finite minds, placed in the midst of the infinite, can not resolve. The Committee would recommend to the Pupils to cultivate a more familiar and less ambitious style; to describe the scenes and characters of actual life, in which exercise they will develop the power of observation, out of which comes originality of thought and individuality of style. (*Annual Examination Report*, 1858, 7)

Many committee reports suggest that, increasingly in the second half of the century, all students were also encouraged to write original text, an 1854 Buffalo committee calling originality "refreshing in days of hackneyed themes." At the same time, the regard for "felicity of sentiment" and "pure and flowing style" that characterized early committee reports gave way to large extent to a regard for "freshness" and "clearness." In 1862, a prize-winning composition was celebrated for its "absence of affectation," and because it was "strikingly original" and "very naturally expressed" (*Annual Circular*, 1862, 29). What the commentary about the student writing suggests to me is that as the nation turned toward more practical concerns, and as the textbooks followed suit, student writing that was chosen by citizens' committees for awards, at least (and even) in these two girls' academies, also reflected these changes.

I point to one final change that I see occurring in the classroom-based writing of nineteenth-century students. In the early part of the century, students wrote about great biblical battles, about the Trojan War, about the Battle of Philippi, and about "war, commerce, and missionary enterprises, as means of civilizing barbarous countries" (Richard Green Parker, *Aids* 397). Some acknowledgment of U.S. political life is visible in early nineteenth-century texts, naming Washington as a hero, for example, or including a model essay about Washington's personal qualities. But in June 1862, Buffalo Female Academy awarded Wilhelmina C. Walbridge, a high school student, a first-prize honor for her essay entitled "Virginia." For today's readers, the language of the essay is sentimental and overstated. The remarkable aspect of the essay is that it is about the Civil War; even more remarkable is that Walbridge wrote the essay in 1862, while the war was in progress. In other words, here is an essay written by a student—in the first person—arguing about a then-contemporary social issue: and the essay won a prize. Tracing Virginia's transition from "a weak colony" to one of the "proudest and most honored among the sisterhood of States," the writer lamented that Virginia, "the Mother of Presidents," became "the Nurse of Traitors": "Angry mutterings of discontent creep through the land like a blight, and Virginia, forgetting her heroes and the proud place they gave her, is among the first to lend a willing ear." Meanwhile, the writer continued,

The loyal North, roused by the many insults heaped upon her name, arises in her might, and strong with God's help and blessing, seeks to crush the rebellion. Again the war-cry sounds through the land. Once more men leave their plows, and work-shops and counting-houses, to respond to it. From the dusty streets of the city, and the green lanes of the country, they come, this time not to repel foreign invasion or oppression, but to save the dear old flag from dishonor and shame. Virginia is the principal theatre of action, and her battle-fields, grown green with the grass of almost a century, are again crimsoned with blood. It was but yesterday that the news came of another terrible battle. All day long had brothers been fighting; all day the cannon had been booming across the field, and Death had been busy claiming his victims, while we sat peacefully at home, little thinking of the hard struggle that was going on in our sister State. . . .

But O, Virginia! we shall yet claim you as our own. Already the "flag of the free" waves over some of your green valleys and fertile plains; and before June with her crown of roses shall have passed from the land, we hope to receive you, wounded and bleeding though you be, into the sisterhood you have so unnaturally deserted; and in after years, should trouble come upon us, to see you rally by *our* banner, thanking God that you can once more fight beneath the Stars and Stripes. (*Annual Circular*, 1862, 27–29)

It is, of course, impossible to know the source of this student's opinion; perhaps she was expressing an opinion she had heard or read second- or third-hand. And as I noted, the language, by contemporary standards, smacks of sentiment. But these disclaimers aside, it is nonetheless true that a student was writing not about universal or moral principles, not about grand historic events from the classical era. Rather, she was writing about a then-contemporary social problem: about men leaving their plows and workshops and counting houses; about crimson fields; about brother fighting brother. Although imperfectly, I see this essay as a representation of the ways that, at least in some cases, complex contemporary issues broke through into nineteenth-century, classroom-based writing as early as 1862.

From the time of Ben Franklin, the two-pronged practice of encouraging competition among students and awarding prizes for the most successful performances—a practice known as "emulation"— was popular in many schools, but not without detractors. And as Nancy Green points out in "Female Education and School Competition: 1820–1850," many of the detractors, both women and men, were especially opposed to encouraging competition among girls because of what they saw as the dangers to the nineteenth-century understanding of the role of women. According to Green, George Emerson, principal of Boston's English Classical School for boys from 1821 to 1823 and later principal of a private school for girls, argued that emulation would "unfit females for the duties of their sex" and encourage "boldness, vanity and selfishness at the expense of humility, devotion to duty, and the desire to do right for its own sake" (qtd. in Nancy Green 134). Echoing this argument, J. C. Warren, another popular educator in the 1830s, wrote, "The application of the system of rivalry to the softer sex . . . appears to me fraught with mischief (qtd. in Nancy

Green 135). So during a time in history when more girls than ever before had the opportunity to attend school beyond the earliest grades and when girls had the opportunity to see their writing in print, there were those who would have silenced the girls' voices in a particular way. The *Common School Journal* of 1840 even published a letter from a young girl who criticized the emulation system. The twelve-year-old wrote in part, "And as to prizes, they scarcely ever fail to create some degree of bad feeling. People must have but a poor opinion of our motives for writing and studying if they think that the hope of obtaining a prize would be any inducement to great effort" (qtd. in "Prizes" 76). That the Albany and Buffalo Female Academies resisted this silencing not only by awarding prizes for themes but also by publishing the girls' writing was, of course, valuable to their students; because the emulation system allows us a window on the evolution of nineteenth-century, classroom-based writing and, in particular, to see that the inclusion of women in school helped to change the way writing developed, it is also valuable to us.[9]

A second value of these reports and the student writing they include is that they complicate Miriam Brody's reading of nineteenth-century rhetoric and composition instruction as "manly." Quoting Dennis Baron that "women's use of [English] was often considered a direct threat to its virility" (101), Brody argues that nineteenth-century school and college composition texts, following Edward Channing's advice in his *Lectures*, equated excellence in writing with manly virtues of "strength" and "purpose" and "directness." For her argument, Brody relies primarily on a reading of college texts and popular school texts, and in these arenas, I believe she is persuasive. A gap in her work is that she does not include sample student writing in her discussion, or lesser-known school texts, or, most importantly, student writing from a female academy. Student texts from the Albany and Buffalo Female Academies allow us to see that in these scenes of writing, qualities other than those associated with "manliness" were valued—and these are the same qualities that represent the move away from writing about the transcendent to writing about the immanent. At the end of the nineteenth-century, Elizabeth Cady Stanton frequently argued that women were denied a voice in government. To

a Senate committee in 1892, she maintained that "Shakespeare's . . .
Titus Andronicus contains a terrible satire on woman's position in the
nineteenth century—'Rude men seized the king's daughter, cut out her
tongue, cut off her hands, and then bade her to call for water and wash
her hands.' What a picture of woman's position!" (qtd. in Baynton 75).
But while women had no voice in nineteenth-century government,
greater numbers of girls and young women attended school in the
nineteenth-century and had a voice in school settings. And the record
of that public voice was preserved in their school compositions. (See
appendix 4 for an account by Elizabeth Cady Stanton of writing a
composition—and its impact on her growth and development.)

Finally, the reports from these two girls' academies are valuable
for the perspective they provide on nineteenth-century evaluation of
student writing: they reveal that the committees understood the complexities involved in judging student work, an 1868 group allowing as
how their judgments were necessarily "one-sided and partial" because
it was "impossible for them to know many things which might tend to
modify or entirely change their decision"; they could not know, for
example, the extent to which one student labored over a paper, the
extent to which another student wrote "hastily at odd moments" (*Annual Examination Report*, 1868, 10). And because the reports suggest
that, overall, the committees were pleased with the quality of the student writing, they complicate our reading of the Harvard reports, especially the 1892 report written by Charles Francis Adams, Edwin
Lawrence Godkin, and Josiah Quincy that is well known for discred-
iting the way schools prepared students for college writing.[10] Occasionally, the Albany and Buffalo reports praised sentence-level correct-
ness: in 1855, a committee admired the compositions of the youngest
students for their "grammatical accuracy and considerable skill in the
structure of sentences" (*Annual Examination Report*, 1855, 5). And occasionally, a committee criticized sentence-level problems: the 1855
Buffalo Female Academy report noted, "One fault, indeed, is too common not to be branded: it respects a loose and unlearned punctuation"
(*Annual Circular*, 1855, 39). But on the whole, unlike the Harvard
reports, these reports focused on the substantive features of essays.
"Perspicuity of thought," "Originality," "Arrangement": these were

criteria cited again and again for determining winning essays. An 1853 committee report from the Albany Female Academy noted "abundant evidence that the instructors . . . have paid much attention to the important subject of English Composition, and that their pupils have profited by their lessons" (*Annual Examination Report*, 1853, 4). And an 1854 report from Buffalo Female Academy explained, the committee members were "highly gratified by the industry and talent evinced in the compositions submitted to them for their inspection" and determined that because "the hardest lesson for young minds, is *learning to think*, it seemed best to make the *degree of thought* evinced in each [theme], the test of excellence" (*Annual Circular*, 1854, 37).

One way to catch a glimpse of writing instruction in nineteenth-century schools is to read the textbooks. Another is to read the student writing included in textbooks or in prize books or in commencement programs; another is to read the reports written by the committees that evaluated student writing. Here I've been suggesting that still another way to read nineteenth-century writing instruction is to read these documents in concert: what these "ways in" share is that they address formal, classroom-based writing, and read next to each other, they reveal striking consistencies among what the textbooks were asking for, what students were producing, and what public opinion and the schools were rewarding. In particular, they suggest that classroom-based writing reflected nineteenth-century educational reforms and that the reforms in the early part of the century are easily visible in the writing of young students and in the writing from students in girls' schools. While some schools continued to prepare students for college and for careers in law or ministry or medicine, the number of schools preparing students for nonprofessional careers increased dramatically in the second half of the nineteenth century. The goal of schools, as they were initially constituted for younger students, but also as uniform high schools became part of the U.S. landscape toward the end of the century, was to prepare increasing numbers of students for the reading and writing tasks of participating in a democracy. Of course, the emphasis shifted from Latin to English, from the classical world to the contemporary world, and from artful writing to writing that was practical and natural. But while classroom writing assignments continued to be circumscribed by teachers and textbooks and cultural mores, students also began to write essays that reflected, at least in some cases, the circumstances of the writer's own life.

For all these changes, however, school-based writing was not a site for play, for resistance, or for writing about writing. For representations of these writerly stances, I turn to student texts from the extracurriculum.

Extracurricular Writing at Home: Letters and Memoirs

> France has acted very badly in refusing so long to pay a debt which she had acknowledged to be due to the United States. . . . But little girls like me had better learn to knit stockings than to be talking about politics.
>
> —Jane Elfreth, letter to her father,
> *Elfreth Book of Letters,* January 20, 1836

> Such horrid Sundays we have here:—fish balls, brown bread, mustard, and doughnuts for breakfast, then half-hours and three quarters to dress, go to Church, sit perked up in the gallery, home to dinner, off immediately to service, then home to stay with your roommate till tea time; after that the visiting quarters, half-hours, and solitude with the victimized roommate, then bed ends the long day. Not a bit of home Sunday life, not one minute of being all together for a good earnest talk; well, I shall know by and by how to value the true Sundays when I get back home to them once more.
>
> —Harriet Chapell Newcomb, *Journal of
> an Abbot Academy Girl,* January 4, 1874

Anne Ruggles Gere points to the value of including alternative literacy sites in the stories of writing instruction and argues for the importance of the writing that adults composed in nonacademic settings, in what she terms, the "extracurriculum." For adults, these sites ranged from gatherings at kitchen tables and in rented rooms where women and men, often with little formal education, gathered to "write down their worlds," to gatherings of the members of a club or society dedicated to solving community-based problems with their writing ("Kitchen Tables," 75–76).

The extracurriculum was also an important site for a youngster's growth in literacy development and also a site that our stories thus far have neglected: at home, students wrote letters, memoirs, and diaries; and in the border space between the classroom and home, they wrote for their school newspaper or literary journal. While students' extracurricular sites for writing were more place-bound than those of adults (students didn't have the freedom to travel around the neighborhood or civic community in the ways that adults did), these sites nonetheless allowed students to write in ways that classroom-based assignments did not.

Most nineteenth-century textbooks included a section on letter writing; "the letter" was frequently considered "an easy form of composition" (John Frost, *EE* 76) and was often the first genre students were asked to write; in addition, textbooks generally gave directives (and often formulas or outlines) for different kinds of correspondence: the friendly letter; the social letter, accepting or declining an invitation, for example; and, later in the century, the business letter. In these sections of their texts, many textbook authors borrowed heavily from letter-writing manuals of the day and replicated the manuals' culturally embedded emphasis on the formal properties of letter writing. Textbooks reassured students that by following the proper guidelines for letter writing, they would demonstrate their good taste, their good breeding, their attention to culturally imposed "niceties." According to Richard Green Parker, when Lord Chesterfield received a letter that was sealed not with wax (the preferred method) but with a wafer, he exclaimed, "What does the fellow mean by sending me his own spittle!" Like Chesterfield, Parker favored wax seals, explaining to students that using a wafer implied "haste, which is inconsistent with the studied courtesies of polished life" (*Aids* 204–5). Unlike the textbooks, I am not concerned with the formal properties of letter writing or with formal letters. Rather, I am interested in the letters that, like diaries, journals, and memoirs, students composed outside of a school setting: these texts address subjects and issues that were rarely included in classroom-based writing, the texts are informal and for the most part, self-sponsored, and the texts had a specific audience (other than a teacher) and most often an intimate audience of family, friends, or the writer's self.

Susan Miller notes that a number of letters from young children appear in the commonplace book collection held by the Virginia Historical Society ("Things Inanimate" 102–6), but in general, of all the nineteenth-century student writing one might hope to read, writing samples from the youngest students, especially samples that are not from a school setting, are most difficult to locate.[11] Edited by Susan Winslow Hodge in 1985, *The Elfreth Book of Letters* is a collection of more than one hundred letters written between 1835 and 1837 by members of a nineteenth-century Quaker family living in Philadelphia. Most of the letters were composed by four Elfreth children, all under ten years old in 1835.

In her introduction to the edition, Hodge notes that Jacob Elfreth, father of the children, gave them a blank book in order that they might "improve in . . . writing and keep memorandums of passing events" (*Elfreth Book* 13). Culturally, the Elfreth letters are noteworthy because they provide a window on Philadelphia life and U.S. politics in the third decade of the nineteenth century, on Quaker values, and on child-rearing practices; they also open a window on the private life and activities of this family and on the affection family members shared for each other. The letters report on the weather (especially snow), visiting relatives, family illness, schoolwork, Bible reading, the birth of a sibling, the purchase of a new stove. Jane, for example, wrote of a trip to the dentist on January 22, 1835, to have two teeth extracted:

Dear Father

This afternoon thee took me to Daniel Neal in Arch Street . . . a dentist who extracted two teeth which were decayed—It hurt me considerably but it it was soon over and I was very glad when it was over and came home much happier than I went—This afternon Mother gave me a set of cups and saucers, a slop bowl, sugar bowl, cream cup & tea pot

and thee brought me home a small box of paints—So I am
very well pleased that my troublesome teeth are out and that
I have received in exchange for them such aceptable presents.

Thy affectionate daughter
Jane P Elfreth (*Elfreth Book* 38)

And in a March 1835 letter to their father, Jane's brother Joseph reported that on a trip into the city to do errands for his mother, he saw
a fire engine he very much admired: "[It] is the prettiest ever I saw her
wheels were all brightened and she is a very nice one when I saw her
she was in the street she stands in Chery street between sixt street and
fith street I which thee had been with me then the could saw her too"
(*Elfreth Book* 73).

The letters also demonstrate ways that, in their out-of-school
writing, children were assimilating and/or resisting dominant values,
in their families and in the larger culture. Jane and Caleb, for example,
wrote of obedience both to their parents and to larger cultural codes.
Jane, age seven, wrote to her father in February 1835, "Thee wanted
me to write a little [in the family letter book] and so I did" (*Elfreth
Book* 59); Caleb, age six, wrote to his grandmother in November 1835,
"None of the boys at our school knew their lessons yesterday but I
intend to learn my lessons and try to be a good boy" (86). More strikingly, the letters offer very early commentary about gender roles and
Jane's resistance to the role she was assigned. In a letter from Jane to
her father in January 1836, she wrote about France's refusal to pay the
debt negotiated at the Treaty of Paris, a topic her father had written
about in an earlier letter. In her text, Jane argued that "France has
acted very badly in refusing so long to pay a debt which she had acknowledged to be due to the United States." But then she went on
in her letter to write, "But little girls like me had better learn to knit
stockings than to be talking about politics" (103). In *Manly Writing*,
Miriam Brody argues that nineteenth-century textbooks reproduced
conventional assumptions about gender roles; the place of men was
one of "privilege" and the place of women was "the special place of the
'angel' by the hearth" (106). What is remarkable about Jane's letter, of

course, is not only her acknowledgment of her prescribed role, but also her articulated resistance to the limitations imposed by her gender and age. Jane probably turned to knit stockings by the hearth, but she didn't do that without comment.

Although several years older than the Elfreth children, Robert Troupe Paine also used informal writing to record the quotidian events of his youth. In Paine's writing—published by his parents after he committed suicide as a twenty-two-year-old Harvard student—are some of his school and college themes as well as personal letters and memoirs. One document that Paine called a "composition" is a lengthy and rambling account (thirty-four typescript pages in the published memoirs) of the sixteen-year-old's daily life during the holiday season of Tuesday, December 23, 1845, to Sunday, January 5, 1846. Paine wrote of receiving a fifteen-volume copy, in French, of *Plutarch's Lives* as a Christmas present from his mother, of playing dominoes and chess with his friends, and of attending various church services, some of which he didn't like. Like Jane Elfreth, Paine also used informal writing as a site for resisting cultural expectations imposed on him. In Paine's case, he had a strong dislike for dancing school: Is dancing "useful" or "beneficial to health"? he asked. "Nay," he concluded; in fact, "it is rather injurious in the mode in which it is now often conducted. In hot rooms, and at late hours. Oh, the folly! Oh, the madness! (351). He also criticized card playing (but not chess), theater, and some religious services. One importance of extracurricular writing, therefore, is that in the first half of the century, it provided a site for writers like Jane Elfreth and Robert Troupe Paine to think and to write outside the lines of customary thought.

Another space that opened in this informal writing that is not evident in school writing until much later in the century was for humor. One of the few textbook assignments that calls for humor appears in Edwin Shaw's 1892 *English Composition by Practice*; the assignment reads, "Soap and water. The wonders they sometimes work. This subject affords an opportunity for a humorous paper" (105). As early as 1835, however, on a page in the Elfreth letter book, a child wrote a few tips for healthy living, including, "If you be living and wish to be dead / Eat a cold apple on going to bed" and, more elaborately, "To miss a meal sometimes is good / It purifies and thins the blood; / Gives nature time to clean her streets / From filth and crudities of meats" (*Elfreth Book* 60). More extensive humor appears in Harriet Chapell Newcomb's journal, a document she wrote and illustrated when she was a student at Abbot Academy from 1874 to 1876. In her record of her school days, Newcomb wrote of her friends, of her teachers, of her recreational activities, of her schoolwork, of the "fish balls, brown bread, mustard, and doughnuts for breakfast" (Newcomb 5). When she accidentally dropped her hymnbook in the mud on her way to service, she decided against soiling her gloves by picking it up; further, she wrote,

> I deliberately stepped on it with my hundred and six pounds and left it to an unknown fate. . . . I expect some charitable theologue or other good philanthropist will find, clean, and bring it back to me. I'm sure I hope he won't, for I want a new book and am very glad to get rid of the old one so neatly. (Newcomb 4)

Next to this account, the writer drew an illustration of herself walking along the muddy path, her head in the air, with a young boy following behind her, leaning over to pick up the book from the mud. And next to this illustration, she wrote,

> This appended illustration will give you a faint idea of how the parties concerned appeared at the time. You know I am the South Hall artist, and must sustain my present reputation. It represents me in my brown suit, seal skin jacket, etc., walking triumphantly along, with little Howard bending over to read my name. (Newcomb 4)

Later, she wrote of a church service so crowded that she and her friends were seated directly under the pulpit, her chair too large for the space and thus tipped on two legs. Her comment was, "Then when we wanted to see Prof. Park [the preacher] we had to roll our eyes up like Murillo's picture of the Madonna, only more so, and it was not one bit pleasant, I assure you" (Newcomb 9). In describing a school scene, Newcomb made fun of herself, but she also made fun of a religious painting, a marker of the freedom students claimed in their out-of-school writing.

In Gere's defense of the extracurriculum as an important scene of writing, she urges us to value "the amateur" ("Kitchen Tables" 88), writing that is composed outside of a formal setting and is motivated by desire rather than obligation. I see two reasons to value the amateur writing produced by nineteenth-century students in the forms of letters and memoirs. First, this amateur writing provided a site for self-expression and for resistance that was not ordinarily available in classroom-based writing. For all the educational reform that occurred in the century, schools replicated the culture's dominant values, including the value that children were to be obedient creatures, seen and not heard. Even the experience-based writing that students did in school was framed by the restrictions of school. Probably because letters and diaries were considered innocuous, children were permitted to use those scenes of writing to contest received wisdom. As early as 1836, three years before John Frost published his groundbreaking *Easy Exercises*, a seven-year-old girl complained about being assigned to knit stockings rather than to discuss politics; before the end of the century, a slightly older student announced her dislike for the crowded conditions of a church service by noting that in order to see the preacher, she had to roll up her eyes like the Madonna in a Murillo painting. While these signs of resistance are minor by today's standards, they were significant in the early nineteenth century, a time when as, Paul Mattingly reminds us, the purpose of education was to create good moral character (xi–xxi), and that would not have included questioning authority. Secondly, this amateur writing is valuable to the composition historian and to today's composition teacher; it allows us to see, firsthand and writ large, that the story of nineteenth-century writing instruction took place, at least in part, outside of the classroom walls and is more layered and more complex than the story that textbooks alone tell.

Extracurricular Writing at School: School Newspapers

> Messrs. Editor: We school-boys are beginning to look forward
> with pleasure to the next vacation. . . . But there is one thing
> which may prevent some from fully enjoying it. I refer to the prac-
> tice of studying during vacation. It is all humbug, and I say it from
> experience. Why, what is vacation for? I have always supposed
> that is given to us for our enjoyment, but if it is meant that we
> should spend our vacation in studying Virgil or learning Greek
> rules, we might as well remain at school. Omega
>
> —Letter to the editor, *The Student's Manual*, March 29, 1851

> The Student's Manual is the title of a small paper issued by the pu-
> pils of the Latin School. It strikes us that a paper of this descrip-
> tion must be of great advantage to the young gentlemen engaged
> in its publication, affording an opportunity for practical writing
> and thinking, which school themes and declamations are not
> likely to admit of.
>
> —from the *Carpet Bag's* review as quoted in
> *The Student's Manual*, April 16, 1851

School newspapers were a second site of extracurricular student writing. Unlike the classroom-based writing that was heavily deter-mined by teachers and textbooks, and unlike the letters and diaries that students wrote, for the most part, on their own and at home, stu-dent newspapers were a liminal site, a site neither as free as home writing nor as tightly bound as classroom-assigned writing. While the students were both editors and writers for these papers, then, as now, faculty members monitored these publications and had the final word in what was published, what was not. But it is also true that modeling their own advice to each other, students wrote more freely, for the most part, in this extracurricular space than they did in their class-room-based writing, and perhaps ever more importantly, students wrote with the self-declared authority of writers, enfranchising them-selves to evaluate writing and to offer advice to others on the compos-ing process.

Published by and for the students of Boston's Latin School, the

Literary Journal is the first student publication from a school that I can document. It appeared in 1829, survived through fourteen issues, and showcased the belletristic writing of students. Like this student publication, some of the other early school papers were primarily belletristic, featuring poems, reviews, and personal essays. The majority of nineteenth-century student newspapers, however, even if they included some belletristic writing, focused more broadly on student news. An editorial in the January 1, 1866 *Satchel*, a later student paper from the Latin School, noted, "It is our intention to devote [the paper] to the incidents and interests of school-boy life, and to fill it, so far as possible, with original contributions from the boys" (2). In addition to an editor's column, most student newspapers included reports of school events (an announcement of breaking ground for a new building, for example); personal accounts of vacations, especially of travel abroad; news of teachers' vacations; short news items about faculty and students (who was sick or who had died); news of school sporting events or competitions; letters from students who were away; a humor/riddle column; and advertisements from local merchants for personal items such as gloves, hats, musical instruments, and stationery. The papers also shared formal and material properties: most were sized at 8 by 11 inches or smaller, appeared monthly, and were about four pages long. Because of financial difficulties, publication of a paper would occasionally cease and after a while resume, sometimes with a new name. In some cases, a school's student publications were dark for one, even two decades; more often the school was without a newspaper for less than a year. In the November 1887 issue of the *Latin School Register*, for example, an editorial encouraging student support for the paper traces its history from its first appearance in 1829 as the *Literary Journal* through several name changes (4).

To my knowledge, no bibliography of these school papers exists, and I have not attempted to compile one, but I have surveyed multiple issues from multiple years of approximately fifty papers (most of them archived in Harvard's Gutman Library), enough to persuade me that student newspapers were a popular extracurricular site for student writing. By 1854, so many school newspapers flourished that a writer in the *Pennsylvania School Journal* announced that "the rapid increase of periodicals . . . designed to give publicity to compositions by pupils in the schools" was, in his words, "remarkable" ("Juvenile Publications" 236). This same writer, however, worried about the dangers of these student publications:

[B]y a system of public display, of which published compositions are only a part, [our children] are actually placed on the stage of action alongside of their parents, in performance of the same parts, and as competitors for the same objects. That such a state of things must be destructive of that decent and modest submission to parental control, and of that safe diffidence which restrains us from *attempts* till our powers are equal to the effort and the occasion requires it, it is not difficult to foresee. ("Juvenile Publications" 237)

This warning notwithstanding, an editorial in an 1877 student paper from the students of St. Mark's School in Southborough, Massachusetts, reported in their first issue of *The Vindex* (February 1877) that because a student paper was a "prominent feature" of large schools, they were launching their publication (1).

In spite of the popularity of this extracurricular writing, most nineteenth-century textbooks had little advice to students about writing for school newspapers; the fullest statement I find appears in W. W. Davis's 1864 *Composition Writing, A Practical Guide*. Davis offered several pages of advice to students who would organize what he called a "school paper," notably that the writing should be original, "not a rich assortment of imported goods," but a "truthful exhibit of fabrics of domestic manufacture" (47) and that a school paper should be not merely a collection of compositions but rather, like the daily gazette, a platform for editorials, news items, letters, advertisements, book notices, and the like. But even Davis did not provide much instruction on how to write for a paper. As Katherine Adams explains, colleges began to offer training in professional journalism at the end of the nineteenth century, and earlier than that, some high schools offered students the possibility of an apprenticeship with a printer, but training in journalism was very much outside the high school curriculum for most of the nineteenth century (99–122). Writing for the school newspaper was most often seen as a form of enrichment, not as professional training, and when students wrote for their school paper, they most often did so as an ad hoc and after-school activity.

One limitation of reading the student writing in these papers is that many nineteenth-century children did not attend school beyond the primary grades. A second limitation is that most of the schools that supported student newspapers in the mid–nineteenth century were private schools—or expensive public schools—and their students were economically privileged. Students wrote about visiting the fountains of Rome, trekking up Vesuvius, wandering the canals of Venice; they wrote about boating parties, playing chess, playing cricket. Although public elementary schools began to take hold by midcentury, and by the end of the century, children of all social classes were attending public school, the public high school was not in place until the end of the century. The children of working-class and middle-class families were not, for the most part, telling their stories in nineteenth-century student papers. In the words of an 1875 editor's column in *Horae Scholasticae*, the student paper from St. Paul's School in Concord, New Hampshire, "The *Horae* offers excellent opportunities for learning to write a good essay or article, which most of us at some time are called upon to do, and which is an art that belongs to the education of every gentleman" (October 2, 1875, 6).

In spite of this limitation—that the student newspapers do not represent all the voices of nineteenth-century children—the papers nonetheless provide another window on nineteenth-century student writing: these newspapers are one of the few sites where I see examples of students reading and responding to each other's texts; where I see students reflecting on or describing the writing process; where I see students assuming the persona of writer. Schools routinely exchanged copies of their school paper with other schools and then acknowledged those papers in a column called "Exchanges." In this column, students sometimes simply listed publications they had received from other schools; in other cases, though, students used this column to comment on publications from other schools. Occasionally, these comments were negative; more often they were positive and often humorous. In the "Exchanges" column, for example, of the January 1889 and February 1889 issues of the *Jabberwock*, the monthly publication of the Girls' Latin School, Boston, the editors commented,

> In the *Academe* are many reports of clubs and societies. We wish we understood them. (January 1889, 6)

> The *Oak, Lily, and Ivy* contains a charming article, "Canoeing up Lake George." (January 1889, 6)

> The December *Cue* contains a thrilling story, which caused one of our editors to have a nightmare after reading it. The January number seems to be overrun with cats. (January 1889, 6)

> The *Stray Shot* has a very good composition on "Boys," written from a little girl's stand-point. It reminds us of a composition we once read on girls, written by a boy, published by Mark Twain. (February 1889, 6)

> We read with interest "A Camping-out Experience" in the *Volunteer*, and we extend our sympathy to the author. (February 1889, 6)

Exchanging school papers allowed students to see their work not as an isolated student publication but, more broadly, as one of many student publications. And the "Exchanges" column provided a site for students to practice, however modestly, responding to the writing in other school papers.

It was in the "Editors' Column," however, a standard feature in most papers, that students wrote more fully about what they expected of writers for their own paper, sometimes even offering suggestions for facilitating the composing process. Often this column appeared on the first page of an issue, and often it began with the editors' report on the financial difficulties of running the paper. One newspaper about to fold wrote, "To those who put down their names as subscribers, but have afterward refused to pay, we can only say that to them belongs the honor of the discontinuance of our sheet" (*Bedford Street Budget*, March 26, 1845, 14). Almost without exception, the editors' next move in these columns was to solicit manuscripts from their readers; the editors of *Jabberwock*, for example, appealed, "Do send more contributions, girls. Do not be afraid of the editorial waste-basket. We have not bought one yet" (March 1888, 2). But even more striking were the editors' repeated requests for "original" materials. In 1866, *Satchel* called for "choice and interesting matter," claiming, "It will not be a difficult task for our talented school-boy friends to send us original contributions" (January 1866, 3); in 1875, editors of the *Horae Scholasticae* wanted their readers "to compose something . . . on some subject that requires some thought," and not to scrawl off "one of the old hackneyed descriptions." The editors wrote,

> Of course it will come pretty hard at first to write anything really original; but in this, as in everything else, practice makes perfect, and the earlier one begins the sooner will he be able to write well. Nearly every one, at some period of his life, has to write some original article, and so every one ought to do his best to learn how to write well; and how can a boy up here at school get a better opportunity than by writing original articles for the *Horae*? (March 1875, 3)

And in the March 1888 *Latin School Register*, no doubt hoping to increase the number of submissions the paper received, A. A. W. Boardman even offered a writing heuristic, "No [student]," he wrote,

> should be disheartened by the utter lack of ideas which seems to overwhelm him at the start. If he will sit down, pen in hand, he will find that ideas will come to him quicker than he could have believed possible, and when the beginning is once made and he has formed a nucleus from which to start, he will discover that nothing is easier than to go straight ahead with his subject. (1–2)

Another incentive editors used to encourage contributions was their belief that writing for the school newspaper would help prepare students for their writing in college. In April 1846, a student wrote to the *Bedford Street Budget*, regretting the lack of submissions:

> We are glad to see many other papers in the different schools, besides our own. . . . We hope the others will continue to flourish, as the habit of composition of all kinds is a very valuable one, and one moreover, from which those boys who hereafter go to College, will derive great advantage, for we have been told that individuals who have been in the habit of writing anything, even a mere journal of the events of their life, get on much better in their Themes, than those who have not written at all until they were compelled to, and thus begin an entirely new study in competition with those who are already advanced in it. (14)

I cite this student writing at some length to suggest the tone of the writing and to challenge the findings of the 1892 Harvard report that schools were inadequately preparing students for college writing. In addition to commentary from the committee members, the 1892 report contains student essays that are rarely cited in our histories. In fact, the student writers themselves document widespread inconsistencies in the amount of writing they did in their high schools. While one student reported that "composition day came once a week," others reported writing once in two weeks, once in four weeks, once in two months, and even, in one case, twice in a semester. But another student noted that although his school gave him no formal preparation for the Harvard entrance exam, newspaper work and the editing of the school paper gave him facility in writing (qtd. in Brereton 80); a student from another school wrote that the students themselves organized a literary society and met once a week to practice essay writing (qtd. in Brereton 81). Students themselves, therefore, challenge the findings of the Harvard reports with their metacommentary, testifying first, to the ways that writing for their school paper helped them to become better writers, and second, to the ways that writing for their school paper helped them to prepare for writing in college. But the students also challenged the findings of the committee more directly with the actual writing they did for their school papers, writing in which they not only reported on school events, but also claimed their place as young composers.

Finally, students used the school paper to work for change in their schools. In letters to the editor, students argued against various school policies, including required summer reading. In an editorial in the March 1888 *Jabberwock*, the student paper of the Boston Girls' Latin School, the students proposed a gymnasium for their school. Following the protocol for a classical argument, the writers gave the history of the problem, stated their proposal, gave their reasons, anticipated objections, and used both ethos and pathos to sway both students and faculty. Here is a portion of their statement of the problem:

> Very often one hears a girl asking her teacher to excuse her from some recitation "on account of a bad headache." With a proper amount of exercise, these girls would soon lose the tired feeling and aching heads of which so many complain. To be sure, a slight attempt is made in that direction in the calisthenics; but what good do three minutes of these simple exercises or a march around the class-room do to girls in tight sleeves and heavy dresses? Some of them cannot lift their arms above their heads: most of them do not try to. They have no interest whatever in these exercises, which are sometimes wrongly called gymnastics. Impeded by the weight of their skirts, they march heavily up and down the aisles to the dull and uninspiring strains of the piano. (*Jabberwock*, March 1888, 1)

The following month, a note in the paper announced that the girls had adopted a costume for their physical exercises, a blouse (we later learn it was flannel) and full skirt (*Jabberwock*, April 1888, 3). Many nineteenth-century school-age students wrote in school and in extracurricular sites. In school, they studied "theme-writing": they wrote formal themes, often on assigned topics, as part of a school curriculum that in the course of the century expanded to include not only exposition and argument, but also forms of description and narration that were grounded in the student's direct experience. Outside the classroom, students wrote at home and/or, in some cases, for their school papers. In these two extracurricular sites, students had greater freedom in selecting their purpose, audience, and genre, greater room for creativity and for experimentation, greater room for thinking of themselves not just as students but also as writers. When nineteenth-century students wrote in classroom-based settings, they wrote regularized, predictable themes that were modeled in textbooks and, in some cases, won prizes. When they wrote in the extracurricular site of their homes, they wrote of their daily lives and their relationship to authority. When they wrote in a second extracurricular site, the school paper, they wrote in a liminal space somewhere between classroom-assigned writing and private writing. Here they authorized themselves to write original text, extolled the benefits of writing frequently, critiqued each other's texts, learned to generate ideas "pen in hand," and, perhaps most significantly, talked about themselves as writers. For different reasons and in different ways, each of these writing sites was important to nineteenth-century students. Finally, however, I believe that the texts students composed in these sites are important to composition historians because they allow us to see not only the range of ways in which writing was instantiated in the lives of nineteenth-century students but also, and more significantly, they allow us to see that nineteenth-century students were writers.

Conclusion

"We Say to Him, Write!"

As soon, then, as the child can form and join his letters, let him commence the practice of composition, and follow it up steadily as long as he remains in school. Few are aware how improvable is the faculty of expressing thoughts upon paper. The gigantic increase of the muscles in a blacksmith's arm, from his wielding the hammer so frequently; the proverbial strength of the memory, by exercise; or the miraculous sleight which the juggler acquires, by practice, with his cup and balls; is not more certain, than that he, who daily habituates himself to writing down his ideas with what ease, accuracy, and elegance, he can, will find his improvement advance, with hardly any assignable limit. Nor will his style, only, improve. It is a hackneyed truth, that, "in learning to write with accuracy and precision, we learn to think with accuracy and precision." Besides this, the store of thought is, in a twofold way, enlarged. By the action of the mind, in turning over, analyzing and comparing, its ideas, they are incalculably multiplied. And the researches, prompted by the desire to write understandingly upon each subject, are constantly widening and deepening the bounds of knowledge. Thus, whether a person wishes to enrich and invigorate his own mind, or to act with power on the minds of others, we say to him, Write!

—Thomas Palmer, *The Teacher's Manual*, 1843

Even by the second half of the nineteenth century when common schools were well established, when public high schools were beginning to sink their roots, and when normal schools were growing in number, not all children had an equal opportunity to attend school.

Most white children attended school for the early grades. But pointing to a class differential, Stuart Blumin uses census data to show that in Philadelphia in 1860, while most children of nonmanual workers were still in school at age fifteen, children of working-class homes were not (190). Carl Kaestle reports that in the nineteenth-century United States, only a "small minority of teenagers attended secondary schools of any kind" (121), and we know that those who did were primarily boys. And he also writes that at the time of the Civil War, blacks in the North had "separate and unequal" school opportunities and that black schools were not affected by early public school reform; that poor blacks and whites in the South lacked common schooling; and that American Indians and Hispanic Americans struggled for educational opportunities (179–80).

Teaching itself was often held in low regard. In a review essay, "The Culture and Politics of American Teachers," Arthur Powell notes that "in the early nineteenth century, the instruction of children rarely offered steady employment, much less a 'career' or even more remotely a 'professional' experience analogous in any sense to the three traditional learned professions" (189). Bruce Kimball reports that in the earliest decades of the century, Anglican clergyman Isaac Fidler toured the United States looking for a schoolmaster's position and was "repulsed by the low status, authority, and remuneration of American teachers" (190). Although teaching began to be called a "profession" in the 1830s—in part, according to Kimball, because of the efforts of teachers Samuel Hall and William Alcott—popular opinion as late as the 1860s was that "persons too lazy to work, and unfit for other profitable employments, were usually engaged as pedagogues" (Kimball 190).

Denied access to law, medicine, and theology, women began to join the ranks of trained teachers by 1860, and after the Civil War, they were admitted to the American Institute of Instruction and the National Teachers' Association. Kaestle estimates that only 10 to 20 percent of teachers were affected by professionalization in the first half of the century. Overall, teachers rarely remained in one school for any length of time, even more rarely for the length of a career; schools opened and closed; teachers moved from one school or district or state to another; and teachers moved in and out of teaching. Kaestle reports, for example, that in Trempeleau County, Wisconsin, in the 1860s "[t]he average teacher had less than two years' experience, and many positions were filled by a 'brigade of irregulars,' who had not taken the certification exam but applied for licenses the weekend before school was to start, in the absence of qualified candidates. The county superintendent labeled these teachers 'vampires' and 'barnacles' " (131–32).

We also know the clichés leveled against nineteenth-century writing instruction: that young students were not thought capable of generating original text; that the instruction was hidebound by rules, and rigid rules at that; that students were taught to write in an "unnatural" way, thinking first, then writing; that students were not taught to use writing to learn; that writing was sometimes assigned to keep students busy; and all the rest. And documentation supports that those rules and formulas and schemes were, indeed, endorsed by members of the profession. In a lecture to a convention of teachers in August 1830, a scholar as prestigious as Samuel Newman explained that he did not "approve of very early attempts in writing." He continued, "Those who attempt to write when very young, almost invariably acquire habits of desultory thinking. They learn to write without connexion or point, and thus all the ease of expression acquired, is dearly paid for" ("On a Practical Method" 180). Like Newman, many nineteenth-century textbooks emphasized "ease of expression" more than composing, and when they did teach composing, they suggested, following John Walker and Richard Green Parker, that it be done according to rigid rules, schemes, outlines. And there was powerful emphasis on error. In 1823, William Russell wrote that "[e]very error ought to be carefully and distinctly shown, and minutely discussed: and the pupil should be required to recite the rule of Syntax, Punctuation, Structure, or Style, which, in any instance, has been violated" (*Grammar of Composition* 67); as late as 1867, J. M. Bonnell wrote that an "essential condition to the highest improvement in this art [writing] is the rigid and faithful correction of every error" (13). It was also difficult to displace the idea that writing was transcription, a vehicle for thought, not a means of generating thought. Alexander Bain saw writing and thinking as separate processes (Brereton 306), and so did some textbook writers for the schools. In John Scott Clark's 1887 *A Practical Rhetoric*, a book for older students, he wrote, "The real thinking . . . should be almost entirely done before the first definite sentence is written" (248). Scattered through nineteenth-century textbooks are many examples of what we, today, would consider hidebound pedagogy—and I have no doubt but that in many classrooms that pedagogy was instantiated.

It would be a mistake, therefore, to assume that every child experienced the instruction in composition or participated in the extracurricular writing that I have elaborated in this book. But it would also be a mistake to assume that composition instruction in nineteenth-century schools was a backwater, or merely a scaled-down version of college writing instruction, or that the small books have nothing to teach us or, worse, nothing to add to our history. My point is that school-based writing instruction in the nineteenth century was a site of tremendous pedagogical innovation—and it is that innovation and the men and women and children who took part in that work that I want to include in our stories of writing instruction.

As I have already noted, writers of First Books, and especially John Frost, are key figures here. Unlike those teachers who advocated long periods of study before writing a single word, Frost, in 1839, taught students to write "freely and boldly" (*EE* 58). And unlike the teachers who pushed students and teachers to check for every error, he wrote,

> If [the student] feel a constant solicitude lest he should make a trifling mistake, this will chill his feelings and give his writing an unpleasant air of stiffness and constraint. When he commences writing it is better that he should say whatever comes into his head in a natural though inaccurate manner, than that he should puzzle himself by hunting after words that do not come readily, or by torturing the commonplace expressions of other people into new and artificial forms. The most common words are the most forcible; and if the idea to be expressed is a good one, it will tell better in short every-

day words than in holyday terms and words of "learned
length and thundering sound." (*EE* 58–59)

In ways that historians have not yet acknowledged, Frost anticipated
the kind of freewriting we associate with Peter Elbow and the cautions
against premature editing advocated by Mike Rose, Linda Flower, and
John Hayes. As an inventional strategy, Enoch Cobb Wines, a colleague of Frost's at Philadelphia's Central High School, recommended,
in his 1839 *Letters to School-Children*, that students keep journals.
"Keeping a journal," he wrote, "of all that you see and hear of any
importance is another extremely useful way of employing your pen.
This not only gives you ease in writing, but it makes you attentive to
what is going on around you, and observant of what you see" (126).
In Boston's Temple Street School, Bronson Alcott required students to
keep journals and resisted correcting every error in these texts. He believed that "petty criticism" kept the art of composition from being developed in children: "[I]f [their writing] is misunderstood, or its
garb criticized, they . . . will be very much tempted to suppress their
own thoughts" (qtd. in Peabody xxxix). Like teachers today, other
nineteenth-century textbook writers pointed to the value of revision.
Charles Morley, for example, counseled, "The habit of rewriting a
composition several times, is one of the best means for improvement"
(*Practical Guide* vi). In conjunction with revising, still others advocated the use of peer response groups. In Gere's work on writing
groups, she argues peer critique was rare in nineteenth-century college curricula and that it moved into high schools even later (*Writing Groups* 14–17). But in texts for younger composers, peer critique
occurred earlier. In 1867, Bonnell recommended in the preface to
his text that students exchange early drafts with each other "for mu-
tual criticism" and then return them to the author for revision (12);
in 1876, Quackenbos suggested the class exchange compositions,
read each other's aloud, then offer their recommendations for revision (*Illustrated Lessons* 161), and in 1892, Shaw wrote, "Occasionally itwill be found of value to let pupils exchange papers for criticism" (x).

In a 1983 study, Shirley Rose suggests sentence combining has a long and rich history, and she cites examples of sentence combining from early twentieth century textbooks. Sentence combining is, however, another example of a contemporary pedagogical practice that was prefigured in nineteenth-century schools. Toward the end of the century, a number of textbooks included a section in which students were asked to combine what writers called "detached sentences" into "well-constructed sentences" (Hart, *First Lessons* 51–53; Swinton, *School Manual* 37–40; Salmon 10–16). And the structure of one book—H. I. Strang and J. Adair Eaton's 1889 *Practical Exercises in Composition*—is almost entirely based in a pedagogy of sentence combining. While the explanations are not as detailed or as linguistically elaborated as the explanations in Francis Christensen's work or in the work of Daiker, Kerek, and Morenberg, the exercises are uncanny in the ways they prefigure contemporary practice. John Hart, for example, in his *First Lessons in Composition*, asks students to combine this group of short sentences: "The boy wrote. He was a good boy. He wrote a letter. He wrote to his father. He wrote from school. He wrote on his birthday. It was a long letter. He wrote it early in the morning. He wrote it before breakfast" (53). William Swinton lists twenty-one independent clauses about Alphonso, king of Sicily and Naples, and then models how students can combine those statements into sentences that are complex, compound, and include, for example, prepositional and participial phrases and adjective clauses (*School Manual* 38–39). Similarly, in Edward Shaw's chapter entitled "Variety of Sentence-Form," he offers exercises in what he calls "Combining Sentences," asking student "to make into one sentence" the catalogue of independent clauses he offers. In addition to teaching sentence variety, these exercises, not unlike those that appear in Joseph Williams's text *Style* or a host of other texts, were teaching students the valances of subordination, that is, how to use the predication of the sentence to carry the central idea of the sentence.

And still other writers encouraged students to assemble and keep their compositions. Simon Kerl urged that compositions be preserved, "like bundles of letters." They would be mementos of school days, he added, and they would allow the pupil to "compare his later with his earlier efforts" (51). W. W. Davis explained that by keeping all their written work, that which was "good or bad," students would have "the satisfaction of tracing their gradual improvement as shown in a long succession of trials"; he went on to recommend that students keep this work in "packages," and that they keep each year's work in a separate package (15). Like Davis, contemporary teachers often ask students to assemble their work; Davis asked them to keep their work in a package; we ask our students to keep it in a portfolio. In both cases, the hope is that students might see the progress in their work by reading it as a whole and over time.

Because these practices anticipate pedagogies that we value today, they stand out and against many others. But there is no reason to suggest they had the same significance to nineteenth-century readers that they do to us. Indeed, because nineteenth-century textbooks were so eclectic, it is highly likely that a text would contain pedagogical practices we would see as repressive as well as those we would see as liberatory. And as is the case today, teachers might have focused on those aspects of the text that they personally found most helpful. Supporting Joseph Harris's argument against a narrative of progress—the claim made by some historians that contemporary pedagogy is an unquestionable and universal improvement over past practice—ample evidence demonstrates that many of the pedagogies that are invoked in writing classes today and widely viewed as recent and innovative carry a history that goes back to the schoolbooks and the classrooms of the nineteenth-century. In *More Than Stories*, Tom Newkirk argues that John Dewey (1859–1952) articulated many of the "cardinal principles" of the writing process: "the constructive model of thought; the primacy of experience; the social nature of learning; the relationship of classroom learning to democratic values" (206). I want to suggest that many of these same principles predate Dewey and, in fact, are rooted in the thought of Pestalozzi and instantiated in early nineteenth-century textbooks used in the schools.

This is not to say that the college writing classrooms were not also innovative. Albert Kitzhaber points out that until 1870, colleges were doing pretty much what they had been doing since the eighteenth century, and James Berlin elaborates the hold that the rhetorics of Campbell, Blair, and Whately and their followers had on college instruction during the century. But other scholars, including John Brereton, JoAnn Campbell, Robert Connors, Sharon Crowley, David Jolliffe, Nan 'Johnson, Susan Miller, Tom Newkirk, and Sue Carter Simmons, suggest that, especially later in the century, college writing instruction was not as monolithic as we once thought. And from my own work, I know that Alexander Bain was familiar with the thinking of Pestalozzi, and that, for example, John Frost's teacher at Harvard, Boylston Professor of Rhetoric and Oratory Edward Tyrrell Channing, lectured about a range of approaches to the composing process. Channing's work, in particular, merits more attention than historians have given it. In his lecture, "A Writer's Habits," for example, he notes that some writers "prefer to do the principal part of their meditation beforehand. . . . Their plan is sketched in every particular"; "Others, on the contrary," he writes, "will tell us that they cannot think without a pen in their hands" (215–16). But I don't hear echoes of Pestalozzian thought or of Channing's work in the college textbooks in the same way I hear them in Frost's work.

For a number of reasons, those I cite and more, the school climate was more encouraging of innovation than the university setting. The sheer numbers of schools in the United States at the end of the century, coupled with the lack of centralization, meant that thousands of teachers were working with thousands and thousands of children and thus exponentially increased the possibility for innovation. And while the British rhetoricians played a role in the school-based instruction, teachers in the schools did not feel obligated, in the way the universities did, to work with a canon of texts. Not all the teachers were themselves university-educated and, thus, were not uniformly familiar with the work, for example, of Campbell and Blair. Before uniform curricula were in place, teachers in independent schools were free to teach what they judged important, and free to teach it as they wished. Unlike the clerics who held chairs in the British or American universities and published their lectures, the school textbook writer's work did not have the same status, and therefore, the writers had greater room for "play," as it were, in their approaches to writing instruction. And while some teachers and textbook writers, especially early in the century, were ministers and teachers, the greater number, especially as the century advanced, were teachers who had a concern for pedagogy that their colleagues in the university did not share.

And so partly because there was less status and less at stake in the schools than in the colleges, the schools were a site for innovation in ways that the colleges were not. The schools were preparing students for what we today call "lifelong learning," equipping students with the knowledge and skills they need to participate in a democratic society; the universities, on the other hand, were preparing students for the professions and, thus, had to conform to external certification measures. That experimentation would take place in textbooks for lower-school students and for students not necessarily bound for college is consistent with Arthur Applebee's 1989 *Study of Book-Length Works Taught in High School English Courses*. In a study of the top ten books on secondary teachers' reading lists over a twenty-year period, Applebee and his colleagues found that most schools were teaching the same literary works that they were teaching twenty years ago and that most of the authors continue to be European American males. The researchers further found that breaks with the traditional canon (in genre, gender, and ethnicity) were most likely to occur in reading lists for junior high and middle school students and for comprehensive students at all levels and that the canon was most codified in college preparatory and advanced placement classes where teachers felt most constrained by conservative assessment forces.

In speculating about why some of what we see as innovative approaches to composing were not widely known or replicated in post-secondary writing classes, several thoughts come to mind. Typically—and wrongheadedly—the educational hierarchy has assigned greater value to what happens at higher levels of education than to what happens at lower levels, and even today, it is rare for innovations in the schools to become part of a curriculum for college students. For the most part, writers of the books I have studied taught in the lower or secondary schools and did not have a ready-made group of students who were preparing for teaching careers and, thus, were likely to use these works in their teaching; often the work of these writers was known only in their own schools. In Frost's case, he even left teaching shortly after the publication of *Easy Exercises* and made writing his full-time career. Before he died in 1859, he and his associates had compiled more than three hundred books for popular use; among them, perhaps the best known was the *Pictorial History of the United States*, which sold more than fifty thousand copies.

In addition, there was no established way for these writers and their work to influence the way writing was being taught in the universities, or, in other words, to trickle up. More often, nineteenth-century educational pedagogies trickled down, and until writers began to understand differences in learning styles between children and adults, assignments for young writers were often modeled on assignments for older students. In the history of school/college collaboration, colleges too often—and wrongly—assumed they were the primary site for generating new understandings for teaching writing (see Schultz, Laine, and Savage), so any kind of immediate cross-pollination or wider distribution of ideas was unlikely if the writers did not themselves move into university teaching and take their ideas with them. My searches, while incomplete, suggest that, for the most part, these writers did not write about their work in the journals of the times and were not themselves the subject of essays in the journals. The avenues we rely on today for naming alternative pedagogical practices—publishing in professional journals or delivering papers at conferences—were not part of the daily lives of the nineteenth-century writers of texts for school-age children. While I have found several cases in which these writers talked about their practice, it was apparently without much notice. In Charles Northend's *The Teacher and the Parent*, a book-length treatise on common school education, he counseled teachers about using concrete subjects to teach composition. And for a short time, John Frost edited both *The Young People's Book* and *The School Master, and Advocate of Education*, and both of these works contain short essays about his approach to teaching writing. It is also true that Frost's work is quoted in an essay by called "Hints and Methods for the Use of Teachers" in a March 1842 issue of the *Connecticut Common School Journal*, but this is the only instance I have found of his work being cited in a journal.

It is also unlikely, however, that university teachers would have been reading any of this secondary work by or about Frost or Northend and just as unlikely that they would have seen any application or relevance of this work to their own teaching situation. I can't imagine, for example, that mid-nineteenth-century university professors would have turned to a book called *Easy Exercises in Composition* for help with writing instruction. And even early twentieth-century teachers' manuals written by college professors for the schools fail to cite these reform educators. I think, for example, of Carpenter, Baker, and Scott's 1903 *The Teaching of English in the Elementary and the Secondary School*, which shows no reference to or acknowledgment of the pioneers who turned our instructional practice in composition in a new direction. Similarly, Franklin T. Baker's entry in Paul Monroe's 1911 *Cyclopedia of Education* entitled "Composition," one of the most comprehensive early descriptions of the activity known as "composition," does not discuss individual practitioners.

For many reasons, many aspects of nineteenth-century writing instruction that we would name as "innovative" remained muted until in a different climate, at a later time, they reemerged and gained a voice. One innovation, however—and that which I deem the most significant—that emerged in the writing classrooms of nineteenth-century schools has had an uninterrupted, if not unquestioned, place in composition pedagogy: the experience-based essay.

Expanding the David Bartholomae–Peter Elbow conversations from the 1980s, debates about the place and/or the value of using experience-based writing in the classroom continue today. Among recent and strongest defenders of autobiographical writing are John Schilb in *Between the Lines*, and Daniel Mahala and Jody Swilky in their essay "Telling Stories, Speaking Personally: Reconsidering the Place of Lived Experience in Composition." In both cases, the writers advocate not just the recounting of experience for its own sake, but the interrogation of experience in support of knowledge-making and the resulting public value. In this same vein, historian Joan W. Scott, in her essay "The Evidence of Experience," argues that crucial to working with experience is interrogating the cultural forces that account for experience. She writes,

It is not individuals who have experience, but subjects who are constituted through experience. Experience in this definition then becomes not the origin of our explanation, not the authoritative (because seen or felt) evidence that grounds what is known, but rather that which we seek to explain, that about which knowledge is produced. (401)

When experience is not considered this way, it falls prey to the criticism that it plays a role in maintaining the status quo by reproducing a subjectivity of the self-made person.

In ways slightly different from Schilb and Mahala and Swilky, Tom Newkirk also supports personal writing in today's composition class. Grounded in the work of Erving Goffman, Thomas Newkirk's 1997 *Performance of Self in Student Writing* argues that experience-based writing is important for young writers because, for them, as they struggle with their present lives and try to imagine their futures, "the achievement of 'self' is more than a theoretical issue." He argues that for young writers, indeed for all of us, to believe that we can "imagine ourselves as coherent selves with coherent histories and can therefore create stories about ourselves" is a powerful means of constructing the self (98–99). And he argues that our writing classrooms need to embrace diverse forms of self-representation and to honor multiple aesthetics and not to mark as "out of bounds" writing that does not conform to a particular orthodoxy or ideology. In other words, for young writers, the representation of experience —even without critical interrogation of cultural assumptions—is the basis for powerful writing.

Students in nineteenth-century schools were, of course, writing as nineteenth-century children, conditioned and restricted by the cultural and historical and social milieus in which they lived. And as I have indicated several times in this book, textbooks reproduced cultural values for their young readers: children were taught to link virtuous living with material success; to privilege white skin over skin of other colors; to privilege some occupations over others; and, naively, to romanticize life in the country or on a farm. In Stuart Blumin's *Emergence of the Middle Class*, he uses a pair of works by John Frost, *The Young Merchant* and *The Young Mechanic*, to argue that while the nineteenth century made a gesture toward valuing physical labor, Frost expresses the culture's—and presumably his own—only slightly veiled "contempt," to use Blumin's word, for manual labor. Frost explains that for the merchant, honest work will reap great rewards, including a "well-ordered home," and civic renown, whereas the "[laborers'] low station, their wants, and their drudgeries, give them a sordidness and ungenerosity of disposition" that presumably will limit their successes (qtd. in Blumin 130–31).

But that acknowledged, schools and their books and their pedagogies were reaching a much broader audience than the universities. And unlike the universities, which until after the Civil War were educating primarily upper-class students for careers in the law and ministry and responding to the neoclassical rhetorics of Campbell and Blair, the schools were preparing students for the world of work, and especially for the trades and professions; and they were responding to a pedagogy of romanticism embodied in the work of Pestalozzi. Early in the century, therefore, writing instruction in the schools was democratized in ways that instruction in the colleges was not. And as part of this democratization of writing, schools were the site where students were first invited to write about their lived experiences. In *Composition-Rhetoric*, Robert Connors writes, "The rhetorical tasks assigned students during the nineteenth century are indeed one long retreat from abstraction and from subjects based outside of immediate cultural and personal experience" (64). An important addition to Connors's statement is that the long retreat from the abstract began not in the colleges, but in the schools. Dozens of books asked students to write about their personal experiences long before John Hart's 1870 *Manual of Composition and Rhetoric*, the book that Connors argues "opened the floodgates to personal writing in composition courses" (*CR* 310). Connors argues that the first summer vacation assignment appeared in Hart's book. In fact, however, as I have already noted, many books for younger students asked for the summer vacation assignment much earlier; Frost's *Easy Exercises*, for example, asked students to "describe your own idea of a pleasant summer holiday" in 1839.

Connors further argues that in the colleges, "The revolt of teachers against abstract subjects did not really begin until after the Civil War," the same time that women began to enter American colleges, and this revolt occurred partly because of the failure of the earlier topics and partly because of the rise of the modal system, which, of course, included the two personal modes of narration and description (*CR* 310). The trail, however, was different in the schools: The rejection of abstract subjects began in the 1830s, and it occurred because of a new understanding of the intellectual development of a child and because of the influence of Swiss education reformer Johann Heinrich Pestalozzi and his commitment to "things" before "words." And the rejection occurred not only in the First Books I study here, it occurred in even lesser-known texts. In 1831, the writer of an article, "Composition in Schools," decried "subjects which would puzzle the brain of a metaphysician" and illustrated a plan for teaching composition based on simple, everyday objects (314–15). In 1841, Sarah L. Griffin, a teacher in Georgia, wrote *Familiar Tales for Children*, a collection of tales intended both to instruct and delight her readers.[1] In the chapter, "The School Composition," Griffin's fictional personae, a girl, Ellen, and her mother, Mrs. H., discuss a theme Ellen wrote for school. Although Ellen's theme, "Industry," was much praised by her teacher, Ellen declares that what she has written is "stupid." Here is part of that theme.

> "Industry is a very great virtue: it is one of the greatest of all virtues; for it leads to all others. How important is it to cultivate it then, to its greatest possible extent. What would the world come to, if there were no industrious people in it? All would soon fall into ruin, and desolation would soon cover the whole earth. . . . It is essential that we should commence the practice of industry early in life, for when our habits are formed, it will be in vain to conquer the indolence which has 'grown with our growth, and strengthened with our strength.' " (128)

Ellen's mother agrees with her daughter's judgment and suggests Ellen write a different paper and in it "describe some pleasant evening's amusement, or a ramble." And thus, Ellen sets out to describe an out-

ing with her cousins in which they made bonnets for sheep out of collard greens:

> then we went into the pasture where the sheep were: we sat
> down under a tree: pretty soon Frank said, "Only see, cousin,
> how the sheep almost shut their eyes; don't you suppose that
> the sun hurts them?" "I don't know, I am sure"; said I, "I
> never noticed it before." So he got up and ran off: pretty
> soon he came back with some large collard leaves and some
> string. . . . "O, I am going to make bonnets for the poor
> sheep"; said he, "for I know the sun hurts them." So he and
> William caught several, and tied the leaves on for bonnets:
> the creatures did not know what to make of it; they tried to
> eat them, but their mouths would not turn over; so they ran
> about sometime with them on, till at last they ate them from
> each other's heads. William tried to catch the old ram, to put
> a bonnet on him; but he soon made him quit that, for he
> butted at him and laid him flat. Willie laughed, and said "the
> ram might burn his eyes out before he made him another
> bonnet." (132–33)

At the end of Sarah Griffin's tale, Ellen takes her experience-based
composition to school and hopes for her teacher's approval, noting
that "there was never anything like it in the school before." Weary of
"Duty," "Industry," and "Truth" as topics, she is determined "to set a
new fashion [in writing] for the girls" (133–34).

When school-based writing included experience—even the experience of making collard green bonnets for sheep—a number of free-
doms opened to the writer. Students were invited to describe the simple objects, places, and scenes of their lives; to write about farming
and fishing and manufacturing and shopkeeping; to recount their own
experiences of friends, family, school, holidays, and reading and writing. And they were invited to give their point of view in this writing,
that is, they were asked to give their thoughts on a subject. I don't
claim that Frost or Sarah Griffin "taught" point of view by asking students to write experience-based essays. I do think, however, that ask-

ing students to write from their own observation and their own experience opened a space for them to take a position, to begin to write,
as Linda Brodkey, says, "on the bias." In other words, writing that
is inflected by lived experience can allow students to take a small
step toward critical thinking by helping them to understand that one
way to internalize knowledge or to understand a concept is to filter it
through the writer's experience.

When nineteenth-century students wrote memorized themes or
themes about abstract topics, they were, of course, reflecting the received wisdom—the point of view—of their culture, whether or not
they were aware of it. For example, in the mid–nineteenth century, a
common belief was that novel reading, especially for adolescents, was
dangerous.[2] In a piece called "Hints to Young Ladies," a writer, in an
1856 edition of the *American Journal of Education* said, "You have no
excuse for reading the profligate and romantic novels of the last century, or the no less profligate and far more insidious romances of the
present day" (Sedgwick 229). And it is not uncommon to read nineteenth-century student essays—especially essays by older students—
that elaborate the dangers of novels. In her 1846 prize-winning essay
called "On Novel Reading," Mary King, a student at the Academy of
the Visitation, wrote that by reading novels, the mind is "poisoned"
and "deceived," and the heart becomes "restless" and "dissatisfied." In
King's essay, an essay that I believe is an important cultural document,
she follows a common writing pattern in formal texts written by nineteenth-century students: she relies on universals to support her position, and her knowledge, at least as she displays it for the reader,
is grounded in external authority rather than personal experience.
While King, of course, may have had experience with novels and with
novel reading, there is no visible trace of that in the essay. Instead, the
essay demonstrates that she had, and very successfully, learned the accepted position on novel reading for nineteenth-century young ladies.
We see no recognition on the writer's part that the values she represents are not universal or transcendent, but are, instead, socially constructed and circumscribed by a particular context. (See figure 12 for
the first page of King's essay in her own handwriting; see appendix 3
for the text of King's essay.)

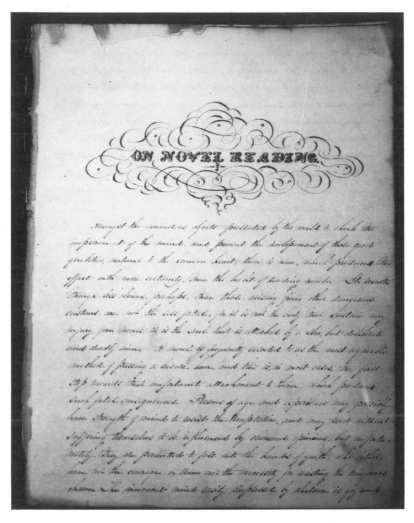

Figure 12. First page of Mary King's 1846 essay, "On Novel Reading."

While King's essay was written from knowledge grounded in external authority, when Frost asked a student for an account of "[your] difficulties in beginning composition, and how they were overcome" (*EE* 72), or when Sarah Griffin's fictional character asked her daughter to "describe some pleasant evening's amusement, or a ramble" (129), they were asking students to write from knowledge rooted in experience. So I would argue that a significant difference in inviting students to write about their own lives and their own experiences is that point of view is made visible, even foregrounded. This kind of writing, in other words, makes space for understanding writing as an interpretive act marked by the writer's subjectivities, however those subjectivities are formed. Thus, even though experience is socially constructed, when the children at the American School for the Deaf were asked to describe a picture, each child's experience of the picture was different, and that experience, of seeing/reading the picture, was no doubt inflected by the child's seeing/reading of her own life. An experience-based essay, therefore, contributes to a different understanding of a writer's authority and how it is constructed, an understanding that the writer's self, even though that self is constructed, is also a site of knowledge making.

I am not prepared to argue that when experience-based writing was introduced in nineteenth-century schools, students were interrogating the social construction of their experiences in the way that some contemporary writers propose; that is, I don't believe the students were using their experience as the basis for cultural analysis. I do, argue, though, that when experience-based writing entered the writing curriculum in the nineteenth century, its role was, at least in some ways to challenge the status quo of writing assignments: no longer was the published writing of accomplished authors the only acceptable model for student writers; no longer were students required to sound like adults in their writing. When experience-based writing entered the curriculum, children learned that what they did outside of school was important in school, and they further learned that their experience could be the basis for knowledge production. Finally, and most significantly, I believe that when students represented their experiences in school-based writing, they were taking the first and necessary step toward the critical use of experience that Schilb and Mahala and Swilky propose. Henry Giroux and Peter McLaren write that "only when we can name our experiences—give voice to our own world and affirm ourselves as active social agents with a will and purpose—can we begin to transform the meaning of those experiences by critically examining the assumptions upon which those experiences are built" (16). The value, thus, of students in the schools writing about their experiences is not simply that they were writing in ways that were in line with their intellectual development; it's that as a discipline, we were taking our first steps toward an understanding that giving voice to experience can help us to interrogate the culture from which that experience springs.

My emphasis on this innovation is not to discredit or deny the value of writing that is not overtly grounded in personal experience; it is rather to say that teaching students (how) to interrogate experience and to use it as a form of evidence and/or as a place from which to start gathering and/or testing other evidence, practices we so take for granted, were a long time coming to writing instruction, and that when they were introduced, they greatly expanded the concept of what writing was, and what it could do. In the nineteenth century, experience-based writing made possible a move, however limited, away from the emphasis on taste that had characterized so much of writing instruction in the eighteenth and early nineteenth centuries and the corresponding emphasis on class, and it made space for students whose lives were situated in the world of manual labor and the world of work. And today, this history also challenges our profession's long-standing and deeply embedded notion that pedagogical innovation always trickles down rather than percolates up.

But just as I do not want to discredit writing that is not grounded in experience, neither, certainly, do I want to credit all writing that is. As the dance comes to life only through the dancer, any classroom-based pedagogy is inflected by the goals and practice of the teacher. And assignments then, like assignments now, when separated from their theoretical underpinnings, atrophy. Consider this. When Richard Whately in 1828, John Frost in 1839, and George Quackenbos in 1851, asked students to write about their summer vacation, a watershed was crossed. What students did outside of school was for the first time valuable in school. Unlike many other writers, these argued that the student's lived experience was content for a composition, that the student, in other words, was a source of authority. And for these writers and their students, the summer vacation assignment instantiated that belief. By the end of the century, however, John Swett advised teachers in a one-room school setting that on the first day of class of a new school year,

> [you should] proceed at once to business by giving out a sheet of paper to all who can use a pen, and require them to write a composition about their last vacation. This will keep them at work an hour at least. . . . The art of the first day is to keep pupils busy. You will avoid much mischief by getting everybody hard at work in ten minutes after school opens. (*Am Public Schools* 309–10)

However sobering this example is, it is also important to notice that the summer vacation assignment, which in other situations was groundbreaking, became, at least for some teachers and their students, busywork. So this caveat: in my pointing to nineteenth-century peda-gogical innovations, I do not mean to suggest they were "pure"; on the contrary, like all writing practices, they were messy, imperfect, incon-sistent, and easily subverted.

The nineteenth century saw the early times of the republic, the beginnings of industrialization, the beginnings of large-scale urban life in the United States, the beginnings of the middle class and of the professions, the settlement of the West. It was also a time when hu-man beings in this country bought and sold other human beings with impunity, and when we fought a Civil War over slavery. And even with slavery's repeal, the century continued to be a time of unequal oppor-tunity for women and peoples of color, of unfair labor practices, of oppression of the poor and the immigrant, and of violence against the Indian nations. Against these social ills, however, it was also the cen-tury that saw the beginnings of universal, public, and free education: of education as we know it in the United States. As it was initiated and as it has developed, this educational system is not without problems—many of them frighteningly serious—but as its founders believed, and as citizens still believe, universal education was and is a hallmark of a democratic society.

In 1977, Alvina Treut Burrows wrote that "one must assume, from present minimal evidence, that composition as we now perceive it simply was not taught [in the 1800s]. Handwriting and spelling, yes; but how to help children set down their ideas and feelings on paper for a live and known audience was ignored in professional references and very probably in the classroom. Not until the early years of the twentieth century did the schools begin this task" (22–23). As recently as 1989, Barbara Finkelstein, in her study of nineteenth-century classroom practice, wrote that from the nineteenth century, "[o]nly rarely do we find allusions to the writing of compositions, and in no instance could I find a description of a teacher who even hinted to his students that writing was an instrument for conveying thoughts and ideas" (67). My own work with nineteenth-century documents challenges the reading of both Burrows and Finkelstein; it also suggests that composition instruction as we know it not only began in the nineteenth-century schools but also, and in noteworthy ways, was innovative. In particular, the schools took the lead in teaching students that experience—not just external authority—could be a basis for knowledge production.

This, then, is my reading—necessarily contingent, perspectival, and partial—of the history of writing instruction in nineteenth-century schools. I am persuaded that we have only begun to explore documents from and about nineteenth-century schools, that these documents have much to teach us, and that many stories remain to be told. Eighteenth-century rhetorician Hugh Blair thought of history as "a record of truth for the instruction of mankind" and argued that the work of good historians was marked with "impartiality" and "fidelity" (398b). Today, Henry Giroux writes of history as "a dialogue among a variety of voices as they struggle within asymmetrical relations of power," and he suggests that traditions are "not valued for their claims to truth or authority, but for the ways in which they serve to liberate and enlarge human possibilities" (122).

In our discipline's ongoing effort to write and revise our histories, I believe our traditions and our stories are liberated and enlarged by including the voices of the men and women who brought writing instruction to the schools. They were not internationally acclaimed rhetoricians; they were teachers. And they were teachers whose work—at once eclectic, derivative, contradictory, and innovative—

for the most part, has not been noticed, and whose voices, for the most part, have been silent in our histories. We know that until the Civil War, most colleges enrolled only a few hundred students, and, of course, had only a handful of professors; we also know that until now, these voices have dominated our stories of writing instruction. Also during that time, however, thousands of teachers were teaching hundreds of thousands of students in the schools. My goal has been to write these teachers and their young composers into our history: to give them voice.

Appendixes
Notes
Bibliography
Index

Appendix 1.

Tables of Contents from John Frost's *Easy Exercises* (1839) and George Quackenbos's *First Lessons* (1851)

These two tables of contents illustrate two different approaches to writing instruction in nineteenth-century schools. John Frost's *Easy Exercises* (1839) represents the innovative approach: beginning with actual writing and with writing in response to illustrations. Quackenbos's *First Lessons in Composition* (1851) represents the part-to-whole approach taken by the better-known texts in the nineteenth century.

CONTENTS.

PART I.

INTRODUCTORY COURSE OF EASY EXERCISES.

PART II.

STRUCTURE OF SENTENCES.

CONTENTS.

PART III.

FIGURATIVE LANGUAGE.

Figure A1.1. Table of contents from John Frost's *Easy Exercises*, 1839.

CONTENTS.

CONTENTS.

LESSON.		PAGE.
XXXIX.	Sentences containing Adverbial and Vocative Clauses,	85
XL.	Different kinds of Sentences,	86
XLI.	Exercise in Sentences,	87
XLII.	Exercise in Sentences,	88
XLIII.	Variety of Arrangement,	89
XLIV.	Variety of Arrangement,	90
XLV.	Variety of Expression,	92
XLVI.	Variety of Expression,	94
XLVII.	Synonymes,	96
XLVIII.	Exercise in Synonymes,	97
XLIX.	Circumlocution,	99
L.	Analysis of Compound Sentences,	100
LI.	Synthesis of Simple Sentences,	102
LII.	Style,	104
LIII.	Purity,	107
LIV.	Propriety,	109
LV.	Precision,	111
LVI.	Clearness,	113
LVII.	Clearness,	115
LVIII.	Strength,	118
LIX.	Strength,	121
LX.	Harmony,	122
LXI.	Unity,	125
LXII.	A Review,	128
LXIII.	Different kinds of Composition.—Analysis of Subjects,	130
LXIV.	Letter-Writing,	133
LXV.	Letter-Writing,	140
LXVI.	Exercise in Letter-Writing,	142
LXVII.	Description,	143
LXVIII.	Exercise in Description,	147
LXIX.	Description of Natural Scenery,	147
LXX.	Exercise in Description of Natural Scenery,	150
LXXI.	Description of Persons,	151
LXXII.	Exercises in Description,	153
LXXIII.	Narration,	153
LXXIV.	Exercise in Historical Narration,	156
LXXV.	Exercises in Historical Narration,	157
LXXVI.	Biographical Sketches,	158
LXXVII.	Exercise in Biographical Narration,	161
LXXVIII.	Fiction,	163
LXXIX.	Essays,	165
LXXX.	Exercise in Essay-writing,	165
LXXXI.	Argumentative Discourses,	166
LXXXII.	Figures.—Simile,	170
LXXXIII.	Metaphor,	172
LXXXIV.	Exercise in Metaphorical Language,	175
LXXXV.	Personification,	176

Figure A1.2. Table of contents from George Quackenbos's *First Lessons*, 1851.

Appendix 2.

Three Student Readings of an Illustration, 1886

Figure A2.1. An old woman and three children.

These three student writers were enrolled at the American School for the Deaf, in Hartford, Connecticut. Their essays were published in the school's 1886 *Annual Report.*

Response 1
   A girl's name is Debby and she is sitting on the floor. The boy tied the string around the yarn. He is kneeling on the chair, and he is holding in his hand. He wants to play with the kitten. The kitten sat under the chair and

sprang and tried to catch the string. Debby is the boy's sister. She is looking at the kitten. She laughs. Her doll is on the stool. She loves the kitten, and the kitten is very sweet and small. The boy's grandma is on the chair, and she sews the stocking. She is looking at the kitten. The other girl's hands are on her grandma's lap. Debby does not see the doll. She hates it perhaps. She does not hate the kitten, and she loves it very much. She is ten years old. The other girl does not see the kitten, and she is reading the book. She laughs. The boy's coat and his hat are on the nail. The kitten is black and white. The boy said to the kitten "you are very funny." His grandma knits every day. She likes to knit. Her hair is gray and she has no teeth.

> —Written by an eleven year-old student whose initials were F. A. P.;
> the student became deaf at nine months and when this was written,
> had been in school 1 2/3 years.

Response 2

I am going to write about this picture. This picture is about an old woman and her daughter and son. The woman is sitting on a chair, and wears a white bonnet and white apron. She holds the cloth and sews it. A pleasant girl is standing near her mother and is reading a black book. She smiles. A boy kneels on a chair, and puts his hand on the chair. He ties a string around a spool of thread and holds it to a white and black cat for he wants to play with it. When the cat sees it it bites the spool and plays with it. The boy likes to look at the cat and laughs. Another girl is sitting on the floor and she wears a white apron. Her hair is long. The girl likes to see the cat playing with the spool. When the mother sees the cat playing, she laughs too. The cat is very pretty. The top of the stool upset and it is lying on the floor. A doll is standing on the stool, and it wears a white dress. Her hair is very black. There is a basket of clothes with a handle on the floor. There are a white plate and cloth on the floor. A white lamp is on the shelf. There are a shawl and a hat hanging on the door. There are a cup of flowers and some things on the shelf. I see a pretty picture on the wall.

> —Written by a thirteen-year-old student whose initials were J. L. C.
> The student was congenitally deaf and when this was written,
> had been in school 2 2/3 years.

Response 3

An old woman lived in a white house. Her name was Mrs. Gray. She had three grand children. One boy's name was Johnny. Two little girls' names were Kate and Mary. One day their grand mother sat down on a chair. She sewed a little cloth. She had a cap on her head, and wore a pair of spectacles on her eyes. She wore a little shawl and an apron. Kate stood near her grand mother, and read a book, when her grand mother sewed because she wanted to learn the book. She seemed to be a cheerful girl. She stood near the fire place. Mary sat down on the floor because she wanted to put a pair of stockings and shoes on her feet. There was a work box on the floor, and some things were on the floor. Some others were on the shelf. There was a kettle on the fire place. Pretty soon Johnny came to the table, and sat down on a chair. He ate some food. When he ate it, a cat named Tabby came to him and looked at him. He saw her and thought that she wanted some milk. He poured it in a saucer. Then he put it on the floor. Tabby licked it. Johnny knelt on the chair, and put his hands over the back of the chair. He wanted to play with Tabby. He asked his grandma to give a ball of yarn to him and told her that he wanted to play with Tabby. She said yes and gave the ball of yarn to him. He let the yarn down to the floor and shook it. Tabby saw him shaking it and ran to it. She played with it. Johnny laughed and his grand mother smiled and said that Tabby was a funny cat. Kate and Mary laughed at her. They thought that she was a smart cat. The cat played with the ball a long time. At last she was tired. The children looked happy.

—Written by a 14-year-old student whose initials were N. G. The student became deaf at nine months of age, and when this was written, had been in school 4 2/3 years.

Appendix 3.
Student Essay: June 20, 1846

The premium book of the Academy of the Visitation in
Washington, D.C., shows that in 1847, Mary King was one
of seven women who received first honors in the "Senior
Circle." Her esssay that follows was handwritten in a note-
book called "First Class Compositions."

On Novel Reading

Amongst the numerous objects presented by the world to check the improvement of the mind, and prevent the developement of those good qualities,
natural to the human heart; there is none which produces this effect with
more certainty than the habit of reading novels. The results though less obvious, perhaps, than those arising from other dangerous customs, are not the
less fatal, for it is not the body that sustain any injury from novels, it is the
soul that is attacked by a slow, but deliberate and deadly aim. A novel is frequently resorted to as the most agreeable method of passing a leisure hour, and
this is, in most cases, the first step towards that unfortunate attachment to
them, which produces such fatal consequences. Persons of age and experience
may possibly have strength of mind to resist the temptations, and may read
without suffering themselves to be influenced by erroneous opinions, but unfortunately they are permitted to fall into the hands of youth who either have
not the courage or know not the necessity for resisting the dangerous charm.
The innocent minds easily impressed by whatever is gay and beautiful, surveys those enchanting pictures with eager delight, one novel after another is
read with increasing interest, and the desire to read grows stronger and
stronger, until at length it becomes an absolute passion. The pursuit of literature is abandoned, it no longer presents any object of sufficient interest to engage the attention. Days and even nights are passed in this manner, the whole
heart and mind absorbed in those pictures of human life as fallen and deceitful
as they are lovely and captivating. Vices and passions are presented under veils
of the most enchanting beauty. Virtue is indeed described as beautiful, but
worthy of pursuit, merely on account of its surpassing beauty, to no higher, no
holier motive is it ascribed, the admirable virtues possessed by a certain por-

tion of mankind are entirely separated from the perfection of that Divine Being for whose love and honor they are practiced. Novels will, therefore, allure the mind from the pursuit of more elevated and useful purposes, and confine it to the contemplation of those imaginary beauties, so far beneath its exalted nature.

Not only is the mind thus poisoned and deceived, but the heart too becomes restless and dissatisfied. Commonplace occurrences, attachments, and pleasures have no longer any power to engage its affections. Deluded by those captivating descriptions of human life, which, if not absolutely fallen, are at least no more than descriptions of the lives and manners of those who must have been destitute of common sense: every amusement becomes dull and insipid, and the heart is tormented with a vain longing to become a partaker of those imaginary scenes of happiness and exiting emotion. None are to be regarded with more compassion than those who suffer themselves to be deluded, because not only do they deprive themselves of peace in this life, but prepare for themselves an eternity of misery. The constant habit of reading novels accustoms them to look no farther than to the accomplishment of their wishes, the present alone is considered, the future presents no prospect of happiness. No idea of death, or of misery beyond the grave, is permitted even to cross the minds, lest it should interfere with those exciting visions of imaginary happiness with which it is perpetually filled. Sin and passion artfully concealed, and clothed in beautiful colours, soon cease to be regarded with the horror they deserve, and there is little reason to hope that one totally indifferent to the dangers of sin, will avoid falling into it, when those, who guard against it, with the utmost caution, scarcely escape. It is frequently urged that *some* novels may be read without injury and even with advantage to the reader, which latter assertion is much to be doubted, for though they may contain nothing that would injure, still they will tend to allure the mind from more solid pursuits, and give a taste for romance and fiction, which will probably tempt them to read every novel, of whatever kind, that falls into their hands.

Nothing can be said in favor of novel reading, good and evil do not often proceed from the same source, and in no light, in which one may view it, can it be productive of any comfort here, and certainly of none hereafter.

Appendix 4.

Excerpt from Elizabeth Cady Stanton's Autobiography, *Eighty Years and More*

Elizabeth Cady Stanton recounts an experience of writing a composition when she was a student at Emma Willard's Seminary at Troy. The event took place in 1830.

I shall never forget one incident that occasioned me much unhappiness. I had written a very amusing composition, describing my room. A friend came in to see me just as I had finished it, and, as she asked me to read it to her, I did so. She enjoyed it very much and proposed an exchange. She said the rooms were all so nearly alike that, with a little alteration, she could use it. Being very susceptible to flattery, her praise of my production won a ready assent; but when I read her platitudes I was sorry I had changed, and still more so in the *denouement*.

Those selected to prepare compositions read them before the whole school. My friend's was received with great laughter and applause. The one I read not only fell flat, but nearly prostrated me also. As soon as I had finished, one of the young ladies left the room and, returning in a few moments with her composition book, laid it before the teacher who presided that day, showing her the same composition I had just read. I was called up at once to explain, but was so amazed and confounded that I could not speak, and I looked the personification of guilt. I saw at a glance the contemptible position I occupied and felt as if the last day had come, that I stood before the judgment seat and had heard the awful sentence pronounced, "Depart ye wicked into my everlasting punishment." How I escaped from that scene to my own room I do not know. I was too wretched for tears. I sat alone for a long time when a gentle tap announced my betrayer. She put her arms around me affectionately and kissed me again and again.

"Oh!" she said, "you are a hero. You went through that trying ordeal like a soldier. I was so afraid, when you were pressed with questions, that the whole truth would come out and I be forced to stand in your place. I am not so brave as you; I could not endure it. Now that you are through it and know how bitter a trial it is, promise that you will save me from the same experience. You are so good and noble I know you will not betray me."

In this supreme moment of misery and disgrace, her loving words and warm embrace were like balm to my bruised soul and I readily promised all she asked. The girl had penetrated the weak point in my character. I loved flattery. Through that means she got my composition in the first place, pledged me to silence in the second place, and so confused my moral perceptions that I really thought it praiseworthy to shelter her from what I had suffered. However, without betrayal on my part, the trick came to light through the very means she took to make concealment sure. After compositions were read they were handed over to a certain teacher for criticism. Miss —— had copied mine, and returned to me the original. I had not copied hers. So the two were in the same handwriting—one with my name outside and one with Miss ——'s.

As I stood well in school, both for scholarship and behavior, my sudden fall from grace occasioned no end of discussion. So, as soon as the teacher discovered the two compositions in Miss ——'s writing, she came to me to inquire how I got one of Miss ——'s compositions. She said, "Where is yours that you wrote for that day?"

Taking it from my portfolio, I replied, "Here it is."

She then asked, "Did you copy it from her book?"

I replied, "No; I wrote it myself."

"Then why did you not read your own?"

"We agreed to change," said I.

"Did you know that Miss —— had copied that from the book of another young lady?"

"No, not until I was accused of doing it myself before the whole school."

"Why did you not defend yourself on the spot?"

"I could not speak, neither did I know what to say."

"Why have you allowed yourself to remain in such a false position for a whole week?"

"I do not know."

"Suppose I had not found this out, did you intend to keep silent?"

"Yes," I replied.

"Did Miss —— ask you to do so?"

"Yes."

I had been a great favorite with this teacher, but she was so disgusted with my stupidity, as she called my timidity, that she said:

"Really, my child, you have not acted in this matter as if you had ordinary common sense."

So little do grown people, in familiar surroundings, appreciate the confusion of a child's faculties, under new and trying experiences. When poor Miss

——'s turn came to stand up before the whole school and take the burden on her own shoulders she had so cunningly laid on mine, I readily shed the tears for her I could not summon for myself. This was my first sad lesson in human duplicity.

This episode, unfortunately, destroyed in a measure my confidence in my companions and made me suspicious even of those who came to me with appreciative words. Up to this time I had accepted all things as they seemed on the surface. Now I began to wonder what lay behind the visible conditions about me. (37–40)

Notes

1. The Beginnings of Composition in Early Nineteenth-Century Schools

1. Early in the century, and before schools were organized by grade levels, many composition textbooks were used by students of a wide age range; in the second half of the century, books began to be more highly focused for students in lower or upper grades. It was not uncommon for nineteenth-century textbooks written for students beyond the primary grades to target multiple audiences, including the student working with a private tutor as a way of preparing for the university. To cite a few examples: Richard Green Parker's 1844 *Aids to English Composition* was intended for "students of all grades"; Henry Noble Day's 1850 *Elements of the Art of Rhetoric* was "adapted for use in colleges and academies, and also, for private study"; and George P. Quackenbos's 1854 *Advanced Course of Composition and Rhetoric* was "adapted to self-instruction, and the use of schools and colleges."

2. For an account of education in the slave quarter community from 1831 to 1865 that is grounded in slave narratives and in stories told by slave descendants, see Thomas L. Webber's *Deep Like the Rivers*. See also works by Donnarae MacCann, especially *White Supremacy in Children's Literature*.

3. Many books construct the history of school in America. Among those I found most interesting from the early part of the twentieth century are John Swett's *American Public Schools*, Clifton Johnson's *Old-Time Schools and School Books*; and Ross Finney's *A Brief History of the American Public School*. Among those I found most helpful to my work are Lawrence Cremin's *American Education: The Colonial Experience*; Cremin's *American Education: The National Experience*; Carl F. Kaestle's *Pillars of the Republic: Common Schools and American Society, 1780–1860*; Michael Katz's *Reconstructing American Education*; Gerald Gutek's *An Historical Introduction to American Education*; David Labaree's *The Making of an American High School*; and Joel Spring's *The American School, 1642–1993*.

For a study of teacher behaviors in nineteenth-century schools, see Barbara Finkelstein's *Governing the Young*; and for studies of nineteenth-century English schools, see Eric Midwinter's *Nineteenth Century Education* and Ian Michael's *The Teaching of English*.

4. Working with nineteenth-century education journals—and there were many—is complex for a number of reasons. Many of the journals changed titles, in some cases several times, and many of the titles are confusingly similar. In addi-

tion, authors of the articles are very often not given, and when they are, they are sometimes pen names. Because the writers were often among the most influential nineteenth-century educators—teachers and public officials who were shaping education as we know it today—knowing their names can be significant. I have found it is sometimes possible to triangulate the data, as it were, and determine an author, and sometimes possible to locate the author behind the pen name, but that work is, at best, both tedious and time-consuming. These challenges notwithstanding, I am persuaded these journals are an important resource we have not sufficiently investigated.

5. Contemporary readers recognize this advice as "Nulla dies sine linea," a quote popularized by Donald Murray in *Write to Learn* (131). According to William Walsh, the line originates with Pliny the Elder, a first-century Roman naturalist, who was describing not writing, but the painting habit of the Greek painter Apelles. In Pliny's *Natural History*, Pliny explained that "it was Apelles' constant habit never to allow a day to be so fully occupied that he had not time for the exercise of his art, if only to the extent of one stroke of the brush" (quoted in Walsh 164).

6. In addition to Ariès's *Centuries of Childhood*, two valuable book-length accounts of the development of the concept and the politicization of "childhood" are Bernard Wishy's *The Child and the Republic*, and N. Ray Hiner and Joseph M. Hawes's edited collection, *Growing Up in America*.

7. As early as 1693, John Locke was critical of an overemphasis on rules and memory in *Some Thoughts Concerning Education*. In section 64, he writes, "And here give me leave to take Notice of one Thing I think a Fault in the ordinary Method of Education; and that is, the charging of Children's Memories, upon all Occasions, with *Rules* and Precepts, which they often do not understand, and constantly as soon forget as given" (38). Arguing that exercising memory did not improve it, he went on to say in section 176, "I do not mean hereby, that there should be no Exercise given to Children's Memories. I think their Memories should be employ'd, but not in learning by rote whole Pages out of Books, which, the Lesson being once said, and that Task over, are delivered up again to Oblivion, and neglected for ever" (155).

8. Others have also written about the interdependence of school and culture; see, for example, Kaestle's chapter on ideology in *Pillars of the Republic*. See also Michael Apple's *Teachers and Texts*; Joel Spring's *Educating the Worker Citizen*; and Kathleen Welsch's dissertation "Nineteenth-Century Composition: The Relationship Between Pedagogical Concerns and Cultural Values in American Colleges, 1850–1890."

9. Although the early nineteenth-century Latin grammar schools and the academies and seminaries and other private schools that followed them had served as what we would think of as college preparatory high schools for the children of the wealthy, the growth of public high schools occurred in the third quarter of the

nineteenth century. Swett records that in 1838 there were fourteen high schools in Massachusetts, and a few scattered in other East Coast cities; by 1896–97, 5,109 public schools were functioning in the United States (*Am Public Schools* 75). For a contemporary account of the development of secondary schools, see William J. Reese's *Origins of the American High School.*

　　10. I think especially of J. R. Sypher's *Art of Teaching School* and *Notes of Talks on Teaching* by Francis Wayland Parker. For an extensive bibliography of texts on pedagogy, see Mariolina Salvatori's *Pedagogy.*

2. First Books of Composition

　　1. A fuller statement of Richard Green Parker's approach to writing instruction appears in his lecture, "On the Teaching of Composition in the Schools," delivered at a meeting of the American Institute of Instruction in Worcester, Massachusetts, August 1837.

　　2. It was not uncommon for nineteenth-century texts for younger students to include "First" in the title. Here are some samples: *First Reader, First Class Reader, First Lessons in Grammar, First Book of Etymology, First Lessons in Language, First Book in Composition, First Lessons in English Grammar and Composition.*

　　3. Citing this text is complex for a number of reasons: there are two 1854 editions, one signed (by this I mean that an author, Amos R. Phippen, is named) and one unsigned (Phippen was the publisher of this edition and pretty certainly the author as well, but no author is named); no historian that I know of has yet called attention to this distinction; and no library that I know of holds a copy of both editions. (The Library Company owns the signed copy; the Library of Congress owns the unsigned copy.) James Green alerted me to the Library Company's ownership of a signed edition, and it is from conversations with him that I understand what I do of this book's publication history. Scholars who have cited the text (Hess, for example) cite the unsigned edition and therefore list no author. There are several interesting differences in the two editions copyrighted in the same year: the unsigned edition includes four illustrations absent from the signed edition, and the signed edition includes one that is absent from the unsigned edition. The quotations that I use in this paper are from the unsigned edition, but I understand Phippen to be the author. I include both 1854 editions of the *Illustrated Composition Book* in my bibliography.

　　4. My thanks to Joseph Harris who pointed out to me that twenty years after Janet Emig wrote this paper, she included it as the first essay in a collection of her works, chronologically arranged, which she called *The Web of Meaning*. Perhaps more interesting, here, however, is that in the reprint Emig does not include the appendix, and it is there that we find her only mention of John Frost and Charles Northend.

3. "No Ideas but in Things"

1. My remarks about Pestalozzi are not intended to offer a complete account of his thought; I omit some aspects of his philosophy (for example, his emphasis on religious and moral instruction) because they are not relevant to this discussion. For additional information about Pestalozzi's life and career, see the often-cited Henry Barnard's *Pestalozzi and His Educational System*; Edward Biber's *Henry Pestalozzi and His Plan of Education*; Robert Downs's *Heinrich Pestalozzi*; Henry Holman's *Pestalozzi*; Hermann Krusi's *Pestalozzi: His Life, Work, and Influence*; Will Monroe's *History of the Pestalozzian Movement in the United States*; and Kate Silber's *Pestalozzi: The Man and His Work*. William Kipnis's dissertation "Propagating the Pestalozzian" is also useful.

2. Other Europeans whose names are associated with school innovation or reform are, of course, Friedrich Froebel (1782–1852) and Johann Friedrich Herbart (1776–1841). Often described as a disciple of Pestalozzi and an advocate of child nurturing, Froebel is best known for the development of the German kindergarten in the 1830s. Following Froebel's model, kindergartens were introduced into the United States in the 1860s and 1870s, largely through the work of Elizabeth Peabody. For an elaboration of Pestalozzi's influence on Froebel (and especially on the importance of physical forms to both educators), see Norman Brosterman's *Inventing Kindergarten*. In Brosterman's text, he emphasizes the importance of the geometry of forms that was an important part of early kindergartens and argues that many of the significant "form-givers" of the modern era—in this group, he includes Frank Lloyd Wright, Le Corbusier, and Paul Klee, for example—were heavily influenced by the "spiritual geometry of early kindergarten" (13). For helping me to identify the Brosterman text, I thank my colleagues Chet Laine and Darwin Henderson.

Herbart developed a five-point plan for classroom instruction (preparation, presentation, association, generalization, and application) and was an important figure in American education especially in the last two decades of the nineteenth century. He is often credited with developing the concept of the lesson plan.

3. For discussions of Comenius's work, see, for example, Will Monroe's *Comenius and the Beginnings of Educational Reform* and John Edward Sadler's *J. A. Comenius and the Concept of Universal Education*.

4. Thanks to John Brereton for pointing out that the "bricks" metaphor appears in Bacon and Milton.

5. This passage from young Louisa May Alcott, as well as all other examples of student writing, appear as originally written; thus many contain misspellings and other errors.

6. In addition to Sheldon's 1863 edition of Mayo, some of the best known of the nineteenth-century books about object teaching include Warren Burton's *Culture of the Observing Faculties*; Norman Calkins's *Manual for Teachers*; J. H. Gladstone's *Object Teaching*; Horace Grant's *Exercises for the Improvement of the Senses*;

William Hailman's *Outlines of a System of Object Teaching*; Anna Johnson's *Education by Doing*; John Keagy's *Pestalozzian Primer*; Norma Litchfield's *Talks about Common Things*; and George Ricks's *Object Lessons*.

In nineteenth-century education journals, articles about object teaching were common. Henry Barnard, an important figure in the history of the American common school, was a promoter of Pestalozzian thought, and under his editorship, both the *Connecticut Common School Journal* (from 1838 to 1842) and the *American Journal of Education* (from 1856 to 1881) frequently published essays about Pestalozzi and object teaching.

7. One of the complexities of reading nineteenth-century composition instruction is that it often appears, as it does here (and, for example, in Daniel Jaudon's *Union Grammar* and in Charles Morley's *Common School Grammar*) tucked into a text that is largely devoted to grammar instruction; sometimes the inclusion of a composition section is mentioned in the explanatory part of the title, sometimes it isn't. Short of turning the pages of every nineteenth-century grammar, I don't know how to sort out those that include composition instruction from those that don't.

8. Another indication of the "silent borrowing" that occurred so frequently in nineteenth-century texts is that John Frost's lists of objects on pages 69 and 70 of *Easy Exercises* in some ways resemble Richard Green Parker's lists on pages 33 and 34 in the 1832 *Progressive Exercises* (see lesson 17, "Definition, and Distinction, or Difference," and lesson 18, "Analogy, or Resemblance"). Unlike Parker, however, who includes both abstract and concrete terms in his lists and refers to the items in the lists as "words," Frost only uses concrete terms and refers to them as "objects"; also unlike Parker who emphasizes analysis, Frost emphasizes the student's powers of observation, and, especially in his lists on pages 71 and 72, he connects the descriptions of objects with writing personal narratives, a move Parker does not make. As I note in this chapter, Parker adds a section on object teaching to the 1844 *Aids to English Composition*; such a section does not exist in the 1832 *Progressive Exercises*.

9. My thanks to my graduate student Gwynda L. Casey for alerting me to the mention of Pestalozzi in Bain's *Education as a Science*.

10. Scudder's essay first appeared in *Every Saturday* in April 1874. It is reprinted in Lane Cooper's *Louis Agassiz as a Teacher*. Cooper's study also includes first-person accounts of studies with Agassiz by Nathaniel S. Shaler, Addison E. Verrill, and Burt G. Wilder. I first learned about Scudder's essay from Toby Fulwiler and Hank Steffens at a "Writing Across the Curriculum" workshop at Shakertown, Kentucky, in the early 1990s. Among the contemporary texts in which the essay is anthologized is *Community of Voices*, edited by Toby Fulwiler and Arthur Biddle. And Robert Scholes discusses Agassiz's teaching goal (that his students will learn "to speak the fish") in a *College English* essay, "Is There a Fish in This Text?"

Ann Berthoff also speaks persuasively about the power of observation. Marjorie Roemer of Rhode Island College tells the story of inviting Berthoff to visit her Brookline High School class some twenty years ago. In addition to the text for her talk, Berthoff brought with her a bag of seaweed and a handful of seashells. Berthoff's advice to the students was this: learn to describe an organic object, for if you look and look again, you see an organic form, and if you write about that organic form, your writing will also have an organic form. In Berthoff's *Forming, Thinking, Writing*, she argues that this kind of observation ("Observing, Observing Your Observations, Observations on Observing") is empowering. To students, she writes, "Deliberately observing your observations and interpreting your interpretations sounds like being self-conscious and, in a sense, it is: you are the one who is aware of what is going on and you are also the one responsible for what is going on; you are the do-er, the agent" (13). And in her text, Berthoff includes bits of student writing with titles like these: "Emily's Walnut Husk," "Bill's Blue Jay Feather," "David's Milkweed Pod," "Martha's Bit of Branch" (16–23). While I am not able to draw a direct link between Pestalozzi's philosophy and Berthoff's teaching, I do see a similarity in their underlying convictions that observation is a powerful tool for learning.

4. The Agency of Textbook Iconography

1. An interesting aside is that C. W. Bardeen, author of the 1884 *A System of Rhetoric*, edited an 1887 English edition of the *Orbis Pictus*. Like Comenius, he argued that the *Orbis Pictus* was an excellent text for preparing students for more advanced studies.

2. For a description of the *New England Primer* and early readers and spellers, see Ruth Freeman's *Yesterday's School Books*.

3. Jane Pomeroy, to whom I am indebted for the explanation of the white-line technique that appears in this chapter, is currently preparing a catalogue raisonné of the engravings of Alexander Anderson, many of which appeared in children's texts. She is identifying the publications he illustrated and describing the illustrations (and his separate prints) on their first appearance. Subsequent appearances of his work in publications will also be included.

4. According to Jane Pomeroy, wood engravings (rather than steel or lithographic images) were used in textbooks because steel or lithographic images had to be printed on presses separate from the press used for the text. That meant more trouble tipping in the sheets when the book was being made up and the expense of additional paper. Wood engravings (the wood blocks), on the other hand, could be put in with the type for the text, and everything rolled through the presses at the same time.

And a note on paper used in these texts. While books from the early part of the century were made from rag paper and thus the pages in many cases remain firm and "unchipped," the bindings were often poor. Books from the latter part of the century were, however, printed on brittle paper, and their pages easily crack and break. Nineteenth-century books that have survived are therefore vulnerable either because of bindings or paper or, in some cases, both. To give researchers access to these texts without risking further wear, Harvard's Gutman Library has microfilmed many of the readers, grammars, and composition books in their textbook collection.

5. Two exceptions I know of are that Whitney, Jocelyn, and Annin engraved the illustrations in Phippen's 1854 *Illustrated Composition Book* and that J. W. Orr identified himself as the engraver of some of the illustrations in Brookfield's 1855 *First Book in Composition*.

6. I have not found any studies dedicated exclusively to the illustrations in children's textbooks. A number of helpful studies focus on illustrations in recreational books for children; they include William Feaver's *When We Were Young*; Philip James's *Children's Books of Yesterday*; Charles Morris's *The Illustration of Children's Books*; Henry C. Pitz's *Illustrating Children's Books*; and Joyce Whalley and Tessa Chester's *A History of Children's Book Illustration*.

7. Here is a sampling of composition books that include illustrations as heuristics; I have arranged them chronologically in order to make more visible the gap in textbook production during the Civil War.

Charles Morley, *A Practical Guide to Composition*, 1838; John Frost, *Easy Exercises in Composition*, 1839; Peter Bullions, *Practical Lessons in English Grammar and Composition*, 1854; Amos R. Phippen, *Illustrated Composition Book*, 1854; F. Brookfield, *First Book in Composition*, 1855; M. E. Lilienthal and Robert Allyn, *Things Taught*, 1862; Hiram Hadley, *Lessons in Language*, 1871; George P. Quackenbos, *Illustrated Lessons in Our Language*, 1876; Thomas W. Harvey, *Elementary Grammar and Composition*, 1880; W. B. Powell, *How To Write*, 1882; Edward Gideon, *Lessons in Language*, 1888; C. C. Long, *New Language Exercises, Part One*, 1889; Alonzo Reed, *Introductory Language Work*, 1891; Edward R. Shaw, *English Composition by Practice*, 1892; William H. Maxwell, *First Book in English*, 1894; Robert C. Metcalf and Orville T. Bright, *Language Lessons, Part One*, 1894; Albert N. Raub, *Lessons in English: A Practical Course of Language Lessons and Elementary Grammar*, 1894; Edward Hawkins, *Language Lessons, First Book*, 1896; Mary F. Hyde, *Practical Lessons in the Use of English*, 1899.

5. Textual Practices of the Young Composers

1. At the turn of the century, a 1902 teachers' guide called *The Conduct of Composition Work in Grammar Schools* already included an entire chapter devoted to publishing student work, the authors Henry Lincoln Clapp and Katharine Huston noting that

> [t]he compositions given here were not written for publication, but have been selected from the best work of each grade as it stood. They are

by no means ideal; they show the immaturity of the writers; they contain crudities without which they would not be children's papers; but they are simple, natural, and show that the writers understood their subjects. (31)

2. See also Robert Connors's discussion of Walker in chapter 7 of *Composition-Rhetoric* and in "Personal Writing Assignments" (170–72).

3. See Crowley's chapter "EDNA Takes Over" in *The Methodical Memory* and, especially, her notes to that chapter for multiple representations of the origin of the modes of discourse. One of the earliest uses of the term "exposition" that I see is in Kerl's 1869 *Elements of Composition and Rhetoric*. See also Robert Connors's chapter on "Discourse Taxonomies" in *Composition-Rhetoric*.

4. Though less frequently, textbook writers cite sources in addition to (or other than) Campbell, Blair, and Whately. Among these less frequently cited sources, for example, are Thomas Dick, author of *On the Mental Illumination and Moral Improvement of Mankind*; Lord Henry Kames, author of *Elements of Criticism*; and Shepherd, Joyce, and Carpenter, authors of *Systematic Education*. Some textbook writers, like Boyd, attribute a specific passage to a specific writer; more commonly, though, writers make no mention of their sources. Or like Richard Green Parker, they include a list of their sources but do not identify the borrowed passages; see for example, Parker's mention of Walker, Booth, and Jardine in the preface to *Progressive Exercises* and his catalogue of sources at the very end of *Aids to English Composition*.

5. Richard Green Parker and George Quackenbos are the textbook authors most frequently cited for their long lists of essay topics. As I have suggested though, listing essay topics, a practice that continues today in some textbooks, was a common feature in nineteenth-century composition texts. Here is just a sample of books with such lists: William Russell's *A Grammar of Composition*, Charles Northend's *Young Composer*, W. S. Barton's *Practical Exercises in English Composition*, Lilienthal and Allyn's *Things Taught*, and Scott and Denney's *Composition-Rhetoric*. In some cases, the concept of the list expanded to become a textbook composed of outlines for student essays; see, for example, Ebenezer Brewer's *Guide to English Composition* and Zander and Howard's *Outlines of Composition*.

6. From Philadelphia's Central High School, a list of prize-winning essays for 1846 reveals that students there were writing exclusively in English, but the titles suggest the essays were still impersonal and, like the essays at the Latin School, were often focused on education. Sample prize-winning titles include "The Influence of the High School," "Education Necessary to the Development of Genius," and "The Public School System."

7. The "extras" that the school offered were Latin, French, German, Italian, and Spanish languages, drawing and painting, piano-forte, guitar, dancing, and the "invigorating and graceful exercise of Horsemanship."

8. The 1855 Buffalo Female Academy report for the "collegiate department" emphasized the importance of higher education for women: "Their [the commit-

tee's] estimate of the infinite value to the sex of correct and complete education for their accomplishment, rejoices to see the age and the country progressively appreciating the advantages that intend and promise the solid glories of America, as identified with the education of her daughters, as well as of her sons" (*Annual Circular* 39).

9. For accounts of composition writing at the Litchfield Female Academy, see the journal entries in Emily Noyes Vanderpoel's *Chronicles of a Pioneer School.* A delightful account of a girl writing about girls of an earlier time participating in a writing competition occurs in *The Schoolfellow.* The 1849 essay is entitled "The Prize at School"; the student writer is Caroline Howard. Here is a piece of her essay:

> On the ensuing day commenced their work of trial. One would have thought that the girls were gazing at invisible objects in the air for inspiration. Whole pages were written by some, and then destroyed as useless; others went into retirement to spout long essays, which sounded well enough with only the silent trees for auditors, but alas! could not stand the nice criticism of a practised ear; others waved away an approaching step, fearing it might put to flight a host of precious ideas; while some imagined that a deep scowl upon the brow, or a hand thrust suddenly through the hair, marring its glossy smoothness, would give birth to ideas worthy of a Socrates or a Locke. But this turning up-side down of all system, and this self-absorption from the rest of creation, was only allowed to continue during one hour in each day. In two weeks the tasks were to be completed, and all the inhabitants of the village were to be invited to hear the reading of the far-famed compositions. (174–75)

10. For the first and fourth of the four Harvard reports written between 1892 and 1897, see John Brereton's *Origin of Composition Studies in the American College, 1875–1925,* a very helpful edition of primary materials including sample curricula, sample student texts, and sections from a range of textbooks, all related to college-level composition.

11. In Susan Miller's essay, she includes a sample letter written by a seven-year-old and, most interestingly, the student's revised version of the letter. For a full-length study of commonplace writing, see Miller's *Assuming the Positions.*

Conclusion: "We Say to Him, Write!"

1. Jane Pomeroy read this text at the American Antiquarian Society. I am grateful to her for alerting me to it, and to the Library of Congress Interlibrary Loan division for mailing me a copy.

2. Many nineteenth-century writers elaborate the dangers of novel reading, especially for young people. In John Walker's 1808 *Teacher's Assistant* (later edi-

tions are titled *English Themes and Essays*), he argues that reading novels wastes time and corrupts morals, manners, and taste. He summarizes,

> The imagination, thus fed with wind and flatulence, loses its relish for truth, and can bear nothing that is ordinary: so that the reading of novels is to the mind, what the drinking of strong liquors is to the body; the palate is vitiated, the stomach is weakened, the juices are corrupted, the digestion is spoiled, and life can be kept up only by that which is super-natural and violent. Nothing, therefore, can be more dangerous to the undersanding, to the morals and the taste, than an attachment to the reading of the generality of these fictitious productions. They glide into the heart through the imagination, and, under the taste of honey, often infuse the strongest poison. (117)

Silently borrowing from Walker, Richard Green Parker uses Walker's arguments as a prompt for a student theme on the dangers of novel reading in his 1832 *Progressive Exercises* (84). In this same vein, J. Mathews cautions students against novels in his 1853 *Letters to School Girls*. Mathews writes,

> Let me warn every school girl against novels. The style is so fascinating, and the love-stories they contain so exciting, that girls who read them at all are apt to become excessively fond of them. They injure both the in-tellectual and moral nature. To read them, is like feeding children on sweetmeats and candies; they soon lose their relish for wholesome food, and their health is injured or destroyed. It is almost impossible to make a good student of a novel-reader. They have an utter aversion to hard study and difficult subjects. If they can slip a novel to read, they will neglect every thing else, and pass through their school-days without ac-quiring any thing useful. (21–22)

Bibliography

Composition and Language Arts
Textbooks, Grammars, and Rhetorics

Abbott, Edwin A. *How To Write Clearly*. Boston: Roberts Brothers, 1875.

Anderson, Jessie McMillan. *Sixty Composition Topics*. New York: Silver, Burdett, 1894.

Andrews, John. *Elements of Rhetorick and Belles Lettres*. Philadelphia: Moses Thomas, 1813.

Arnold, Sarah Louise, and George Lyman Kittredge. *The Mother Tongue, Book I*. Rev. ed. Boston: Ginn, 1908.

Bain, Alexander. *English Composition and Rhetoric: A Manual*. 1866. New York: D. Appleton, 1884.

———. *English Composition and Rhetoric: A Manual*. Enlarged ed. New York: D. Appleton, 1887.

Baldwin, Charles Sears. *The Expository Paragraph and Sentence*. New York: Longmans, Green, 1897.

Bancroft, T. Whiting. *A Method of English Composition*. Boston: Ginn, 1894.

Bardeen, C. W. *A System of Rhetoric*. New York: A. S. Barnes, 1884.

Barton, W. S. *Practical Exercises in English Composition*. Boston: Gould and Lincoln, 1856.

Bentley, Rensselaer. *Introduction to the Pictorial Reader*. New York: George F. Cooledge and Brother, 1847.

Bingham, Caleb. *Juvenile Letters*. Boston: David Carlisle, 1805.

Black, J. *Little Grammarian*. Boston: Munroe and Francis, 1829.

Blair, David. *Universal Preceptor*. 3d American ed. Philadelphia: Edward and Richard Parker, 1819.

Blair, Hugh. *Lectures on Rhetoric and Belles Lettres*. London: W. Strahan, 1785.

Bobins, Helen J., and Agnes F. Perkins. *An Introduction to the Study of Rhetoric*. New York: Macmillan, 1908.

Bonnell, J. M. *A Manual of the Art of Prose Composition*. Louisville, KY: John P. Morton, 1867.

Booth, David. *The Principles of English Composition*. 1831. London: John Taylor, 1840.

Boyd, James R. *Elements of English Composition*. New York: A. S. Barnes, 1871.

———. *Elements of Rhetoric and Literary Criticism*. New York: Harper and Brothers, 1844.

Branson, Levi. *First Book in Composition*. Raleigh, NC: Branson, Farrar, 1863.

Brewer, Ebenezer C. *A Guide to English Composition*. New York: C. S. Francis, 1853.

Briggs, Thomas H., and Isabel McKinney. *A First Book of Composition*. Boston: Ginn, 1913.

Brookfield, F. *First Book in Composition*. New York: A. S. Barnes, 1855.

Brooks, Stratton D., and Marietta Hubbard. *Composition-Rhetoric*. New York: American Book, 1905.

Brown, Goold. *First Lines of English Grammar*. New York: Samuel S. and William Wood, 1826.

Buck, Gertrude, and Elisabeth Woodbridge. *A Course in Expository Writing*. New York: Henry Holt, 1899.

Bullions, Peter. *Practical Lessons in English Grammar and Composition*. New York: Pratt, Woodford, Farmer and Brace, 1854.

Burn, John. *Practical Grammar of the English Language*. Glasgow: J. and A. Duncan, 1805.

Cairns, William B. *Introduction to Rhetoric*. Boston: Ginn, 1900.

Carpenter, George R. *Elements of Rhetoric and English Composition*. New York: Macmillan, 1902.

——. *Exercises in Rhetoric and English Composition*. 6th ed. New York: Macmillan, 1897.

Chambers, William, and Robert Chambers. *Introduction to English Composition*. Edinburgh: Chambers, 1842.

Channing, Edward Tyrrell. *Lectures Read to the Seniors in Harvard College*. 1856. Ed. Dorothy I. Anderson and Waldo W. Braden. Carbondale: Southern Illinois UP, 1968.

Chesterfield's Art of Letter-Writing Simplified. New York: Dick and Fitzgerald, 1857.

Chittenden, L. A. *The Elements of English Composition*. Chicago: S. C. Griggs, 1890.

Christensen, Francis. *Notes Toward a New Rhetoric*. New York: Harper and Row, 1967.

Clark, John Scott. *A Practical Rhetoric*. New York: Henry Holt, 1887.

Cleveland, Helen M. *Letters from Queer and Other Folk*. New York: Macmillan, 1899.

Clippinger, Erle E. *Written and Spoken English*. Boston: Silver, Burdett, 1917.

Collett, Josephus. *Complete English Grammar*. Indianapolis: Indiana School Book, 1891.

Comenius, John Amos. *Orbis Pictus*. Ed. C. W. Bardeen. Syracuse, NY: C. W. Bardeen, 1887.

Conklin, Benjamin Y. *A Complete Graded Course in English Grammar and Composition*. New York: D. Appleton, 1889.

——. *Practical Lessons in Language*. New York: American Book, 1893.

Cooper, Joab. *North American Spelling-Book*. Philadelphia: J. Towar and D. M. Hogan, 1830.

Coppee, Henry. *Elements of Rhetoric*. Philadelphia: E. H. Butler, 1859.

Coppens, Charles. *A Practical Introduction to English Rhetoric*. New York: Schwartz, Kirwin, and Fauss, 1886.

Cruikshank, James. *Analysis, Parsing and Composition*. New York: Sheldon, 1870.

Daiker, Donald, Andrew Kerek, and Max Morenberg. *The Writer's Options*. 5th ed. New York: Harper and Row, 1994.

Davis, W. W. *Composition Writing, A Practical Guide*. Chicago: George and C. W. Sherwood, 1864.

Day, Henry Noble. *The Art of Discourse*. New York: Charles Scribner, 1867.

———. *The Art of English Composition*. 9th ed. New York: Ivison, Blakeman, Taylor, 1867.

———. *Elements of the Art of Rhetoric*. Hudson, NY: W. Skinner, 1850.

———. *Rhetorical Praxis*. Cincinnati: Moore, Wilstach, Keys, 1861.

———. *The Young Composer*. New York: Charles Scribner, 1870.

DeGarmo, Charles. *Language Lessons, Book One*. New York: Werner School Book, 1897.

Duncan, Carson, Edwin Beck, and William Graves. *Prose Specimens*. Boston: D. C. Heath, 1913.

Ellsworth, H. W. *Textbook on Penmanship*. New York: D. Appleton, 1862.

Farrar, Mrs. John. *The Youth's Letter-Writer*. New York: R. Bartlett and S. Raynor, 1834.

Felch, Walton. *A Comprehensive Grammar*. Boston: Otis, Broaders, 1837.

Fernald, James C. *Expressive English*. New York: Funk and Wagnalls, 1918.

Fletcher, J. B., and J. R. Carpenter. *Introduction to Theme-Writing*. Boston: Allyn and Bacon, 1895.

Frazee, Bradford. *An Improved Grammar of the English Language System*. Philadelphia: Sorin and Ball, 1845.

Frost, John, ed. *Abridgment of Elements of Criticism*. By Henry Kames. New York: Samuel Raynor, 1855.

———, *Easy Exercises in Composition*. 2d ed. Philadelphia: W. Marshall, 1839. This is the edition that was stereotyped, and it is the edition from which I quote in this book. Published one month later than the first edition by the same publisher, it includes several more illustrations than the first edition and a short section on dialogue writing that does not appear in the earlier edition.

———. *Elements of English Grammar*. Boston: Richardson and Lord, 1829.

———. *Five Hundred Progressive Exercises in Parsing*. Boston: Hilliard, Bray, Little and Wilkins, 1828.

———, ed. *Lessons on Common Things*. By Elizabeth Mayo. Philadelphia: Thomas T. Ash, 1835.

———, ed. *Lessons on Things*. By Elizabeth Mayo. Philadelphia: Carey and Lea, 1831.

———. *A Practical English Grammar*. Philadelphia: Thomas, Cowperthwait, 1842.

——— [Robert Ramble, pseud.]. *Robert Ramble's Picture Gallery*. Philadelphia, 1838.

Frost, S. A. *How To Write a Composition*. New York: Dick and Fitzgerald, 1871.

Genung, John F. *Outlines of Rhetoric*. Boston: Ginn, 1894.

———. *The Practical Elements of Rhetoric*. Boston: Ginn, 1890.

Genung, John F., and Charles Lane Hanson. *Outlines of Composition and Rhetoric*. Boston: Ginn, 1915.

Gideon, Edward. *Lessons in Language*. Philadelphia: Eldredge and Brother, 1888.

Gilmore, J. H. *Outlines of the Art of Expression*. Boston: Ginn, 1887.

Goodrich, Samuel Griswold. *Peter Parley's Little Reader*. Philadelphia: R. W. Pomeroy, 1837.

Goyen, P. *Principles of English Composition*. New York: Macmillan, 1894.

Greene, Samuel. *First Lessons in Grammar*. Philadelphia: Thomas, Cowperthwait, 1848.

Griffin, Sarah L. *Familiar Tales for Children*. Macon, GA: Benjamin F. Griffin, 1841.

Hadley, Hiram. *Lessons in Language*. Chicago: Hadley Brothers, 1871.

Hall, William D. *Rand McNally English Grammar and Composition*. Chicago: Rand, McNally, 1898.

———. *Rand McNally Primary Grammar and Composition*. Chicago: Rand, McNally, 1897.

Harper, Mary J. *Practical Composition*. New York: Charles Scribner, 1869.

Hart, John S. *First Lessons in Composition*. Philadelphia: Eldredge and Brother, 1886.

———. *A Manual of Composition and Rhetoric*. 1870. Philadelphia: Eldredge and Brother, 1891.

Harvey, Thomas W. *Elementary Grammar and Composition*. New York: American Book, 1880.

———. *An Elementary Grammar of the English Language*. Cincinnati: Van Antwerp, Bragg and Company, 1869.

Haven, E. O. *Rhetoric: A Text Book*. New York: Harper and Brothers, 1869.

Hawkins, Edward. *Language Lessons, First Book*. Indianapolis: Indiana School Book, 1896.

Hazen, Edward. *Hazen's Composition Book*. New York: J. S. Redfield, 1847.

Hepburn, A.D. *Manual of English Rhetoric*. Cincinnati: Van Antwerp, Bragg, 1875.

Herrick, Robert, and Lindsay Todd Damon. *Composition and Rhetoric for Schools*. Chicago: Scott, Foresman, 1899.

Hill, Adams Sherman. *The Foundations of Rhetoric*. New York: Harper and Brothers, 1897.

———. *The Principles of Rhetoric and Their Application*. New York: Harper and Brothers, 1880.

Hill, David J. *The Elements of Rhetoric and Composition*. New York: Sheldon, 1878.

———. *The Science of Rhetoric*. New York: Sheldon, 1877.

Hitchcock, Alfred M. *Practice Book in English Composition.* New York: Henry Holt, 1906.

Hope, M. B. *The Princeton Text Book in Rhetoric.* Princeton, NJ: John T. Robinson, 1859.

Huffcut, Ernest. *English in the Preparatory Schools.* Boston: D. C. Heath, 1892.

Hyde, Mary F. *Practical Lessons in the Use of English.* Boston: D. C. Heath, 1899.

Illustrated Composition Book. New York: A. R. Phippen, 1854. (See also Phippen.)

Illustrated Primer. New York: George F. Cooledge and Brother, 1847.

Irving, David. *Elements of English Composition.* Philadelphia: Jacob Johnson and Thomas L. Plowman, 1803.

Jameson, Henry W. *Rhetorical Method.* St. Louis: G. I. Jones, 1879.

Jamieson, Alexander. *A Grammar of Rhetoric.* 4th ed. New Haven, CT: A. H. Maltby, 1826.

Jaudon, Daniel. *A Short System of Polite Learning.* Philadelphia: M'Carty and Davis, 1835.

———. *The Union Grammar.* 4th ed. Philadelphia: Towar and Hogan, 1828.

Juvenile Primer. Baltimore: Bayly and Burns, 1837.

Kames, Henry Home. *Elements of Criticism.* London: G. Cowie and Poultry, 1824.

Kavana, Rose M., and Arthur Beatty. *Composition and Rhetoric.* Chicago: Rand, McNally, 1902.

Keeler, Harriet L. *Studies in English Composition.* Boston: Allyn and Bacon, 1892.

Kellogg, Brainerd. *A Textbook on Rhetoric.* New York: Maynard, Merrill, 1894.

Kerl, Simon. *Elements of Composition and Rhetoric.* New York: Ivison, Phinney, Blakeman, 1869.

Kirkham, Samuel. *English Grammar.* 25th ed. New York: M'elrath and Bangs, 1831.

Kittredge, George Lyman, and Sarah Louise Arnold. *The Mother Tongue, Book II.* Rev. ed. Boston: Ginn, 1908.

Knighton, F. *The Young Composer.* Philadelphia: Robert F. Peterson, 1853.

Knox, Samuel. *A Compendious System of Rhetoric.* Baltimore: Swain and Matchett, 1809.

Laidley, Mary Fontaine. *Our English: A Textbook in Composition and Grammar, Book Two.* Cincinnati: American Book, 1922.

Leonard, Arthur W., and Claude M. Fuess. *Good Writing.* New York: Harcourt, Brace, 1922.

Lewis, Edwin Herbert. *A First Book in Writing English.* New York: Macmillan, 1899.

———. *A First Manual of Composition.* New York: Macmillan, 1902.

Lewis, Frances W. *Inductive Lessons in Rhetoric.* Boston: D. C. Heath, 1900.

Lewis, William D., and James Fleming Hosic. *Practical English for High Schools.* New York: American Book, 1916.

Lilienthal, M. E., and Robert Allyn. *Things Taught.* Cincinnati: W. B. Smith, 1862.

Little One's First Book. Philadelphia: Davis, Porter and Coates, [18—?].

Lockwood, Sara. *Lessons in English.* Boston: Ginn, 1890.

Long, C. C. *New Language Exercises, Part One*. New York: American Book, 1889.

Mathews, J. *Letters to School Girls*. Cincinnati: Swormstedt and Poe, 1853.

Maxwell, William H. *First Book in English*. New York: American Book, 1894.

——. *Primary Lessons in Language and Composition*. New York: A. S. Barnes, 1886.

Mayo, Elizabeth. *Lessons on Common Things*. Ed. John Frost. Philadelphia: Thomas T. Ash, 1835.

——. *Lessons on Objects*. 1830. London: Sealey and W. Burnside, 1832.

——. *Lessons on Shells*. New York: Peter Hill, 1833.

——. *Lessons on Things*. Ed. John Frost. Philadelphia: Carey and Lea, 1831.

McElroy, John G. R. *The Structure of English Prose*. New York: A. C. Armstrong, 1890.

Mead, William Edward. *Elementary Composition and Rhetoric*. Boston: Leach, Shewell, and Sanborn, 1894.

Meiklejohn, J. M. D. *English Grammar*. Boston: D. C. Heath, 1894.

Metcalf, Robert C., and Orville T. Bright. *Language Lessons, Part One*. New York: American Book, 1894.

Mills, Abraham. *Outlines of Rhetoric and Belles-Lettres*. New York: R. B. Collins, 1854.

Morley, Charles. *Common School Grammar*. Hartford, CT: Henry Benton, 1836.

——. *A Practical Guide to Composition*. 1838. New York: Robinson, Pratt, 1839.

Murray, Donald. *Write To Learn*. 5th ed. New York: Harcourt, Brace, 1996.

Murray, Lindley. *Abridgment of Murray's English Grammar*. Brooklyn: T. Kirk, 1808.

——. *English Grammar*. New York: Collins, Perkins, 1807. (The first edition of Murray's *English Grammar* was published in England in 1795. The first American edition appeared in 1800.)

——. *First Book for Children*. New York: Collins, Perkins, 1805.

Newcomer, Alphonso G. *A Practical Course in English Composition*. Boston: Ginn, 1893.

Newman, Samuel P. *A Practical System of Rhetoric*. 60th ed. 1827. New York: Ivison, Phinney, 1862.

Northend, Charles. *The Young Composer*. Portland, ME: Sanborn and Carter, 1848.

O'Hare, Frank. *Sentence Combining*. Urbana, IL: NCTE, 1973.

Oram, Elizabeth. *First Lessons in English Grammar and Composition*. New York: Daniel Burgess, 1855.

Parker, Richard Green. *Aids to English Composition*. Boston: Robert S. Davis, 1844.

——. *Progressive Exercises in Composition*. Boston: Lincoln and Edmands, 1832.

Pearson, Henry Carr. *The Principles of Composition*. Boston: D. C. Heath, 1897.

Pearson, Henry Carr, and Mary Frederika Kirchwey. *Essentials of English, First Book*. New York: American Book, 1914.

——. *Essentials of English, Second Book*. New York: American Book, 1915.

Phippen, Amos R. *Illustrated Composition Book*. New York: Henry W. Law, 1854.

Pinneo, T. S. *Pinneo's Analytical Grammar*. Cincinnati: Winthrop B. Smith, 1850.

———. *Pinneo's Guide to Composition*. Cincinnati: Wilson, Hinkle, 1877.

Powell, W. B. *How To Write*. Philadelphia: Cowperthwait, 1882.

Quackenbos, George P. *Advanced Course of Composition and Rhetoric*. 1854. New York: D. Appleton, 1855.

———. *First Lessons in Composition*. New York: D. Appleton, 1851.

———. *Illustrated Lessons in Our Language*. New York: D. Appleton, 1876.

Raub, Albert N. *Lessons in English: A Practical Course of Language Lessons and Elementary Grammar*. Chicago: Werner, 1894.

———. *Practical Rhetoric and Composition*. Philadelphia: Raub, 1887.

Raymond, George L., and George P. Wheeler. *The Writer*. New York: Silver, Burdett, 1893.

Reed, Alonzo. *Introductory Language Work*. New York: Effingham Maynard, 1891.

Reed, Alonzo, and Brainerd Kellogg. *Graded Lessons in English*. New York: Maynard, Merrill, 1901.

———. *Higher Lessons in English*. New York: Charles E. Merrill, 1909.

———. *A One-Book Course in English*. New York: Maynard, Merrill, 1895.

Rippingham, John. *Rules for English Composition, and Particularly for Themes*. Poughkeepsie, NY: Paraclete Potter, 1816.

Roux, Alphonse. *New Zetetic Method*. New York: Spalding and Shepard, 1847.

Russell, William. *A Grammar of Composition*. New Haven, CT: A. H. Maltby, 1823.

Salmon, David. *Longmans' School Composition*. New York: Longmans, Green, 1890.

Scott, Fred Newton, and Gertrude Buck. *A Brief English Grammar*. Chicago: Scott, Foresman, 1906.

Scott, Fred Newton, and Joseph Villiers Denney. *Composition-Rhetoric*. Boston: Allyn and Bacon, 1897.

Scott, Fred Newton, and Gordon A. Southworth. *Lessons in English, Book One*. Boston: Benj. H. Sanborn, 1906.

———. *Lessons in English, Book Two*. Boston: Benj. H. Sanborn, 1906.

Shaw, Edward R. *English Composition by Practice*. New York: Henry Holt, 1892.

Sheldon, Edward A. *Lessons on Objects*. New York: Charles Scribner's Sons, 1863.

Shepherd, William, Jeremiah Joyce, and Lant Carpenter. *Systematic Education*. London: Longmans, 1815.

Smith, J. K. *Juvenile Lessons*. Keene, NH: J. and J. W. Prentiss, 1832.

Smith, Roswell. *English Grammar on the Productive System*. Boston: Richardson, Lord and Holbrook, 1831.

———. *Intellectual and Practical Grammar, in a Series of Inductive Questions*. Providence, RI: H. H. Brown, 1829.

Smith, Mrs. Spencer. *First Lessons in English Composition*. Boston: Hickling, Swan and Brown, 1856.

Smithdeal, Grace H. *Smithdeal's Practical Grammar, Speller and Letter-Writer*. [Richmond, VA]: G. M. Smithdeal, 1895.

Spalding, Elizabeth H. *The Principles of Rhetoric*. Boston: D. C. Heath, 1906.

Strang, H. I., and J. Adair Eaton. *Practical Exercises in Composition.* Boston: Educational Publishing, 1889.

Swinton, William. *Language Lessons.* New York: Harper and Brothers, 1877.

———. *School Composition.* New York: Harper and Brothers, 1874.

———. *A School Manual of English Composition.* New York: Harper and Brothers, 1889.

Sykes, Frederick Henry. *Elementary English Composition.* Toronto: Copp, Clark, 1900.

Tarbell, Horace S. *Lessons in Language.* Boston: Ginn, 1891.

Taylor, J. Orville. *A Help to Young Writers.* New York: American Common School Union, 1838.

Thorndike, Ashley, and Katherine Mose. *The Elements of Rhetoric and Composition.* New York: Century, 1918.

Tower, David B., and Benjamin F. Tweed. *Grammar of Composition.* New York: Daniel Burgess, 1855.

Waddy, Virginia. *Elements of Composition and Rhetoric.* Cincinnati: Van Antwerp, Bragg, 1888.

Walker, John. *The Teacher's Assistant in English Composition.* 1801. Carlisle, PA: G. Kline, 1808.

Webster, Noah. *A Grammatical Institute of the English Language.* New York: Robert Wilson, 1798.

Weld, Allen H. *The Progressive English Grammar.* Rev. by Sidney A. Norton. Portland, ME: Bailey and Noyes, 1863.

———. *Weld's English Grammar.* Buffalo, NY: H. and E. Phinney, 1849.

Welsh, Alfred H. *Complete Rhetoric.* Chicago: S. C. Griggs, 1885.

———. *English Composition.* New York: Silver, Burdett, 1896.

Wendell, Barrett. *English Composition.* First published as *Eight Lectures*, 1891. New York: Frederick Ungar, 1963.

Whately, Richard. *Elements of Rhetoric.* 1828. Boston: James Munroe, 1843.

Williams, William. *Composition and Rhetoric.* Boston: D. C. Heath, 1894.

Wines, Enoch Cobb. *Letters to School-Children.* Boston: Marsh, Capen and Lyon, 1839.

Wooley, Edwin C. *Handbook of Composition.* Boston: D. C. Heath and Company, 1907.

Worcester, Samuel. *A Primer of the English Language.* Boston: Hilliard, Bray, Little, and Wilkins, 1826.

Zander, H. J., and T. E. Howard. *Outlines of Composition.* Boston: Robert S. Davis, 1869.

Student Writing

Alcott, Bronson. "Principles and Methods of Intellectual Instruction Exhibited in the Exercises of Young Children." *American Annals of Education and Instruc-*

tion 2 (January 1832): 52–56; (November 1832): 565–570; and (May 1833): 219–23. (Contains writing samples from Alcott's students.)

Annual Circular and Catalogue and Commencement Proceedings (Buffalo [NY] Female Academy) 1854–1865.

Annual Examination Report, Circular and Catalogue (Albany [NY] Female Academy) 1844–1875.

Annual Report of the American School for the Deaf (Hartford, CT) 1817–1882. (Founded as the American Asylum for the Education and Instruction of the Deaf and Dumb.)

"Appendix." Peabody 177–98. (Unedited student journal entries from Bronson Alcott's Temple School, 1817–1882.)

Arms Student (Arms Academy, Shelburne Falls, MA) 1889.

Bedford Street Budget (Boston Latin) 1845–1846.

Bell, Emily. Miscellaneous composition books. Philadelphia, 1859–1865.

Crescent (Young Ladies Collegiate Institute, New Haven, CT) 1849–1850.

The Elfreth Book of Letters. Ed. Susan Winslow Hodge. Philadelphia: U of Penn. P, 1985.

Fredonia Alchemist (Fredonia Academy, Fredonia, NY) 1857.

Gleaner (Lawrence Academy, Groton, MA) January 1852.

Greer, Mabel. Miscellaneous composition books. Philadelphia, 1891–1892.

High School Gazette (Salem High School, Salem, MA) January–March, 1861.

High School Index (Wellesley High School, Wellesley, MA) 1888–1893.

High School Life (Melrose High School, Melrose, MA) 1892.

High School Record (Troy High School, Troy, NY) 1887.

High School Review (Hamilton High School, Hamilton, OH) 1898.

Horae Scholasticae (St. Paul's School, Concord, NH) 1873–1882.

Howard, Caroline. "The Prize at School." *The Schoolfellow: A Magazine for Girls and Boys* (Athens, GA; ed. and publ. William C. Richards) 1849: 171–77.

Jabberwock (Girls' Latin School, Boston, MA) 1888–1895.

King, Mary L. E. "On Novel Reading." Essay. Academy of the Visitation, Washington, DC, 1847.

Lassell Leaves (Lassell Seminary, Auburndale, MA) 1887.

Latin School Register (Boston Latin) 1881–1888; 1890–1891.

Literary Journal (Boston Latin) 1829.

Newcomb, Harriet Chapell. *The Journal of an Abbot Academy Girl, 1874–1876.* Ed. Flora Mason. Taunton, MA: Charles W. Davol, 1927.

"Our Best Prize Offers for April." *Common School Education* 4 (April 1891): 148–49.

"Our Prize Reproduction Stories." *Common School Education* 5 (May 1891): 194.

Oxonian (Horner School, Oxford, NC) 1897.

Paine, Robert Troupe. *Memoir.* New York: John Trow, 1852.

Philo Mirror (Phillips Academy, Andover, MA) 1882–1885.

Prize Book of the Publick Latin School. 6 vols. Boston: Cummings and Hilliard, 1820–1826.

"Prizes." *Common School Journal* 2.5 (March 1840): 76.
Putnam Record (Putnam Free School, Newburyport, MA) July–November 1857.
Quaas, Charles. *Miscellaneous composition books.* Philadelphia, 1839.
RMTS Register (Rindge Manual Training School, Cambridge, MA) 1899.
Satchel (Boston Latin) 1866.
Student's Aid (Lawrence Academy, Groton, MA) 1878–1888.
The Student's Manual (Boston Latin) 1851.
Students' Repository (Union Literary Institute, Spartanburg, IN) 1863–1864.
Vermont Academy Life (Saxton's River, VT) 1886.
Volunteer (Concord High School, Concord, NH) 1892–1893.
The Vindex (St. Mark's School, Southborough, MA) 1877–1882.
Waif (Girls' High School, Boston) 1867.

Other Sources

Abbott, John. *The Child at Home.* New York: American Tract Society, 1833.
Adams, Charles Francis, Edwin Lawrence Godkin, and Josiah Quincy. *Report of the Committee on Composition and Rhetoric.* Cambridge: Harvard U, 1892. Brereton 73–100.
Adams, Katherine H. *A History of Professional Writing Instruction in American Colleges.* Dallas: Southern Methodist UP, 1993.
Alcott, Louisa May. *Journals.* Ed. Joel Myerson and Daniel Shealy. Boston: Little, Brown, 1989.
Apple, Michael. *Teachers and Texts.* New York: Routledge and Kegan, 1986.
Applebee, Arthur N. *Study of Book-Length Works Taught in High School English Courses.* Report Series 1.2. Albany: Center for the Learning and Teaching of Literature, SUNY, 1989.
Ariès, Philippe. *Centuries of Childhood.* Trans. Robert Baldick. New York: Knopf, 1962.
Bain, Alexander. *Education as a Science.* 1879. New York: D. Appleton, 1896.
———. *On Teaching English.* New York: D. Appleton, 1887.
Baker, Elizabeth Whitemore. *The Development of Elementary English Language Textbooks in the United States.* Nashville: George Peabody College for Teachers, 1929.
Baker, Franklin T. "Composition." *Cyclopedia of Education.* Ed. Paul Monroe. Vol. 2. New York: Macmillan, 1911. 165–68.
Barnard, Henry. "Educational Labors in Connecticut: Modes of Ascertaining Conditions of the Schools, as to the Measure and Results." *American Journal of Education.* Supplement to 1 (1855–56): 685–97.
———. *Pestalozzi and His Educational System.* Syracuse, NY: C. W. Bardeen, 1874.
Barney, William L. *The Passage of the Republic.* Lexington, MA: D. C. Heath, 1987.
Baynton, Douglas. *Forbidden Signs.* Chicago: U of Chicago P, 1996.

Berger, John, and Jean Mohr. *Another Way of Telling*. New York: Vintage, 1995.

Berlin, James A. "Octalog: The Politics of Historiography." *Rhetoric Review* 7 (fall 1988): 8–49.

———. "Revisionary Histories of Rhetoric." Vitanza 112–27.

———. *Writing Instruction in Nineteenth-Century American Colleges*. Carbondale: Southern Illinois UP, 1984.

Berthoff, Ann E. *Forming, Thinking, Writing*. Montclair, NJ: Boynton/Cook, 1982.

Besig, Emma. "The History of Composition Teaching in Secondary Schools Before 1900." Diss. Cornell U, 1935.

Biber, Edward. *Henry Pestalozzi and His Plan of Education*. London: John Sauter, 1831.

Blumin, Stuart M. *The Emergence of the Middle Class*. Cambridge: Cambridge UP, 1989.

Brereton, John C., ed. *The Origins of Composition Studies in the American Colleges, 1875–1925*. Pittsburgh: U of Pittsburgh P, 1995.

Brodkey, Linda. *Writing Permitted in Designated Areas Only*. Minneapolis: U of Minnesota P, 1996.

Brody, Miriam. *Manly Writing*. Carbondale: Southern Illinois UP, 1993.

Brosterman, Norman. *Inventing Kindergarten*. New York: Abrams, 1997.

Bullock, Henry Allen. *A History of Negro Education in the South*. Cambridge: Harvard UP, 1967.

Burrell, Edward William. "Authors of English Textbooks Published in the United States, 1845–1855." Diss. Harvard U, 1964.

Burrows, Alvina Treut. "Composition: Prospect and Retrospect " *Reading and Writing Instruction in the United States*. Ed. H. Alan Robinson. Urbana, IL: ERIC/ International Reading Association, 1977. 17–43.

Burton, Warren. *The Culture of the Observing Faculties*. New York: Harper, 1865.

Butler, George P. *School English*. New York: American Book, 1894.

Butts, R. Freeman, and Lawrence A. Cremin. *A History of Education in American Culture*. New York: Henry Holt, 1953.

Calkins, Norman A. "The History of Object Teaching." *American Journal of Education* 12 (1862): 633–45.

———. *Manual for Teachers*. Boston: L. Prang, 1877.

Campbell, JoAnn. "Controlling Voices: The Legacy of English A at Radcliffe College 1883–1917." *College Composition and Communication* 43 (December 1992): 472–485.

Carpenter, Charles. *History of American Schoolbooks*. Philadelphia: U of Penn. P, 1963.

Carpenter, George, Franklin Baker, and Fred Scott. *Teaching of English in the Elementary and Secondary School*. 1903. New York: Longmans, 1927.

Carr, Jean Ferguson. "Interchanges: Rereading the Academy as Worldly Text." *College Composition and Communication* 45 (February 1994): 93–97.

"Chapter on Autography." *Graham's Magazine* 19 (November 1841): 224–34.

Child, Lydia Maria. *The Mother's Book*. Boston: Carter, Hendee and Babcock: 1831.

Clapp, Henry Lincoln, and Katharine Huston. *The Conduct of Composition Work in Grammar Schools*. Boston: D. C. Heath, 1902.

Cohen, Sol, ed. *Education in the United States: A Documentary History*. Vol. 3. New York: Random, 1974.

Coleman, Michael. *American Indian Children at School*. Jackson: UP of Mississippi, 1993.

Comenius, John Amos. *The Great Didactic*. Ed. M. W. Keating. London: Black, 1896.

"Composition." *American Journal of Education* 5.15 (May 1830): 235.

"Composition." Letter to the editor. *Common School Assistant* 1 (January 1836): 36.

"Composition in Schools." Part 2. *American Annals of Education and Instruction*. 1.7 (July 1831): 313–20. (This article continues in the November 1831 issue of this journal, 1.11: 532–37.)

Connors, Robert J. *Composition-Rhetoric*. Pittsburgh: U of Pittsburgh P, 1997.

——. "Dreams and Play." *Methods and Methodology in Composition Research*. Ed. Gesa Kirsch and Patricia A. Sullivan. Carbondale: Southern Illinois UP, 1992. 15–36.

——. "Personal Writing Assignments." *College Composition and Communication* 38 (May 1987): 166–83.

——. "The Rhetoric of Explanation: Explanatory Rhetoric from Aristotle to 1850." *Written Communication* 1 (April 1984): 189–210.

——. "Textbooks and the Evolution of the Discipline." *College Composition and Communication* 37 (May 1986): 178–94.

——. "Writing the History of Our Discipline." *An Introduction to Composition Studies*. Ed. Erika Lindemann and Gary Tate. New York: Oxford UP, 1991.

Cooper, Lane. *Louis Agassiz as a Teacher*. Ithaca, NY: Comstock, 1945.

Corbett, Edward P. J. "John Locke's Contributions to Rhetoric." *College Composition and Communication* 32 (1981): 423–33.

Cremin, Lawrence A. *American Education: The Colonial Experience*. New York: Harper and Row, 1970.

——. *American Education: The National Experience*. New York: Harper and Row, 1980.

Crowley, Sharon. *The Methodical Memory*. Carbondale: Southern Illinois UP, 1990.

Cubberly, Ellwood. *Public Education in the United States*. Boston: Houghton, 1919.

Currie, James. *The Principles and Practice of Early School Education*. New York: E. L. Kellogg, 1887.

Davis, Emerson. *The Teacher Taught*. Boston: Marsh, Capen, Lyon, and Webb, 1839.

Dick, Thomas. *On the Mental Illumination and Moral Improvement of Mankind*. Philadelphia: Key and Biddle, 1836.

Downs, Robert B. *Heinrich Pestalozzi*. Boston: Hall, 1975.

Early Children's Books and Their Illustrations. New York: Pierpont Morgan Library, 1975.

Elson, Ruth Miller. *Guardians of Tradition*. Lincoln: U of Nebraska P, 1964.

Emig, Janet. "The Relation of Thought and Language Implicit in Some Early American Rhetoric and Composition Texts." Unpublished qualifying paper. Harvard U, 1963.

——. "The Relation of Thought and Language Implicit in Some Early American Rhetoric and Composition Texts." *The Web of Meaning*. Ed. Dixie Goswami and Maureen Butler. Upper Montclair, NJ: Boynton/Cook, 1983. 1–45.

Feaver, William. *When We Were Young*. New York: Holt, Rinehart, and Winston, 1977.

"Fifty Troubles of a Teacher." *American Annals of Education* 7 (September 1837): 409–10.

Finkelstein, Barbara. *Governing the Young*. New York: Falmer, 1989.

Finney, Ross. *A Brief History of the American Public School*. New York: Macmillan, 1927.

Fowle, William. "English Grammar." *Common School Journal* 14 (December 1852): 374–75.

Franklin, John Hope. *From Slavery to Freedom*. 5th ed. New York: Knopf, 1980.

Freeman, Ruth. *Yesterday's School Books*. Watkins Glen, NY: Century House, 1960.

Frost, John. *Pictorial History of the United States*. Philadelphia: B. Walker, 1844.

——, ed. *The School Master, and Advocate of Education*. Assisted by W. R. Johnson, J. M. Keagy, W. Russell, and J. B. Walker. Philadelphia: W. Marshall, 1836.

——. *Young Mechanic*. New York: Saxton and Miles, 1843.

——. *Young Merchant*. Philadelphia: R. W. Pomeroy, 1839.

——, ed. *The Young People's Book*. Philadelphia: Morton M'Michael, 1842.

Fulwiler, Toby, and Arthur Biddle, eds. *Community of Voices*. New York: Macmillan, 1992.

Gallaudet, Thomas Hopkins. "School Room Arrangements." *American Annals of the Deaf and Dumb* 2 (1849): 74–81.

Gere, Anne Ruggles. "Kitchen Tables and Rented Rooms: The Extracurriculum of Composition." *College Composition and Communication* 45 (February 1994): 75–92.

——. *Writing Groups: History, Theory, and Implications*. Carbondale: Southern Illinois UP, 1987.

Gilligan, Carol. *In a Different Voice*. Cambridge: Harvard UP, 1982.

Gilligan, Carol, Jill McLean Taylor, and Amy M. Sullivan. *Between Voice and Silence*. Cambridge: Harvard UP, 1995.

Giroux, Henry. *Border Crossings*. New York: Routledge, 1992.

Giroux, Henry, and Peter McLaren. "Writing from the Margins: Geographies of Identity, Pedagogy, and Power." *Journal of Education* 174 (November 1992): 7–30.

Gladstone, J. H. *Object Teaching*. New York: E. L. Kellogg, 1888.

Grant, Horace. *Exercises for the Improvement of the Senses*. Boston: Lee and Shepard, 1887.

Green, J. A., ed. *Pestalozzi's Educational Writings.*London: Edward Arnold, 1916.

Green, Nancy. "Female Education and School Competition." *History of Education Quarterly* 18 (summer 1978): 129–42.

Gutek, Gerald Lee. *An Historical Introduction to American Education.* 2d ed. Prospect Heights, IL: Waveland, 1991.

———. *Pestalozzi and Education.* New York: Random, 1968.

Hailman, William. *Outlines of a System of Object Teaching.* New York: Ivison, Phinney, Blakeman: 1866.

Haley-Oliphant, Ann E. "Classroom Ecology in a Science Class: A Description of Interaction Patterns in the Margins of Lessons." Diss. U of Cincinnati, 1989.

Hall, Samuel R. *Lectures to School-Masters on Teaching.* 4th ed. Boston: Carter, Hendee and Company, 1833.

Halloran, S. Michael. "From Rhetoric to Composition: The Teaching of Writing in America to 1900." *A Short History of Writing Instruction.* Ed. James J. Murphy. Davis, CA: Hermagoras, 1990. 151–82.

Hamilton, Sinclair. *Early American Book Illustrators and Wood Engravers.* Princeton: Princeton U Library, 1958.

Harris, Joseph. *A Teaching Subject.* Upper Saddle River, NJ: Prentice Hall, 1997.

Hess, Glenn. "An Analysis of Early American Rhetoric and Composition Textbooks from 1784 to 1870." Diss. U of Pittsburgh, 1949.

Hiner, N. Ray, and Joseph M. Hawes, eds. *Growing Up in America.* Urbana: U of Illinois P, 1985.

"Hints and Methods for the Use of Teachers." *Connecticut Common School Journal* 4 (March 1842): 53–60.

Holman, Henry. *Pestalozzi.* London: Longmans, 1908.

Hootman, A. M., and M. D. Mugan. *English Training Course.* Chicago: O. M. Powers, 1891.

"How To Teach Composition." *Connecticut Common School Journal* 11 (January 1864): 7–15.

"Influence of the 'Picture System' of Education." *American Annals of Education and Instruction* 4 (May 1834): 206–7.

James, Philip. *Children's Books of Yesterday.* London: The Studio, 1933.

Jardine, George. *Outlines of a Philosophical Education.* Glasgow: A. and J. Duncan, 1818.

Jarratt, Susan C. *Rereading the Sophists.* Carbondale: Southern Illinois UP, 1991.

Jedan, Dieter. *John Heinrich Pestalozzi and the Pestalozzian Method of Language Teaching.* Bern: Peter Lang, 1981.

Jeffreys, Montagu V. C. *John Locke.* London: Methuen, 1967.

Johnson, Anna. *Education by Doing.* New York: E. L. Kellogg, 1891.

Johnson, Clifton. *Old-Time Schools and School-Books.* New York: Macmillan, 1904.

Johnson, Nan. *Nineteenth-Century Rhetoric in North America.* Carbondale: Southern Illinois UP, 1991.

Jolliffe, David. "The Moral Subject in College Composition: A Conceptual Framework and the Case of Harvard, 1865–1900." *College English* 51 (February 1989): 163–73.

"Juvenile Publications." *Pennsylvania School Journal* 2 (February 1854): 236–37.

Kaestle, Carl F. *Pillars of the Republic: Common Schools and American Society, 1780–1860.* New York: Hill and Wang, 1983.

Katz, Michael. *Reconstructing American Education.* Cambridge: Harvard UP, 1987.

Keagy, John M. *An Essay on English Education.* Harrisburg, PA: Wyeth, 1824.

———. *The Pestalozzian Primer.* Harrisburg, PA: John Wiestling, 1827.

Kellner, Hans. "After the Fall." Vitanza 20–37.

Kellogg, Amos. *Teacher's Manual, No. 18: The Writing of Compositions.* New York: E. L. Kellogg, 1892.

Kimball, Bruce. *The "True Professional Ideal" in America.* Cambridge, MA: Blackwell, 1992.

Kipnis, William. "Propagating the Pestalozzian." Diss. Loyola U of Chicago, 1972.

Kitzhaber, Albert. *Rhetoric in American Colleges, 1850–1900.* Introd. John T. Gage. Dallas: Southern Methodist UP, 1990.

Krusi, Hermann. *Pestalozzi: His Life, Work, and Influence.* Cincinnati: Wilson, Hinkle, 1875.

Labaree, David. *The Making of an American High School.* New Haven: Yale UP, 1988.

Labaree, Leonard W., ed. *The Papers of Benjamin Franklin.* Vol 4. New Haven: Yale UP, 1961.

Lehmann-Haupt, Hellmut. *The Book in America.* New York: R. R. Bowker, 1939.

Litchfield, Norma. *Talks about Common Things.* New York: Teachers Publishing, 1891.

Locke, John. *Some Thoughts Concerning Education.* 1693. Cambridge: Cambridge UP, 1899.

Lyman, Rollo. *English Grammar in American Schools Before 1850.* Chicago: U of Chicago Libraries, 1922.

MacCann, Donnarae. *White Supremacy in Children's Literature.* New York: Garland, 1998.

Mahala, Daniel, and Jody Swilky. "Telling Stories, Speaking Personally: Reconsidering the Place of Lived Experience in Composition." *Journal of Advanced Composition* 3 (1996): 363–89.

Makler, Andra. "Imagined History: 'A Good Story and a Well-Formed Argument.' " *Stories Lives Tell.* Ed. Carol Witherell and Nel Noddings. New York: Teachers College P, 1991. 29–47.

Mann, Mary Peabody (Mrs. Horace), and Elizabeth P. Peabody. *Moral Culture of Infancy.* 1863. New York: J. W. Schemerhorn, 1869.

Mattingly, Paul. *The Classless Profession.* New York: New York UP, 1975.

Mayo, Charles. *Pestalozzi and His Principles.* 3d ed. London: Home and Colonial School Society, 1873.

McCord, Phyllis Frus. "Reading Nonfiction in Composition Courses." *College English* 47 (November 1985): 747–62.

McCormick, Kathleen. *The Culture of Reading and the Teaching of English.* Manchester, UK: Manchester UP, 1994.

McCuskey, Dorothy. *Bronson Alcott, Teacher.* New York: Arno, 1969.

Michael, Ian. *The Teaching of English.* Cambridge: Cambridge UP, 1987.

Midwinter, Eric. *Nineteenth Century Education.* London: Longmans, 1970.

Miller, Susan. *Assuming the Positions.* Pittsburgh: U of Pittsburgh P, 1998.

———. "Things Inanimate May Move: A Different History of Writing and Class." *College Composition and Communication* 45 (February 1994): 102–7.

Mitchell, W. J. T. *Picture Theory.* Chicago: U of Chicago P, 1994.

Monroe, Paul. *A Text-Book in the History of Education.* New York: Macmillan, 1911.

Monroe, Will S. *Comenius and the Beginnings of Educational Reform.* New York: Charles Scribner's Sons, 1900.

———. *History of the Pestalozzian Movement in the United States.* Syracuse, NY: C. W. Bardeen, 1907.

Morris, Charles. *The Illustration of Children's Books.* London: Library Association, 1957.

Myers, Miles. *Changing Our Minds.* Urbana, IL: NCTE, 1996.

Newkirk, Thomas. "Barrett Wendell's Theory of Discourse." *Rhetoric Review* 10 (fall 1991): 20–30.

———. *More Than Stories.* Portsmouth, NH: Heinemann, 1989.

———. *The Performance of Self in Student Writing.* Portsmouth, NH: Heinemann, 1997.

Newman, Samuel P. "On a Practical Method of Teaching Rhetoric." *American Institute of Instruction, Proceedings, 1830 Annual Meeting.* Boston: Hilliard, Gray, Little and Wilkins, 1831. 163–182.

Nietz, John A. *The Evolution of American Secondary School Textbooks.* Rutland, VT: Charles E. Tuttle, 1966.

———. *Old Textbooks.* Pittsburgh: U of Pittsburgh P, 1961.

Northend, Charles. *The Teacher and the Parent; A Treatise upon Common School Education.* Boston: Jenks, Hickling, and Swan, 1853.

Oberholtzer, Ellis Paxson. *The Literary History of Philadelphia.* Philadelphia: George W. Jacobs, 1906.

"On the Use of Pictures in School Books." *American Annals of Education* 4 (November 1834): 508–13.

Palmer, Joseph. *Necrology of Alumni of Harvard College, 1851–52 to 1862–63.* Boston: John Wilson, 1864.

Palmer, Thomas. *The Moral Instructor.* Philadelphia: Thomas, Cowperthwait, 1841.

———. *The Teacher's Manual.* Boston: Thomas H. Webb, 1843.

Parker, Francis Wayland. *Notes of Talks on Teaching.* New York: E. L. Kellogg, 1883.

Parker, Richard Green. "On the Teaching of Composition in the Schools." *Proceedings and Lectures of the American Institute of Instruction.* Boston: James Munroe, 1838. 182–207.

Peabody, Elizabeth Palmer. *Record of a School.* Boston: Russell, Shattuck, 1836.

Peet, Harvey. "Memoir on the Origin and Early History of the Art of Instructing the Deaf and Dumb." *American Annals of the Deaf and Dumb* 3 (April 1851): 129–60.

Pestalozzi, Johann Heinrich. *Letters on Early Education.* 1819. Syracuse, NY: C. W. Bardeen, 1898.

Pitz, Henry C. *Illustrating Children's Books.* New York: Watson-Guptill, 1963.

Powell, Arthur. "The Culture and Politics of American Teachers." *History of Education Quarterly* 18 (summer 1978): 187–94.

"Preventive Discipline." *Common School Journal* 11 (September 1849): 257–60.

Questions to Candidates. *Common School Journal* 9 (December 1847): 378–81.

Reese, William J. *The Origins of the American High School.* New Haven: Yale UP, 1995.

Ricks, George. *Object Lessons.* Boston: D. C. Heath, 1895.

Rose, Shirley K. "Down from the Haymow: One Hundred Years of Sentence-Combining." *College English* 45 (September 1983): 483–91.

Rousseau, Jean Jacques. *Émile; or Education.* 1762. New York: Dutton, 1911.

Russell, William. *Suggestions on Education.* New Haven: A. H. Maltby, 1823.

Sadler, John Edward. *J. A. Comenius and the Concept of Universal Education.* New York: Barnes and Noble, 1966.

Salvatori, Mariolina, ed. *Pedagogy.* Pittsburgh: U of Pittsburgh P, 1996.

Schilb, John. *Between the Lines.* Portsmouth, NH: Boynton/Cook, 1996.

Scholes, Robert. "Is There a Fish in This Text?" *College English* 46 (November 1984): 653–64.

Schultz, Lucille M., Chester Laine, and Mary Savage. "Interaction among School and College Writing Teachers: Toward Recognizing and Remaking Old Patterns." *College Composition and Communication* 39 (May 1988): 139–53.

Scott, Joan W. "The Evidence of Experience." *Lesbian and Gay Studies Reader.* Ed. Henry Abelove, Michele Aina Barale, and David M. Halperin. New York: Routledge, 1993. 397–415.

Scudder, Samuel H. "In the Laboratory with Agassiz." *Every Saturday* 16 (April 4, 1874): 369–70. Rpt. in Lane Cooper's *Louis Agassiz as a Teacher.*

Sedgwick, C. M. "Hints to Young Ladies as to What To Read and How To Read." *American Journal of Education* 2 (1856): 227–29.

Shannon, Patrick. *The Struggle to Continue.* Portsmouth, NH: Boynton/Cook, 1990.

Silber, Kate. *Pestalozzi: The Man and His Work.* 2d ed. London: Routledge, 1965.

Simmons, Sue Carter. "Critiquing the Myth of Current Traditional Rhetoric: Invention in Writing Instruction at Harvard." Penn. State Conference on Rhetoric and Composition. University Park, PA, July, 1991.

Spalding, Elizabeth H. *The Problem of Elementary Composition.* Boston: D. C. Heath, 1896.

Spring, Joel. *The American School 1642–1993.* 3d ed. New York: McGraw-Hill, 1994.

———. *Educating the Worker Citizen.* New York: Longmans, 1980.

Stanton, Elizabeth Cady. *Eighty Years and More: Reminiscences, 1815–1897*. 1898. Boston: Northeastern UP, 1993.

Swett, John. *American Public Schools*. New York: American Book, 1900.

——. *Methods of Teaching*. New York: Harper, 1886.

Sypher, J. R. *The Art of Teaching School*. Philadelphia: J. M. Stoddart, 1872.

Thornton, Tamara Plakins. *Handwriting in America: A Cultural History*. New Haven: Yale UP, 1996.

U.S. Bureau of Education. *Indian Education and Civilization*. 1888. Millwood, NY: Kraus Reprint, 1973.

Vanderpoel, Emily Noyes. *Chronicles of a Pioneer School: From 1792 –1833*. Cambridge, MA: University Press, 1903.

Vitanza, Victor, ed. *Writing Histories of Rhetoric*. Carbondale: Southern Illinois UP, 1994.

Wallis [William B. Fowle]. "English Grammar." *Common School Journal* 12 (January 1850): 5–7.

Walsh, William. *International Encyclopedia of Prose and Poetical Quotations*. Philadelphia: John Winston, 1921.

Webber, Thomas L. *Deep Like the Rivers*. New York: Norton, 1978.

Welsch, Kathleen. "Nineteenth-Century Composition: The Relationship Between Pedagogical Concerns and Cultural Values in American Colleges, 1850–1890." Diss. U of Pittsburgh, 1996.

Whalley, Joyce, and Tessa Chester. *A History of Children's Book Illustration*. London: John Murray, 1988.

Williams, Joseph. *Style*. Chicago: U of Chicago P, 1990.

Williams, Raymond. *Problems in Materialism and Culture*. London: Verso, 1980.

Wishy, Bernard. *The Child and the Republic*. Philadelphia: U of Pennsylvania P, 1968.

Woods, William. "The Reform Tradition in Nineteenth-Century Composition Teaching." *Written Communication* 2 (1985): 377–90.

Woodson, Carter G. *Education of the Negro Prior to 1861*. 2d ed. Washington, DC: Association for the Study of Negro Life and History, 1919.

Index

LUCILLE M. SCHULTZ is an associate professor in the Department of English at the University of Cincinnati. In the range of composition courses she teaches, her particular interest lies in building bridges between the academic and civic communities. Her essays have appeared in journals including *Assessing Writing, College Composition and Communication, Rhetoric Review*, and *Written Communication*, as well as in edited collections.

Her main argument:

the pedagogical innovation in these first books of comp.

(19th cent. not all that dominated by current — traditional.)

the need for practical caused by increased enrollments 30

Parker's book the first in history to emphasize practice (activities + exercises, etc.)
1832

Reform pedagogy appeared in 1830s.

Influence of Pestalozzi: writing about objects, concrete descriptions of things and experiences. Child-centered. NOT rule-governed. Found mostly in Mayo and Frost, not in texts for college-age. P. contributed to the democratization of education.

- 1st major shift: from memory - based instruction to practice.
- Change in concept of Childhood 24 accompanied by significant developments in the art of printing 27
- early in the century, "taste" a cultural trope & common writing topic.
- abstract topics replaced by "lived experience"
- on deaf education and the imp. of visual aids 98
- the hidden curriculum 102-03
  the moral lesson as/more imp. than the comp. lesson.

- assignments atrophy when sparated from their theoretical underpinnings 162